Peter and Paul in Acts

Peter and Paul in Acts

David Spell

Wipf & Stock
PUBLISHERS
Eugene, Oregon

PETER AND PAUL IN ACTS

ISBN: 978-1-49824-834-1

Cataloging-in-Publication Data:

Spell, David
        Peter and Paul in Acts.

viii + 212p.; 23 cm.

Includes bibliography
ISBN: 1-59752-784-X

1. Bible. N.T. Acts—Criticism, interpretation, etc. 2. Bible. N.T. Acts—Theology. 3. Paul, the Apostle, Saint. 4. Peter, the Apostle, Saint. I. Title.

BS2510 .564 2006

Contents

Acknowledgements

No work of this magnitude would be complete without thanking those who have supported or encouraged me in some way. First of all, thanks to my beautiful wife, Annie, and our daughters, Sarah and Rachel. Thanks for your patience, understanding, and support. I love you all so much!

Thanks to my father-in-law, Dr. George W. Keitt, Jr. You were an excellent sounding board in the early stages of this study and I appreciate all of your helpful suggestions. Thanks to my parents, Charles and Pat Spell. Your encouragement, example, and support have never wavered. I am blessed to have parents like you.

Thanks to Pastors Dean Sweetman and Catherine Reynolds at Christian City Church, Lawrenceville. You provided the spark that I needed to undertake this endeavor. It is an honor and pleasure serving with you.

Introduction

WHILE the New Testament book of Acts is traditionally known as "The Acts of the Apostles," it is primarily the story of only two apostles, Peter and Paul.[1] Luke lists all of the apostles by name in Acts 1:13. After that, however, there are only passing references to any of the others, such as John and James, the sons of Zebedee.[2] The apostles are referred to throughout the rest of Acts only in a group context. A few examples should suffice. In Acts 5:12 Luke says, "The apostles performed many miraculous signs and wonders among the people." They were arrested as a group in Acts 5:18. The apostles sent Peter and John to Samaria in Acts 8:14. The apostles were present at the Jerusalem Conference in Acts 15:2, 22-23. This is also the last time that the apostles are mentioned as a group in Acts.

After the initial listing of the Twelve in Acts 1:13, John and James, the sons of Zebedee are the only other apostles listed by name besides Peter and Paul. John is shown in two different passages working with Peter. John and Peter are together in Acts 3–4 where Luke recounts Peter's healing of the lame man at the Temple, and then their subsequent hearing before the Sanhedrin. Peter and John are also sent to Samaria together in Acts 8 to pray for the new believers so that they might receive the Holy Spirit. Cullman says that in both of these narratives, John, "plays little more than the role of an extra."[3] In each of these passages, Peter does all the speaking and generally dominates the scene. John's brother, James, is later mentioned by name, but only as the first apostle to be martyred in Acts 12:2.[4]

---

[1] I. Howard Marshall, *The Acts of the Apostles,* Tyndale New Testament Commentaries, (Grand Rapids: Eerdmans, 1980) 34. "Luke's story is very much structured on the careers of the two Christian leaders, Peter and Paul."

[2] David J. Williams, *Acts,* New International Biblical Commentary, (Peabody, Mass.: Hendrickson, 1995) 14, "Of the original twelve apostles, we read a good deal of Peter, a little of John, James, Judas, and nothing at all of the others, except for an occasional mention of 'the apostles.'"

[3] Oscar Cullman, *Peter: Disciple, Apostle, Martyr,* trans. Floyd V. Filson (London: SCM, 1962) 35.

[4] F. F. Bruce, *The Book of the Acts,* The New International Commentary on the New Testament (Grand Rapids: Eerdmans, 1988) 233, Bruce says that James, "experienced the fulfillment of Jesus' promise to him and his brother John that they would both drink from his cup and share his 'baptism' (Mark 10:39)."

As one works their way through the Book of Acts, it becomes evident that instead of documenting the ministries of all the apostles, Luke chose to structure his book around the ministries of only two of them, Peter and Paul. Even though Luke only shows Peter and Paul both being present at the Jerusalem Council in chapter 15,[5] and never shows them working together, he does show them "as parallel figures" in the early church.[6] Gundry echoes this thought in the way that he outlines Acts. He sees chapters 1–12 as being devoted to Peter's ministry to the Jews and chapters 13–28 as being devoted to Paul's ministry to the Gentiles.[7] While this may be a convenient way to outline Acts, a thorough study of the book shows that there was quite a bit of overlap in the target audiences that both men were trying to reach. Paul, in his efforts to reach the Greek world, never completely abandoned his attempts to win the Jews,[8] and even though Peter's ministry was primarily to the Jews, he was the first apostle to take the Gospel to a Gentile audience.[9]

This book will examine the apostolic ministries of Peter and Paul within the framework of The Acts of the Apostles. While other New Testament writings will not be ignored, Acts will be the primary source that we will examine. The primary question that will be guiding the study is, "How do the ministries of Peter and Paul, as discussed in the Book of Acts, compare and contrast with each other?" There are also a number of other questions that will be explored:

1. What is the basic purpose behind the writing of Acts?

---

[5] Luke records that Paul met "the apostles" in Jerusalem with Barnabas' help after his conversion. (Acts 9:26-30) There is no specific mention of any of the other apostle's names, however, Hemer makes a strong case that this passage in Acts is a parallel to what Paul said in Galatians 1:18-19 where he said he spent fifteen days with Cephas. "Luke says Paul had apostolic contact: Paul tells us whom he saw," *The Book of Acts in the Setting of Hellenistic History* (Winona Lake, Ind.: Eisenbrauns, 1990) 249.

[6] Johannes Munck, *The Acts of the Apostles,* Anchor Bible (New York: Doubleday, 1967) lv. See also, Williams, 14, "Luke quite deliberately draws a series of parallels, between Peter in the first half of the book and Paul in the second . . ."

[7] Robert H. Gundry, *A Survey of the New Testament* (Grand Rapids: Zondervan, 1970) 219. See also Gerhard Krodel, *Peter in the New Testament*, ed. Raymond E. Brown, (Minneapolis: Augsburg, 1973) 40, "It has often been observed that Peter dominates the story of the spread of Christianity narrated in the first half of Acts (he is not mentioned after Acts 15), while Paul dominates the story in the second half."

[8] Paul is shown in Acts routinely starting in the synagogue of the cities that he is attempting to reach and Acts closes with Paul reasoning with a group of Roman Jews in 28:23-29.

[9] Acts 10. "Peter supports the gentile mission, but it is largely carried out through Paul and his companions, according to Acts." See Robert C. Tannehill, "The Functions of Peter's Mission Speeches in the Narrative of Acts," *New Testament Studies* 37 (1991) 412.

2. What is the basic message of Acts and how does this affect the way that Peter and Paul are depicted?

3. What does Acts reveal about Peter's practices of evangelism and church planting?

4. What does Acts reveal about Paul's practices of evangelism and church planting?

5. What were the areas of similarity between Peter and Paul?

6. What were the areas of dissimilarity between Peter and Paul?

7. Were the ministries of Peter and Paul largely complementary or contrasting?

As these questions are answered, the reader should go away with a greater understanding of how the apostles conducted their ministries. These insights from the first Century should provide us with invaluable revelations that can be applied to our ministries in the twenty-first Century.

PART ONE

The Book of Acts in Critical Perspective

Critical Issues Associated With Acts

Because Acts is going to be the foundation for this study, it is important that some of the historical/critical issues that are associated with the book be discussed. This material may be more appropriate for the scholar as opposed to the average lay person. However, it is important for the lay reader to understand those areas in which Acts has been attacked and how it has withstood these attacks. An understanding of the critical issues associated with Acts will carry over into the rest of the New Testament as well.

Acts is the only book in the New Testament that is devoted to the history of the early church and its value as a source for early church history continues to generate discussion and debate among scholars.[10] This debate does not diminish the importance of the book for New Testament study. Foakes-Jackson acknowledges the importance of Acts when he says, "Without it, had we even the rest of the New Testament, the origin of the Christian church would be a subject for ingenious conjecture."[11]

The first group of scholars that will be discussed are those who consider Acts as having little, if any, historical significance. These are generally regarded as being liberal in their view of the Scriptures. F. C. Baur and the "Tübingen School" are examples of this type of thought.[12] While Baur himself never completely rejected all of Acts, believing that some of the material may have been inspired by genuine traditions, he laid the groundwork for his followers, Albert Schwegler and Eduard Zeller, who

---

[10] Hemer, 1. See also W. Ward Gasque, "The Historical Value of Acts," *Tyndale Bulletin* 40 (1989) 136.

[11] F. J. Foakes-Jackson, *Acts,* The Moffatt Commentary (New York: Harper and Brothers, 1931) ix.

[12] Gasque, 136. See also Samuel Sandmel, *The Genius of Paul: A Study in History* (Philadelphia: Fortress, 1979) 149.

did.[13] They dated Acts in the 110–150 AD period and according to Hemer, "there is no room in these writers for any connection with authentic traditions deriving from a companion of Paul."[14] Baur and his followers attempted to apply Hegelian philosophy to Christian history in order to understand how the early church developed. In so doing, the Tübingen School became "a historical-critical approach to the Bible that completely ignored the divine element in it."[15]

One of the main ideas that Baur and his followers subscribed to was that Acts was written in an effort to reconcile Petrine and Pauline theology. It was believed that there had been a split between Peter and Paul while they were living and that Acts was written in an effort to heal this rift between their followers.[16] Baur based this on 1 Corinthians 1:12, where Paul described one of the problems in the Corinthian church. Some were aligning themselves with Christ, others with Cephas, others with Apollos, and still others with Paul.[17] It will be demonstrated in chapter 2 that the New Testament does not give any concrete evidence of a long-term conflict between Peter and Paul, nor does it provide the basis for the "two churches" or "two missions" that some scholars describe.

While Baur and his followers lived about 150 years ago, their influence is still felt in some circles today.[18] There are contemporary scholars who do not accept Acts as an accurate account of early church history and seem to have been influenced by Baur and his followers. One modern scholar who exemplifies this is Gerhard Krodel. In one of his commentaries on Acts, he states that Acts is neither chronological, nor historically accurate, and is what he refers to as an example of "biblical history which

---

[13] Hemer, 308–9.

[14] Ibid., 309.

[15] R. V. Pierard, "Tübingen School," http://www.mb-soft.com/believe/bxc/Tübingen.htm (May 22, 2003).

[16] French L. Arrington, *The Acts of the Apostles* (Peabody, Mass.: Hendrickson, 1988) xxxiv. See also, Sandmel, 157. See also Willam R. Cannon, "The Book of Acts," http://www.religion-online.org/cgi-bin (May 22, 2003); Luke's motive for writing Acts, "was to present to posterity a harmonious and unified picture of Christianity by playing down all controversies and differences of opinion, especially those between Peter and Paul, the one the protagonist of Judaism and the other the champion of the rights of the gentiles."

[17] E. Earle Ellis, *Paul and His Recent Interpreters* (Grand Rapids: Eerdmans, 1961) 18. Ellis says that in this verse, Bauer found his "interpretive key . . . conflict between Paul, the apostle to the Greeks . . . and the narrow Jewish Christianity of the original apostles."

[18] Horton Harris, *The Tübingen School: A Historical and Theological Investigation of the School of F. C. Baur* (Grand Rapids: Baker, 1990) 1, "No single event ever changed the course of Biblical scholarship as much as the appearance of the Tübingen School."

proclaims the mighty acts of God."[19] By relegating it to "biblical history," it does not matter to Krodel if Acts is accurate historically or not.[20] Krodel also seems to accept Baur's premise that Luke wrote to heal rifts between the followers of Peter and Paul.[21]

A Pauline scholar who acknowledges the value of the Tübingen School is Samuel Sandmel. He believes that Baur and his students were "on the threshold of the correct solution," in how to treat Acts.[22] While agreeing with most of the their conclusions regarding Acts, Sandmel thinks that the Tübingen scholars' biggest mistake was in their attempt to force their findings into a Hegelian framework.[23]

Unlike many Pauline scholars who only focus on Pauline traditions, Sandmel also discusses Petrine tradition in Acts. He believes that the only valid Petrine tradition in the New Testament is that which Paul wrote in Corinthians and Galatians.[24] As a scholar who holds to the Tübingen ideals, Sandmel believes that Luke's Peter is created as "the hammer with which one blunts the sharp edge of Pauline doctrine."[25]

J. Christiaan Beker is another modern scholar who appears to have been influenced by the Tübingen School. He says that Acts is composed of "a mixture of oral reports, memories, and legends . . ."[26] Beker believes that Luke's Paul is presented in a way that shows continuity with the original apostles and he is shown working hard to maintain a harmonious relation-

---

[19] Gerhard Krodel, *Acts,* Proclamation Commentaries (Philadelphia: Fortress, 1981) 2. Krodel also says, "We should recognize that Luke's silence about Paul's problems with his churches or with Peter in Antioch is theologically motivated and his theology determines his writing of history," 110.

[20] Harris, xxiii–xxiv, Baur felt that anything that had to do with God, "should be excluded from all historical events, so that history is treated as *pure* history, as *purely* historical, with no admixture of supernatural factors or forces."

[21] Krodel, 102.

[22] Sandmel, 146.

[23] Ibid., 147.

[24] Ibid., 157.

[25] Ibid., 158. Sandmel goes on to say, "Acts is no more reliable for the 'Petrine' tradition than it is for the Pauline."

[26] J. Christiaan Beker, *Heirs of Paul: Their Legacy in the New Testament and the Church Today* (Grand Rapids: Eerdmans: 1991) 64.

ship with them.[27] In Beker's view, the Paul we see in Acts is a product of Luke's creativity.[28]

Another contemporary scholar who holds to the Tübingen idea that Acts was written to reconcile Peter and Paul is Michael Goulder. He says, "Acts is in fact a doubtful asset, for it was Luke who invented the united virginal church theory, and Acts is his steady attempt to paper over all the cracks."[29] Goulder goes to great lengths in his book to establish the fact that the two very different missions of Peter and Paul played a significant role in the development of the church.[30]

Many modern scholars have attempted to find some middle ground concerning Acts. One example of this is Marion Soards. While he does not accept Acts as a primary source for establishing a chronology for Paul's life, he does believe that the book has value as a secondary source. Soards says that Acts, "may be used cautiously as a supplement to the primary materials when it is not in conflict with the letters."[31] He believes that it is important that both sources be used, Paul's letters and Acts, when attempting to develop a chronology of Paul's life and ministry.[32]

Johannes Munck also acknowledges that both Acts and Paul's letters are important if one wants to gain a clear picture of the early church, especially where Paul was concerned. However, Munck does believe that Paul's letters hold more weight than Acts even though he argues that in many places Acts is a valid primary source for information on the early church.[33] In arguing strongly against the Tübingen point-of-view of Acts, Munck says,

---

[27] J. Christiaan Beker, *The Triumph of God: The Essence of Paul's Thought* (Minneapolis: Fortress, 1990) 10, "Thus the thought of the apostle was reduced and domesticated to a minimum for the sake of harmonizing his witness with that of the other apostles, with the result that Paul's theological influence in the patristic period was minimal."

[28] Ibid.

[29] Michael Goulder, *St. Paul versus St. Peter: A Tale of Two Missions* (Louisville: Westminster John Knox, 1994) x.

[30] Ibid., ix–x, "The two missions were agreed about the supreme significance of Jesus, but they disagreed about almost everything else . . ."

[31] Marion L. Soards, *The Apostle Paul: An Introduction to his Writings and Teachings* (New York: Paulist, 1987) 9.

[32] Ibid., 34.

[33] Johannes Munck, *Paul and the Salvation of Mankind*, trans., Frank Clarke (Richmond: John Knox, 1959) 80–81.

Freed from the load of tradition, [Acts] gives us a much clearer picture of primitive Christianity, and that its presentation of Jewish Christianity does not open between Paul and Jerusalem the deep chasms that the Tübingen School took for granted . . .[34]

C. K. Barrett is another scholar who appears to occupy this middle ground concerning Acts. While Barrett accepts much of Acts as a valid source for how the early church developed, he is much more critical in the way he examines Luke's presentation of Paul. Barrett concludes that Luke's Paul is so different from the Paul that one sees in his own letters, that Luke resorted to "degrees of fictitiousness."[35] Barrett believes that if the author of Acts were actually a personal companion and admirer of Paul his presentation of him would be more consistent with the Paul who wrote the letters.[36]

The speeches that are put in the mouths of Peter and Paul are another area in which Barrett believes the author of Acts exercised creativity. Barrett is one of many scholars who thinks that Luke attempted to create a speech that Peter or Paul might have spoken, but he believes that Luke completely missed the mark with Paul's speech at the Areopagus in Athens in Acts 17.[37] Barrett believes that Paul would never have preached a message like this and there does not appear to be any flexibility in Barrett's thinking that Paul might have preached in different ways to different audiences.[38]

Barrett's conclusion concerning the historicity of Acts is interesting. He appears to contradict his own views when he says,

> We cannot prove that it happened in the way that Luke describes, but if it did not it must have happened in a similar way or the result could not have been what it was—the result that a Christian church came into being in Jerusalem, and that in tentative, diverse, uncoordinated ways it spread out into the Mediterranean world . . .[39]

A third group of scholars that will be mentioned are those that are conservative in their outlook and have continued to treat Acts as an accurate historical narrative of the growth of the early church. They also hold to

---

[34] Ibid., 84.

[35] C. K. Barrett, "The Historicity of Acts," *Journal of Theological Studies* 50 (1999) 526.

[36] Ibid., 527.

[37] Ibid., 528.

[38] C. K. Barrett, *Paul: An Introduction to His Thought* (Louisville: Westminster John Knox, 1994) 7, "Paul was a great theologian; the author of Acts was not, and if on some important issues he misunderstood Paul he was certainly not the last to do so."

[39] Barrett, "The Historicity of Acts," 534.

the traditional view that it was written by Luke, the companion of Paul.[40] This has been the accepted tradition of Acts throughout church history. The first mention of Luke's authorship goes back to the Muratorian Canon in AD 190.[41] The traditional view went unchallenged until the end of the eighteenth century and the rise of the Tübingen School. While most scholars who hold to the traditional view of Acts would acknowledge that there are problems in developing a chronology of events based on Acts, they do not see these conflicts as insurmountable. Colin Hemer, for example, does not see Acts as an exhaustive history of the early church but rather a framework for the historian to build on.[42] By accepting this view of Acts as a framework, it is much easier to answer the arguments of those who believe that Luke was not an adequate historian because he was so selective in what he recorded. Luke never intended for his work to be a comprehensive account of church history.

Hemer also challenges the notion that Paul's letters are unbiased and that Acts is not a trustworthy source. The argument can be made that Paul also had an agenda in his writings and it would have affected his objectivity to the events that he was describing. He was not an unbiased observer, for example, in the meetings with the apostles in Jerusalem that he writes about in Galatians. Both Acts and Paul's letters must be used and tested by the canons of historical criticism.[43] Hemer also argues that the "we" sections in Acts should be included in the primary source category. The author's participation in the narrative elevates the material from a secondary to a primary source.[44]

Another important point to remember when dealing with Paul's writings is the fact that even in his "autobiographical" passages, he was not attempting to write a chronology for his readers. In these passages, he is attempting to make certain points, not present a history of his life. In Galatians 1:13—2:10, for example, Paul is interested in showing his independence from the Jerusalem apostles, not in providing a detailed chronology for his early life.[45]

---

[40] Riesner, 7.

[41] D. A. Carson, Douglas J. Moo, and Leon Morris, *An Introduction to the New Testament* (Grand Rapids: Zondervan, 1992) 186.

[42] Hemer, 20.

[43] Gasque, 142. In this article, Gasque not only reviews scholarship since F. C. Baur, he also gives a thorough review of Hemer's book.

44 Hemer, 316.

[45] Jack T. Sanders, "Paul's 'Autobiographical' Statements in Galatians 1–2," *Journal of Biblical Literature* 85 (1966) 343. See also Peter Ricahrdson, "Pauline Inconsistency: I Corinthians 9:19-23 and Galatians 2:11-4," *New Testament Studies* 26 (1979–1980) 359,

W. M. Ramsay, while accepting Acts' accuracy, acknowledges that Luke was not interested in documenting everything that the modern reader wishes he would have. "He dismisses ten years in a breath, and devotes a chapter to a single incident. His character as an historian, therefore, depends on his selection of topics."[46] This idea of Luke's being selective in his choice of topics is one that will be dealt with later on when the focus of the study turns more specifically to Peter and Paul. It was Ramsay whose archaeological research at the end of the nineteenth century marked the end of Tübingen School's "reign" in the theological world.[47] Ramsay's research verified the historicity of much of Acts and even over one hundred years after it was first published, continues to hold its own among modern scholarship and research.

Another scholar who holds to the traditional view concerning Acts is Luke Timothy Johnson. While readily acknowledging that Luke was a selective writer, he concludes that,

> Taking into account his fidelity to the one source we can check, his general accuracy in matters we know about from archaeological or documentary sources, and the overall agreement between his description of Paul's movements and the description in the Pauline letters, we conclude that Luke is accurate in what he tells us.[48]

In Johnson's view, Luke did have an agenda that motivated his writing both a Gospel and an account of the early church. Merely having an agenda, however, does not make Luke a bad historian. It just means that he only covered the part of the story that fit with his purposes.[49] One example of this is that Acts is devoted almost exclusively to the ministries of Peter and Paul. There were other apostles and missionaries in the early church, but Luke was not concerned with telling their story. Martin Hengel echoes this idea when he says, "In reality, the writers in the New Testament make their proclamation by narrating the action of God within a quite specific period of history, at a particular place and through real men, as a historical report."[50] In his writings, Luke selects the times, places and people that

---

"The selection of material in Galatians 1 and 2 is shaped by the need to demonstrate that Paul does *not* please men."

[46] W. M. Ramsay, *St. Paul The Traveller and the Roman Citizen* (Grand Rapids: Baker, 1951) 18.

[47] Marshall, 34.

[48] Luke T. Johnson, *The Writings of the New Testament: An Interpretation* (Philadelphia: Fortress, 1986) 201.

[49] Ibid., 203–4.

[50] Martin Hengel, *Acts and the History of Earliest Christianity*, trans. John Bowden (1980;

he feels are the most important for his purposes. Leon Morris takes this thought a step further when he says, "Luke is not simply a historian narrating history, though there is history here. He is first and foremost a believer. He is writing about how God worked in the early church to accomplish His purpose."[51] Luke is not just recording history; he is interpreting it.

I. Howard Marshall is another conservative scholar who makes a strong case that among the historians of his day, "Luke acquits himself very creditably. In matters of detail his historical stature is high."[52] Marshall accepts the premise that Luke chose to follow only one strand in the history of the early church, that being the one from Jerusalem to Rome. This simplified view of church history, however, does not mean that Luke was inaccurate or faulty as a historian; it merely means that he was only interested in that particular strand of history. Marshall also observes that Luke would rather present the reader with typical incidents of life in the early church than to attempt to paint the broad panorama of the "Big Picture."[53]

Luke's portrayal of Paul versus the way that Paul portrays himself in his letters is one of the areas that has caused scholars much debate. Luke had no intention of reconciling his work with Paul's letters when he wrote Acts. If Acts was written at an early date, as some scholars believe, it is possible that Luke had little or no contact with Paul's letters. Many modern scholars, however, being unable to reconcile the Paul of Acts with the Paul of the epistles have rejected Luke as a credible historian.[54] The differences appear to be too great to reconcile them. Marshall, however, would take strong exception to this rejection of Luke as a historian where Paul is concerned. Marshall accepts that there are differences between the Paul that is seen in Acts and the Paul that is seen in his letters. Rather than seeing these differences as grounds for accusing Luke of fictionalizing his account of Paul, however, Marshall makes the case that, "a man's self-portrait

---

reprinted, Eugene, Ore.: Wipf and Stock, 1979) 43.

[51] Leon Morris, *The Cross in the New Testament* (Grand Rapids: Eerdmans, 1965) 108. See also Jacob Jervell, *The Unknown Paul: Essays on Luke-Acts and Early Christian History* (Minneapolis: Augsburg, 1984) 19, Jervell takes Morris' thought a step further. Luke was not only a believer. He is also a, "preacher and theologian describing past situations with relevance for the situation of his own readers."

[52] I. Howard Marshall, *Luke: Historian and Theologian* (Grand Rapids: Zondervan, 1970) 69.

[53] Ibid., 74. See also John T. Squires, *The Plan of God in Luke-Acts* (Cambridge: Cambridge University Press, 1993) 21, While, "Luke himself has carried out the historian's task of carefully scrutinizing his sources, it is clear that he has arranged them according to his own purposes."

[54] I. Howard Marshall, "Luke's View of Paul," *Southwestern Journal of Theology* 33 (1990) 36.

(even when unconsciously undertaken) will not necessarily agree with the impression of him received by other people."[55] Marshall, like many other scholars who hold the traditional view of Acts, believes that Paul's life and ministry, as seen in Acts, can be harmonized in general terms with what is seen in his letters.[56] Foakes-Jackson tends to agree with Marshall when he says, "it is impossible to construct the story of the sequence of events out of a collection of letters, which weighty as they undoubtedly are, are very brief, and allusive rather than informative in regard to events."[57] One must also remember that Paul was not an unbiased, objective writer in his letters. He had his own biases and agenda for writing. Even Paul's own memory of events would have been slanted by his unique perspective.[58]

Haenchen, in his commentary, sees the discrepancies between Luke's Paul and the Paul of the epistles to be threefold.[59] First of all, Luke describes Paul (and Peter as well) as a great miracle-worker. In Paul's letters, however, he never gives any examples of miracles that he performed. A second discrepancy is that in Acts, Luke portrays Paul as a great orator in several places. Paul's speeches are powerful instruments that lead to the conversions of many. ". . . he is never at a loss for the right word. He is a born orator, imposing himself with eloquence of a Demosthenes."[60] The real Paul, according to Haenchen, admitted that he was a weak and unimpressive speaker. The last discrepancy that he discusses is that of Paul's apostleship. In Acts, only the Twelve are understood to be apostles. They were the only ones who met the requirements listed in Acts 1:21-22. Paul, however, constantly referred to himself as an apostle in his letters and on several occasions pointedly defended his apostleship. Each of these points will be addressed.

In responding to Haenchen's first point about Luke's portrayal of Paul as a great miracle-worker, passages from two of Paul's undisputed letters need to be examined. In Romans 15:18-20 Paul discusses what Christ has accomplished through him among the Gentiles. Paul referred to "the power of signs and miracles, through the power of the Spirit," as being a major

---

[55] Marshall, *Luke: Historian and Theologian*, 75. See also F. F. Bruce, "Is the Paul of Acts the Real Paul?" *Bulletin of John Rylands Library* 58 (1976) 282. Bruce feels that both portraits of Paul, the one in Acts and the one in his letters must be carefully examined to get "the real Paul."

[56] Marshall, 75.

[57] Foakes-Jackson, ix.

[58] Keathley, 68.

[59] Ernst Haenchen, *The Acts of the Apostles: A Commentary*, trans. Bernard Noble et al. (Philadelphia: Westminster, 1971) 113–15.

[60] Ibid., 114.

reason that so many people turned to God. Even though he does not provide a list of miracles that he performed, Paul is clearly referring to the miraculous aspects of his apostolic ministry. These miracles were catalysts that led people to faith, and also served to validate his apostleship. The focal point of Paul's ministry was, "Jesus Christ and him crucified," not the miracles that he performed in the course of his ministry.

A second passage in which Paul himself mentions the miraculous in his ministry is 2 Corinthians 12:12 where he describes the signs that mark an apostle: "signs, wonders, and miracles." He says that these, "were done among you with great perseverance." He reminds the Corinthian believers that when he was with them, they saw the miraculous in Paul's ministry. Even though Paul does not provide specifics, it is likely that this passage would have served as a reminder to those who read it of miracles that they had seen Paul perform.

Even though Paul does not devote much space in his letters to discussing the miraculous aspects of his ministry, there is no reason to dismiss Luke's portrayal of him as a miracle-worker. Paul's purpose in his letters was to teach, correct, and exhort. He was not interested in boasting about his accomplishments. In alluding to miracles that he performed, Paul could remind his readers that the signs of an apostle were evident in him. Luke, however, was interested in showing the miraculous side of Paul's ministry. It fit his purpose in Acts and he devoted a significant amount of space to providing examples of the miracles that Paul performed. While Paul did not feel comfortable "tooting his own horn," Luke was happy to describe miracles that Paul performed in great detail.

The second discrepancy that Haenchen sees between Luke's Paul and the "real" Paul is that of oratory skill. Without a doubt, the Paul in Acts is never at a loss for words and is an excellent public speaker in whatever arena he finds himself. In his letters, however, Paul makes some comments that appear to make him look weak as a public speaker. 2 Corinthians 10:10 is the verse that Haenchen uses to make his point. In this verse, however, Paul actually quotes his opponents who say that, "His letters are weighty and forceful, but in person he is unimpressive and his speaking amounts to nothing." Paul is not denigrating himself in this verse but merely quoting his opponents. In the next verse, he actually defends himself from their charge. "Such people should realize that what we are in our letters when we are absent, we will be in our actions when we are present."[61] Paul seems to be saying that when he comes back to Corinth, his preaching is going to be as strong as the letters that he had sent to them. To be fair to Paul, this

_____

[61] 2 Corinthians 10:11.

observation by his opponents should not be the verse used to evaluate his public speaking skills.

The last discrepancy that was mentioned concerns Paul's claim of apostleship. There is no question that in Acts Luke portrays the Twelve in a significant position. In the very first chapter of Acts Luke outlines their unique requirements. They had to have been around Jesus and His followers from the beginning, from the time of John's baptism until the time that Jesus was taken up. Obviously, Paul did not meet these requirements. Paul's understanding of his own apostleship, however, was that he received it directly from Jesus when He appeared to him on the Damascus road. This special appearance of Jesus to Paul qualified him as an apostle. Paul understood that the Twelve was a unique group that he could never be a part of, but he saw himself as an apostle nonetheless. While Luke only refers to Paul as an apostle once in Acts (14:4), he nevertheless validates his apostolic ministry. Luke's portrayal of Paul's ministry parallels that of Peter's in many ways. Paul is shown doing the same kinds of things that Peter does. Luke seems to be implying that Paul's apostolic ministry was just as valid as that of the Twelve.

Conclusion

As has been seen in this brief overview, scholars take a number of different views when it comes to the accuracy and historicity of Acts. The goal here has not been to conduct an in-depth study of the different viewpoints but to highlight the most prevalent ones. In examining many of the various views concerning the reliability of Acts, it has been noted that there are extreme differences of opinion over whether or not Luke's work can be trusted.

While the Tübingen School and its proponents are at the extreme end of liberal scholarship and not nearly as influential as they were in the past, there are still those who hold to some of Baur's tenants. Baur and his followers rejected an early date for Acts and felt that the author fictionalized the characters that he wrote about, primarily Peter and Paul. Specific discrepancies were raised by Haenchen between the Paul of Acts and the Paul of the epistles. By digging a little under the surface, however, these discrepancies can easily be resolved. While those scholars who reject the historicity of Acts do bring up valid points, they still do not present enough evidence to overturn the traditional view. As Neil points out, "The traditional view has not been conclusively proved to be wrong, and many of us would prefer to give more weight to the tradition of the Church than to the hypotheses of individual scholars."[62]

The work of a number of scholars who hold to the traditional view regarding Acts, i.e., that it was written by Luke, the companion of Paul was also highlighted. By the standards of his day, Luke can be considered a reliable historian who carefully investigated the things that he wrote about. Luke even describes his method of writing by acknowledging the "eye-witnesses and servants of the word"[63] from whom he got much of his material. It can be acknowledged that Luke did have an agenda for his writing without rejecting his work. Even though Luke only focused on one part of the expansion of the early church, it does not take away from his reliability as a historian.[64] He may have been selective in the story that he presented but the case has been made that what he presented can be trusted as an accurate account of early church history.[65] Further evidence of the historicity of Acts will be presented in the next section as attention is focused on some of the literary concerns that are associated with the book.

Literary Issues Concerning Acts

Authorship

Before moving on to an examination of the apostolic ministries of Peter and Paul, it is important to focus on some of the literary issues that are present in Acts. The first issue that will be addressed is that of its authorship. It is important to remember that Acts is part of a two-volume work, commonly referred to as "Luke-Acts."[66] There is little debate in the scholarly world that the same author composed both the Gospel of Luke and

---

[62] Willam Neil, *The Acts of the Apostles,* The New Century Bible Commentary (Grand Rapids: Eerdmans, 1973) 22. See also Carson, Moo, and Morris, 190, "We have shown that there is no convincing reason to deny that the author of Acts was a companion of Paul. That he was his companion is the natural implication of the "'we'" passages. That this companion was none other than Luke "'the beloved physician'" is the unanimous opinion of the early church. We have good reason, then, to conclude that Luke was the author of Acts."

[63] Luke 1:2

[64] Hengel, 36, "He certainly knew a good deal more than he put down; when he is silent about something, there are usually special reasons for it."

[65] Hemer, 69, "Facts do not come in sealed packets untouched by human hand: selection and interpretation, at however rudimentary stage, are inseparable from historical information, and it is none the worse for it."

[66] Joseph B. Tyson, *A Study of Early Christianity* (New York: Macmillan, 1973) 204, "Any evaluation of the Gospel of Luke must recognize the unity of the two books and consider the material in Acts as having a direct bearing on the meaning of the Gospel."

the Book of Acts.[67] There does continue to be much debate and discussion over who that author was. The traditional view of authorship states that Luke, the companion of Paul, wrote both volumes. Scholars who hold to this view believe that the evidence clearly points to one of Paul's coworkers. If this is the case, Luke would be the leading candidate, based on tradition and textual evidence from Luke-Acts, as well as Paul's letters.[68]

Krodel represents the view of many scholars in his rejection of the traditional view of authorship. In his understanding, there are too many historical discrepancies between what is written in Acts and what is written in Paul's own letters. Some of these same discrepancies were raised by Haenchen and discussed in the previous section. Krodel says, "that not much is gained by affirming the traditional view on the authorship of Acts by a travel companion of Paul if simultaneously the discrepancies which have been noted are not glossed over."[69] Some of these same issues that concern authorship were also discussed in the previous section relating to critical issues concerning Acts and bear reiterating here.

To address Krodel's statement about the discrepancies in Acts, it is important to remember that there will always be some discrepancies between biographical writing and autobiographical writing.[70] A biographer's perception of Paul will always be different from Paul's perception of himself. Events that Paul considered important, Luke did not mention, and vice versa. Munck argues the case that even if Acts were not written by Luke, it had to have been written by another of Paul's companions. He believes that there are too many vivid eyewitness accounts in Acts for it to have been written by someone who was not there.[71] He points out that, "In historical sources from other fields such discrepancies are no surprise to the scholar, nor do they make him doubt the historical reliability of the accounts . . ."[72]

---

[67] Charles H. Talbert, *Reading Acts: A Literary and Theological Commentary on the Acts of the Apostles*, (New York: Crossroad, 1997) 2–3, Talbert, for example, argues for the unity of the two books based on the similar prefaces, the architecture of the two books, and the theological themes. See also Hengel, 37, "Acts cannot be separated from the Third Gospel: both books must be understood as a historical and theological unity."

[68] Mark Allan Powell, *What Are They Saying about Acts?* (New York: Paulist, 1981) 32–33.

[69] Krodel, 111.

[70] See note 57 above.

[71] Munck, xxxv.

[72] Ibid., xxxiv. See also, Merrill C. Tenney, *New Testament Survey* (Grand Rapids: Eerdmans, 1961) 231, "The reliability of Acts has often been challenged, but it has never been successfully impugned."

Munck argues that the traditional view of Lukan authorship should not be dismissed lightly. It is safer, in his view, to accept the traditions and look for supporting testimony in the written sources.[73] Hemer also saw the strength behind the traditional view:

> There is no apparent reason why the early church should have chosen to ascribe the two longest books in the New Testament, together some two-sevenths of its total bulk, to so relatively obscure a person unless it preserved sound tradition.[74]

The argument can be made that the historicity of Acts does not necessarily depend on whether or not its author was Luke, the companion of Paul. It is unlikely that those who hold to the traditional view believe that Luke was an eyewitness to the events that took place in his gospel or in the first half of Acts.[75] The first "we" passage occurs in Acts 16:10 and they continue sporadically throughout the rest of the book indicating that he was an eyewitness for much of what took place. For the first half of the book, however, the author had to have had other sources. This was alluded to in the preface to the Gospel of Luke, "just as they were handed down to us by those who from the first were eyewitnesses and servants of the word."[76] The author of Luke-Acts is clearly claiming that he is presenting a reliable, historical account. Not only does he acknowledge his use of sources, he, "emphasizes that the authors who preceded him were eyewitnesses 'from the beginning.'"[77] Even though the reliability of Acts does not hinge on Lukan authorship, the reader will "probably have more confidence in the accuracy of the narrative if they could be reasonably certain that the author was in one way or another in close contact with the people and places that feature in his story."[78]

While it is impossible to say with certainty that Luke, the companion of Paul is the author of Luke-Acts, the strongest evidence points in that direction. The earliest traditions of the church acknowledged him as the author. The internal evidence of his writings point to someone that was close to the apostles and Paul in particular, and was also an eyewitness for much that he wrote about in Acts. As of yet, no one has been able to provide a better alternative to Luke.

---

[73] Ibid., xxxiii.

[74] Hemer, 308.

[75] Neil, 18.

[76] Luke 1:2.

[77] Squires, 20–21.

[78] Neil, 22.

Date

The whole issue of dating Acts is closely related to the issue of authorship. The earlier the date that is assigned to Acts, the more likely it is that Luke, the companion of Paul, was the author. On the other hand, if a later date is chosen, it is much less likely that Luke was the author.

The most common time period that is accepted for the authorship of Luke-Acts is from AD 60 to 150.[79] The case has been made previously that the traditional view of Lukan authorship is the most viable. If Luke was the author of Acts, it is reasonable to set it between AD 60 and 85.[80] Obviously, there are many scholars who will continue to reject Lukan authorship and an early date for his writings. The following discussion will highlight some of the strongest arguments for an early dating of Luke-Acts.

Hemer argues for an early date of AD 62.[81] He bases this date on five key points.[82] First of all, there is no mention in Acts about the fall of Jerusalem, which took place in AD 70. In Acts, Luke clearly believed that Jerusalem was the center of early Christianity. It would be very surprising if Jerusalem had fallen and Luke did not mention it. Another point that Hemer makes for his early dating of Acts is that there is no mention of the outbreak of the Jewish War, which started in AD 66. In Acts, the relationship between the Jews and the Romans was still fairly cordial. A third point is the fact that the church's relationship with Rome has not deteriorated in Acts. Paul felt comfortable in appealing to Caesar and truly believed that he would be treated fairly. The fourth argument that Hemer makes for an early date for Acts is the fact that the author displays no knowledge of Paul's letters. This has often been one of the criticisms leveled against the historicity and accuracy of Acts. If the author were a companion of Paul's then he would have surely made some reference to Paul's letters. An early dating of Acts, however, eliminates this argument because few of Paul's letters would have been in circulation when Acts was written. The last point that Hemer makes is that Luke gives no hint as to the death of James, the brother of Jesus. He was martyred around AD 62. While this is an argument from silence, it is still a reasonable argument. James occupied a fairly large role in Acts as the leader of the church in Jerusalem. It would be surprising that Luke would not have said anything about his

---

[79] A. J. Mattill, Jr., "The Date and Purpose of Luke-Acts: Rackham Reconsidered," *Catholic Biblical Quarterly* 40 (1978) 335.

[80] Ibid., 336.

[81] Hemer, 408.

[82] Ibid., 376–78.

death. While Hemer's argument may not provide *prima facie* evidence for an early date, it probably comes as close as can be reasonably expected.

There are also a number of other arguments that can be made for an early dating of Acts. One of these has to do with the death of Paul. If Luke had known of the death of Paul, it is unlikely that he would not have mentioned it. He never failed to mention the deaths of other key figures in the church in his writings. Luke reported the deaths of John the Baptist, Jesus, Judas, Stephen, and James, the brother of John.[83] With the exception of Jesus, none of these figures occupied a role as large as that of Paul in Luke's writing, yet their deaths were recounted. Luke drew a number of parallels between Jesus and Paul in Acts.[84] Luke's failure to show Paul's death after his last journey to Jerusalem must have meant that he had not been martyred yet.[85]

One last argument that will be mentioned for an early date for Acts has to do with its ending. When Acts ends, Paul is still in Roman custody waiting for his appeal to be heard. Those who hold to a later dating of Acts have difficulty explaining why Luke ended his book as he did. If Acts was written later, why did Luke not tell his audience what happened to Paul? If he was released or if he was executed when his appeal was finally heard, why would the author not say? Paul's reputation had been solidly established by the end of Acts. Neither his release nor his martyrdom would have tarnished his image. The most likely reason that Luke does not tell what happened to Paul was because his book was written before Paul's case came up before Caesar.[86]

Relationship Between Luke's Gospel and Acts

The relationship between the Gospel of Luke and Acts is strong. It appears that the books were intended to tell a single story.[87] There is a strong unity between the two books. The Gospel details the life of Christ and includes a blend of narrative, miracles, and teachings. Acts details the life of the early church. It also includes a blend of narrative, miracles, and teachings.[88] Jesus

---

[83] Ibid., 338.

[84] Carson, Moo, and Morris, 192, "Would not Paul's execution have made a fitting parallel to the execution of James earlier in Acts (12:2) and brought Acts to a similar climax as the gospel of Luke, with its narrative of Jesus' death?"

[85] Mattill, 336.

[86] Ibid., 338–39.

[87] J. Dawsey, "The Literary Unity of Luke-Acts: Questions of Style—A Task for Literary Critics," *New Testament Studies* 35 (1989) 48.

[88] John A. Hardon, "The Miracle Narratives in the Acts of the Apostles," *Catholic Biblical*

is the central figure in the Gospel; Peter and Paul are the central figures in Acts.

Luke's style of writing comes closer to that of the ancient Greek classical writers than any other New Testament writing.[89] The prologues to the Gospel of Luke and Acts are good examples of this.[90] Luke appears to be writing to a Greek audience that has some knowledge of Judaism. In both of his works, he makes repeated references to the Septuagint version of the Old Testament. Drury says that Luke relied heavily on the Septuagint and, "There is scarcely a verse which is uncolored by them [i.e., the Septuagint Scriptures]."[91] Morris echoes this when he says, "It seems that Luke thought of the style of the Septuagint as good biblical style and most appropriate for the kind of narrative he was composing."[92]

Both the Gospel of Luke and Acts deal with many of the same themes:

Prayer—Luke shows Jesus at prayer more than any other writer.[93] He is shown spending the night in prayer before selecting His twelve apostles.[94] There is also some extended teaching by Jesus on prayer in Luke 11. In Acts, "the church faced one crisis after another with prayer."[95] When Peter

---

Quarterly 16 (1954) 305–6.

[89] Craig A. Evans, *Luke*, New International Biblical Commentaries, (Peabody, Mass.: Hendrickson Publishers, 1990) 5.

[90] Bruce, *The Book of the Acts*, 29–30, "Such dedications were common form in contemporary literary circles." See also, Evans, 17–19.

[91] John Drury, *Tradition and Design in Luke's Gospel* (Atlanta: John Knox, 1976) 49. See also J. L. Houlden, "The Purpose of Luke," *Journal for the Study of the New Testament* 21 (1984) 62, Houlden says of Luke that, "he is at home in the language and content of the Septuagint and perhaps other Jewish literature."

[92] Leon Morris, *The Gospel according to St. Luke*, Tyndale New Testament Commentaries (Grand Rapids: Eerdmans, 1974) 27. See also Hengel, 52, "Luke is evidently influenced by a firm tradition with a religious view of history which essentially derives from the Septuagint. His imitation of the style of the Septuagint shows that he wants quite deliberately to be in this tradition."

[93] Ibid., 46.

[94] C. F. Evans, *Saint Luke*, Trinity Press International New Testament Commentaries (Philadelphia: Trinity, 1990) 318–19, Evans feels that Luke is drawing a deliberate parallel here between Jesus praying before selecting His apostles, and the account of Matthias being added to the Eleven in Acts 1:14-26. Matthias was chosen during a time of corporate prayer.

[95] Arrington, xlii.

was arrested, the church prayed for his release.[96] When Paul and Silas were arrested in Philippi, they prayed and sang hymns.[97]

The Holy Spirit—From the first chapter of his Gospel where Mary was told she would be overshadowed by the Holy Spirit to where Elizabeth is seen to be filled with the Holy Spirit while pregnant with John, until the last chapter where Jesus tells His disciples they would be "clothed with power from on high," Luke emphasizes the work of the Holy Spirit.[98] Acts shows the Holy Spirit coming upon disciples on the Day of Pentecost and then guiding and directing the early church as it grew and spread.[99] The disciples were repeatedly "filled with the Spirit." Luke emphasized the work of the Holy Spirit more than any other New Testament writer.[100]

The Poor and the Outcast—Only Luke records the story of the angels appearing to the shepherds in the infancy narrative, the parable of the rich man and the beggar, Lazarus, and the account of the widow's gift of two small coins.[101] In Acts, Peter and John healed a lame beggar at the temple, the church administrated the feeding of widows, and Paul and Barnabas brought a financial gift for the famine-stricken Palestinian church from the church at Antioch.

The Kingdom of God—Luke's Gospel opens with Gabriel's promise to Mary that her Son would, "reign over the house of Jacob forever; and His kingdom will have no end." (Luke 1:33) Jesus began His ministry by proclaiming the Kingdom of God. The Kingdom message was one that Jesus regularly proclaimed.[102] Acts opens with the disciples asking if the resur-

---

[96] Williams, 212. Acts 12:5, informs the reader that the church was praying "fervently" for Peter's release. This is reminiscent of Jesus praying "fervently" in Gethsemane in Luke 22:44.

[97] Marshall, *The Acts of the Apostles*, 271, "The prayers offered may have been simply of praise to God; there is no suggestion that the prisoners prayed for release . . ."

[98] C. F. Evans, 85, "The Spirit occupies a crucial position in the structure of the two volumes."

[99] Arrington, 21, According to Arrington, this outpouring of the Holy Spirit on Pentecost became the pattern for how the church would move forward. The church would only continue to grow as the believers walked in the fullness of the Holy Spirit.

[100] Roger Stronstad, *The Charismatic Theology of St. Luke* (Peabody, Mass.: Hendrickson, 1984) 34–35. See also, F. F. Bruce "The Holy Spirit in the Acts of the Apostles," *Interpretation* 27 (1973) 168, According to Bruce, the difference between the Holy Spirit's ministry in Luke's Gospel and Acts is the fact that in the Gospel, the Holy Spirit's works are, "seldom explicitly mentioned, but they are implied throughout." In Acts, however, with Jesus physically gone, the Holy Spirit has a much more prominent role in the lives of the believers.

[101] Morris, 41–42.

[102] C. F. Evans, 98, "From his sources Luke inherited a double strand of teaching about the kingdom- that it was to come in the future, and that it was already operative in the

rected Jesus was going to restore the kingdom to Israel.[103] Peter's Pentecost message emphasized the fact that Jesus had fulfilled the Old Testament prophecies, especially regarding David's unending kingdom. Peter's sermon at Cornelius' house characterizes Jesus' revelation of the kingdom in Acts 10:38: the healing and deliverance of those who were under the power of the Devil.[104] Acts closes with Paul, "testifying about the kingdom of God" to a group of Roman Jews. As the Anointed One in Luke, Jesus exercised His authority over the kingdom of Satan. In Acts, the apostles proclaimed Jesus as the Anointed One who was still wreaking havoc on the kingdom of darkness.[105]

It appears that Luke used the same literary template for both of his books. They have a similar structure and it appears that Luke designed the Gospel and Acts to be parallel parts to the story that he was telling.[106] Below are examples of a few of these parallels.[107]

1. In Luke 3:21, Jesus is shown praying at His baptism. In Acts 1:14, the disciples are shown in prayer as they await their baptism with the Holy Spirit.

2. Luke 3:22 tells of the Holy Spirit coming upon Jesus as He prayed.[108] Acts 2:1-13 shows the Holy Spirit filling all of those in the upper room as they were praying.[109]

---

activity of Jesus." See also, Ralph P. Martin, "Salvation and Discipleship in Luke's Gospel," *Interpretation* 30 (1976) 373, "The ministry of Jesus centers on the proclamation of God's kingdom."

[103] Williams, 21, The disciples ask this question before Pentecost. After Pentecost they will preach the Kingdom message themselves from a new perspective.

[104] Martin, 373–374.

[105] Susan R. Garrett, *The Demise of the Devil: Magic and the Demonic in Luke's Writings* (Minneapolis: Fortress, 1989) 64.

[106] C. F. Evans, 43. According to Evans, these parallels, "are deliberate, and show Luke's work to have an architectonic design based on the principle of balance, which may be detected in other writings of the period."

[107] Talbert, 11–12.

[108] Morris, 99, "Luke is the only one of the Evangelists who tells us that the descent of the Spirit occurred as Jesus *was praying*" [author's italics].

[109] Arrington, 19, "Physical manifestations accompanied the coming of the Spirit at Pentecost. At the Jordan the Spirit's descent was in bodily form, and at Pentecost his presence was seen in the dividing of tongues similar to fire and in the disciples' speaking in other tongues. The similarity between what happened at Jesus' messianic anointing and at Pentecost strongly indicates that the disciples received the power of the Spirit by which Jesus had preached the gospel, healed the sick, and cast out demons."

3. Luke 4:16-30 describes the opening of Jesus' ministry with a sermon that focused on Him as the fulfillment of the Old Testament prophets and then ended with Him being rejected by those who heard it.[110] It appears that Jesus was rejected because He challenged the idea of Jewish exclusivism by recounting God's dealings with the Zarephathite widow and Naaman the Syrian.[111] Acts 7 shows Stephen preaching a message that traced God's dealings with the nation of Israel but also challenged the notion of Jewish exclusivism. Stephen pointed out that Abraham was called out of Mesopotamia, Joseph was used mightily by God in Egypt, and God's call of Moses came while he was living in Midian.[112] Stephen's message was rejected and he was stoned to death. Luke goes to great lengths in both the Gospel and in Acts to emphasize the universality of God's salvation.[113]

4. In Luke 10:1-12, Jesus sent the 70 out on a missionary trip to preach, heal, and cast out demons.[114] Jesus told His disciples in Acts 1:8 that they would be His witnesses, "to the ends of the earth." The first half of Acts shows Peter and Philip, in particular, begin this process. In Acts 13–20, Paul and others went on several mission trips, eventually taking the Gospel all the way to Rome.[115]

5. In Luke 9:51—19:28, Jesus made a final journey to Jerusalem. It was done under divine prompting and not understood by the disciples.[116] Paul made a final visit to Jerusalem in Acts 19:21—21:17.

---

[110] Evans, 70, "Luke wishes to make it clear that Jesus' ministry begins in the power of the Spirit as he taught in their synagogues (see 1:35; 3:22; 4:1), which parallels the inauguration of the apostolic preaching and teaching in Acts 2."

[111] Ibid., 72, "What makes all of this preaching so 'unacceptable' is that the people of Jesus' time expected Messiah to come and destroy Israel's enemies, not minister to them."

[112] John R. W. Stott, *The Message of Acts: The Spirit, the Church and the World,* The Bible Speaks Today (Downers Grove, Ill.: InterVarsity, 1990) 133–38.

[113] Morris, 36.

[114] Evans, 169, "Whereas the Twelve may represent the reconstitution of the twelve tribes of Israel, the Seventy may represent the seventy Gentile nations of the world, founded by the sons of Noah after the flood . . ."

[115] Fred Jonkman, "The Missionary Methods of the Apostle Paul," http://www.thirdmill. org/paul2/missionary_methods.asp (Oct. 11, 2001) 1, "It was Paul's mission activities (Acts 13–28) that contributed remarkably towards the Christian church's move from the limited sphere of Judaism to the broader frame of the Gentile world. It then becomes, for all religious history, a preeminent model for missionary outreach."

[116] Evans, 161, Luke says that Jesus "resolutely set His face to go to Jerusalem." (Luke 9: 51) This has several Old Testament parallels. One of the most obvious is Ezekiel 21:2, "Son

It also was done under divine prompting and not understood by Paul's friends and co-workers.[117]

6. Luke 22:54 shows a mob seizing Jesus. Acts 21:30 shows a mob seizing Paul.[118]

7. In Luke 24:45-49, Jesus' ministry ended on the note of the fulfillment of Scripture. In Acts 28: 25-31, Paul's ministry ended on the note of the fulfillment of Scripture.

These parallels between the Gospel of Luke and Acts give some idea of what Luke thought was important. They also serve to develop a clear picture of Luke's theology. Marshall says that Luke should not be labeled as only a "historian," or as only a "theologian." He is both, and according to Marshall, should be called "evangelist," for that term encompasses both of the others.[119] Martin also sees strong pastoral concerns in Luke's writings, specifically in the area of discipleship.[120] This aspect of discipleship is paralleled in both the Gospel and in Acts. Luke's use of parallels will be seen even more clearly when the study focuses more specifically on the apostolic ministries of Peter and Paul.

---

of man, set your face toward Jerusalem, and speak against the sanctuaries, and prophesy against the land of Israel." Moessner sees this final journey as more of a type of a new Exodus. "Luke will tell his readers that as Jesus progresses through the "'towns and villages of Israel, teaching in their streets'" (13:22) the crowds continue to swell around him until these "'myriads'" become a "'multitude of crowds'" (11:29; 12:1; 14:25). As the prophet like Moses Jesus gathers all Israel on their Exodus to Jerusalem," David P. Moessner, "'The Christ Must Suffer': New Light on the Jesus-Peter, Stephen, Paul Parallels in Luke-Acts," *Novum Testamentum* 28 (1986) 239.

[117] Arrington, 209, "The solemn prophetic admonitions were understood by Paul to be the definite guidance of the Holy Spirit to go to Jerusalem, the place where the purpose of God would be carried out.

[118] Luke records that after Paul was seized by the mob, "they dragged him out of the temple; and immediately the doors were shut." Bruce sees significance in the shutting of the temple doors. "For Luke himself, this may have been the moment when the Jerusalem temple ceased to fill the honorable role hitherto ascribed to it in his two-fold history. The exclusion of God's message and messenger from the house once called by his name sealed its doom: it was now ripe for the destruction which Jesus had predicted for it many years before (Luke 21:6)," *The Book of the Acts*, 410.

[119] Marshall, *Luke: Historian and Theologian*, 18. This is in direct contradiction with C. K. Barrett who does not feel that the author of Acts was a very good theologian. See note 45 above.

[120] Martin, 377.

The Purpose of Luke-Acts

As with the study of any Biblical writing, it is important to understand the purpose behind the author's work. Unlike the other Evangelists, Luke provides the reader with some idea of why he was writing:[121]

> Inasmuch as many have undertaken to compile an account of the things accomplished among us, just as those who from the beginning were eyewitnesses and servants of the Word have handed them down to us, it seemed fitting for me as well, having investigated everything carefully from the beginning, to write it out for you in consecutive order, most excellent Theophilus; so that you might know the exact truth about the things you have been taught. (Luke 1:1-4)

The prologue found in Acts refers back to the Gospel and is also written to Theophilus, tying the two works together.

> The first account I composed, Theophilus, about all that Jesus began to do and teach, until the day when He was taken up, after He had by the Holy Spirit given orders to the apostles whom He had chosen. To these He also presented Himself alive, after His suffering, by many convincing proofs, appearing to them over a period of forty days, and speaking of the things concerning the kingdom of God. (Acts 1:1-3)

It appears that the preface for the gospel applied to the work as a whole. The shorter preface in Acts was more like a chapter heading referring the reader back to the earlier preface.[122]

Aside from the obvious aspect of linking the Gospel of Luke and Acts together, the two prologues provide much insight into what the author was trying to accomplish through his writings. One first notices that both books are addressed to the enigmatic Theophilus. It has been generally assumed that each of the gospels was written to a different Christian community to provide needed spiritual instruction.[123] Luke, however, says that he is writing to an individual. Other scholars have discussed in-depth who this Theophilus might be. What is important to us is the fact that Luke tells Theophilus what his goal is in writing. Luke says that he wants Theophilus to, "know the exact truth about the things he has been taught." Many scholars believe that Theophilus was a new believer and that Luke was writ-

---

[121] Evans, 17.

[122] J. Dawsey, "The Literary Unity of Luke-Acts: Questions of Style—A Task for Literary Critics," *New Testament Studies* 35 (1989) 50.

[123] C. F. Evans, 121.

ing to provide him with a better understanding of what the Christian life was all about.[124] Some have speculated that Luke may have even intended his work to be a catechism for Theophilus and the others that would have access to it.[125] It is also apparent from the scope of the work and the way in which Luke wrote it that he intended for it to have a larger audience than just Theophilus.[126] While there may be a number of primary and secondary reasons put forth for why Luke wrote his two volumes, the safest route is to accept Luke's own purpose for writing. He wanted, "to give Theophilus a comprehensive, accurate, historical account of the matters concerning Christianity in order that he may be assured of the reality of the things which he has been taught."[127]

In a similar way, W. Ward Gasque sees four purposes in Luke's writings that emerge from a study of the prologues.[128] First of all, the prologues outline Luke's *literary* pretensions. He tells his reader how he is going to write. Luke's prefaces also show *historical* pretensions. He is organizing an "orderly account" of the story that he is telling. Luke also has a *theological* purpose to his writing. He wants to tell what God has done: "the things that have been fulfilled among us." The last area that Gasque mentions concerns the fact that Luke is writing his book to a Gentile Christian audience who need to be assured that what they have been taught is accurate and true. This fourth purpose, then, is *pastoral* in nature.

There are several other possible purposes for Luke-Acts that have been put forward and deserve consideration. These look beyond just the prologues and take into account the entirety of both books. The first of these that will be mentioned is the one that was set forth by Hans Conzelman in *The Theology of St. Luke*. Conzelman understood Luke's central theme to be responding to the delay of the Parousia.[129] The anticipation of a quick re-

---

124 Darrell L. Bock, *Luke,* The NIV Application Commentary (Grand Rapids: Zondervan, 1996) 42, "Theophilius was probably a new believer, who as a Gentile found himself in what had started out as a Jewish movement." See also, Marshall, *The Acts of the Apostles,* 56, "Theophilus was probably already a Christian, and Luke wrote his book to help him and others like him to have a reliable account of the beginnings of Christianity."

125 Morris, 66.

126 Hiebert, 130, "While writing for the personal benefit of Theophilus (Luke 1:4), Luke clearly intended for his work to have a much wider circulation."

127 Ibid., 132, He goes on to say that Luke's "ultimate aim is to convey these truths to Gentile readers and to awaken and deepen their faith in Jesus as the God-sent Savior for all mankind."

128 W. Ward Gasque, "A Fruitful Field: Recent Study of the Acts of the Apostles," *Interpretation* 42 (1988) 119–20.

129 Hans Conzelman, *The Theology of St. Luke,* trans. Geoffrey Buswell, (New York: Harper & Row, 1961) 131.

turn of the Lord gave way to disillusionment in some segments of the early church. Luke understood this and as a pastor he wrote to provide encouragement that everything was proceeding according to God's predetermined plan. By showing the unfolding of world history from the viewpoint of God's unfolding revelation of Himself, Luke lets his readers know that the delayed Parousia is not really delayed at all.[130] God's plan was worked out in the life of Jesus and now is being worked out in the life of the church.[131] There is no indication in either of the prologues that Luke was writing to explain the delay of the Lord's return. Conzelman does make a strong case, however, that this was one of the subsidiary purposes that Luke was attempting to demonstrate.

A second purpose that has been set forth for Luke-Acts is that of an apologetic work intended to offset the charges that Christianity was politically antagonistic towards the Roman government.[132] While this does not appear to have been a primary purpose for the writing of Luke-Acts, it could have been a secondary one. Luke notes that Pilate declared the innocence of Jesus three times.[133] The Roman authorities declared the innocence of Paul on three occasions.[134] Rosenblatt argues that this is one of the primary themes for Acts. She believes that Luke deliberately shows Paul as, "the witness and the accused- who must press forward from synagogue to courtroom to give his testimony, ultimately before governors and kings."[135] According to her, in Acts, Paul's judicial confrontations gradually assume dominance in the narrative and Acts ends with Paul defending the Gospel to the Roman world.[136] While Rosenblatt does make a good case that this apologetic aspect of Luke's writing is one of the purposes for his writing, she seems to overstate it by making this the primary reason. Luke does not even hint in either one of his prologues that he is planning on writing an apology for Christianity. As has been shown, Luke seemed to have several purposes for writing and apologetics is only one of them.[137]

---

[130] John Navone, "Three Aspects of the Lucan Theology of History," *Biblical Theology Bulletin* 3 (1973) 115.

[131] Conzleman, 132, "As the End is still far away, the adjustment to a short time of waiting is replaced by a 'Christian life' of long duration, which requires ethical regulation and is no longer dependent upon a definite termination."

[132] Hiebert, 133.

[133] Luke 23: 4, 14, 22.

[134] Acts 23:29; 25:25; 26:31.

[135] Marie-Eloise Rosenblatt, *Paul the Accused: His Portrait in the Acts of the Apostles* (Collegeville: Liturgical, 1995) xvii.

[136] Ibid., 95.

[137] Marshall, *The Acts of the Apostles*, 21–22, "We are not denying that Luke had an

Another purpose for Luke-Acts that will be examined specifically relates to the material that is recorded in Acts. Many scholars believe that one of Luke's reasons for writing was to address the problems that developed between the Jewish and the Gentile believers in the early church.[138] It is easy to build a case for this theory based on the text of Acts. Luke records a number of instances that directly relate to this issue. These include the story of Peter and Cornelius, along with Peter's subsequent defense of his actions in chapters 10 and 11 and the issue of the Judaizers in Antioch and the Jerusalem Council in chapter 15. Paul's arrest in chapter 21 was directly related to his trying to appease the Jewish believers of the Jerusalem Church who thought he was teaching Jews to disobey the Law. This appears to be another valid subsidiary purpose for the writing of Acts.

A last purpose that will be mentioned for Luke-Acts is put forth by Carson, Moo, and Morris in *An Introduction to the New Testament*. They argue that Luke wrote to edify and build up Christians by showing how God's plan was first fulfilled in Jesus. The plan of God had then "continued to unfold in the history of the early church."[139] In his two-volume work, Luke clearly shows how Jesus was the fulfillment of the Old Testament prophecies. In essence, history culminated in Christ but continued to move forward through the apostles and then, "the church as the eschatological people of God."[140] This understanding of the purpose for Luke-Acts will become even clearer as Peter and Paul's ministries are compared and contrasted.

The Message of Acts

Because Luke's second volume is going to be the primary source for this study on Peter and Paul, this chapter will end by looking briefly at the basic message that is presented there. First of all, it is apparent that Acts is a continuation of the third Gospel. What Jesus did in the Gospel of Luke, He continued to do through His church in Acts.[141] After the apostles

---

apologetic motive in the composition of Luke-Acts, especially in the case of Acts. But it is a subordinate aim as compared with the main theme of the presentation of the historical basis for the Christian faith."

[138] David Gooding, *True to the Faith: A Fresh Approach to the Acts of the Apostles* (London: Hodder & Stoughton, 1990) 12–13.

[139] Carson, Moo, and Morris, 210.

[140] Ibid. See also, Squires, 153, "Thus, Luke's history of Jesus and the church is driven by the fulfillment of prophecies."

[141] Bruce, 30, "The implication of Luke's words is that his second volume will be an account of what Jesus *continued* to do and teach after his ascension—no longer in visible presence on earth but by his Spirit in his followers" [author's italics]. See also Arrington, xxxviii, "Luke's

were filled with the Holy Spirit on the day of Pentecost, they began to do the same things that they had seen Jesus do when He was with them: preaching, teaching, healing, raising people from the dead, and casting out demons.[142]

A second element of Luke's message, as seen in Acts, is that of the church. Luke traced the birth and development of the church and showed how it grew into a worldwide movement in about thirty years.[143] In his Gospel, Luke gives a detailed account of the birth of Christ and some aspects of His childhood before moving on to discuss His ministry. In a similar way in Acts, Luke describes the birth and infancy of the church. He then goes on to describe how it grew into "adulthood."[144]

Included in this theme of showing the way the church grew, Luke makes it a point to show some of the "growing pains" that were associated with it. One of the main issues that Luke attempted to resolve was that of Jewish/Gentile relations. Luke wrote Acts in such a way that chapter 15, the center of the book, dealt with the question of whether or not Gentiles would have to be circumcised before being accepted into the church.[145] A further aspect of the problem was concerned with table fellowship between the two groups. Could a Jewish believer share a meal with a Gentile believer? While Luke did touch on this subject, it was much more fully developed in the writings of Paul.[146]

The third component of Luke's message in Acts that will be mentioned is the fact that the Gospel is a universal message.[147] No longer were

---

second volume makes clear that what Jesus began to do during his ministry, he continued to do through his witnesses (Acts 1:1)."

[142] Stronstad, 49, "By this transfer of the Spirit, the disciples become the heirs and successors to the earthly charismatic ministry of Jesus; that is, because Jesus has poured out the charismatic Spirit upon them the disciples will continue to do and teach those things which Jesus began to do and teach (Acts 1:1)."

[143] Gundry, 220, He says that Acts shows, "the extension of Christianity in early Church history so as to convince readers by the irresistible advance of the Gospel that God through His Spirit really is working in human history for the redemption of all men."

[144] Talbert hints at this connection (*Reading Acts: A Literary and Theological Commentary on the Acts of the Apostles*, 3ff.), however, there did not appear to be any other scholars who saw a connection between the birth and infancy narratives in the Gospel, and the early days (infancy) of the church.

[145] Frank Stagg, *The Book of Acts: The Early Struggle for an Unhindered Gospel* (Nashville: Broadman, 1955) 13, "The problem of accepting uncircumcised Gentiles became increasingly difficult for Jewish Christians, leading eventually to the self-exclusion of the Jews from the Christian community." See also Marshall, 29–32.

[146] Stagg, 13–14.

[147] Marshall, 50, "Luke demonstrates that in the purpose of God there can be *no racial*

the Gentiles to be excluded. Now they were to be numbered among the people of God. The universal message that was hinted at in Luke's Gospel is developed much more fully in Acts.[148] In Acts, Luke legitimized the new movement by showing its Jewish origins and by, "emphasizing the divine providence which was reflected in every aspect of the development and expansion of the early church."[149] This is seen taking place progressively through the course of Acts. Philip, and later Peter and John, evangelize in Samaria. Peter, shortly after that, is instructed by a heavenly vision to go to the centurion Cornelius' house where he ministers to a Gentile audience. A church is later established in Antioch that is composed both of Gentile and Jewish believers. It is from this base that the Apostle Paul and others take the message of Christ throughout the Roman Empire.[150] By the end of Acts, Luke has made the case that Christianity is "an independent religious movement in the process of emerging from Judaism to which it is its legitimate successor."[151]

Conclusion

The second part of this first chapter has highlighted many of the literary issues that are associated with the writings of Luke, and Acts in particular. First of all, the authorship of Acts was discussed. While many scholars do not accept the traditional view that Luke, the companion of Paul, wrote Acts no one has been able to present enough evidence to successfully refute it. Tradition and internal evidence point towards Lukan authorship.

The dating of Acts was examined next. Authorship and dating are closely related. If Acts is given a late date, such as the early to middle of the Second Century, as many scholars do, then the traditional view of authorship is effectively nullified. If Luke was the author of Acts, then an early date of 60 to 85 AD is not unreasonable. A date in the early to mid-60's seems to make the most sense in the light of the internal evidence that was presented.

---

discrimination within the church" [author's italics].

[148] Hiebert, 257, "It shows how Christianity, which arose out of Judaism, was led step by step to recognize God's purpose that it can be an intrinsically universal body."

[149] David E. Aune, *The New Testament in its Literary Environment,* Library of Early Christianity (Philadelphia: Westminster, 1987) 137.

[150] F. F. Bruce, "The Significance of the Speeches for Interpreting Acts," *Southwestern Journal of Theology* 33 (1990) 28, The gospel message that Luke presents in Acts is, "freed from national restrictions to be accepted by all nations, and therefore entitled to be granted the liberty enjoyed by Jewish communities throughout the world."

[151] Aune, 140.

The relationship between Luke's Gospel and Acts was the next area that was discussed. A number of themes that are common to both works were discussed. There are numerous literary parallels between the two books. Several of these were highlighted.

The purpose for Luke-Acts was the next literary topic that was examined. The primary purpose for both works is found in the prologues. There, are, however, numerous other subsidiary purposes that have been set forth as to why Luke wrote these volumes. Several of these were mentioned. The last literary issue that was discussed was the basic message of Acts.

The next chapter will start the process of looking specifically at Peter and Paul. The focus will be on their relationship to each other in the early church and whether or not they should be considered friends or foes. It will look beyond Acts to their respective letters to see what they had to say about each other.

2

Peter and Paul: Opponents or Fellow Workers in the Early Church?

B EFORE Peter and Paul's ministries are examined in Acts, their relationship in the New Testament will be explored and discussed. Paul mentions Peter in two of his letters, Galatians and 1 Corinthians. Peter refers to Paul in one of his letters, 2 Peter. These passages will be looked at in an effort to determine what kind of relationship the two men had. As was discussed in the previous chapter, there are some scholars, primarily those influenced by Baur and the other scholars that made up the Tübingen school, who see a deep division between the two apostles and their followers. This is based in large part on the passages in 1 Corinthians and Galatians that will be examined. In their view, Acts was written in an attempt to heal the division that existed between the two men and their followers.[1]

The passages in Galatians that discuss the relationship between Peter and Paul will be examined first. The reason that Galatians will be discussed first is because it is commonly accepted to be one of Paul's earliest letters.[2] From an autobiographical point-of-view, Galatians also deals with an early period in Paul's Christian life.[3] We will look at Galatians 1:18-21, Galatians 2:1-10, and Galatians 2:11-14. As the passages are examined in Galatians, there will be some reference to the related passages in Acts, but the goal will not be to necessarily harmonize them with what Luke wrote. The intent

---

[1] Nicholas M. van Ommeren, "Was Luke an Accurate Historian?" *Bibliotheca Sacra* 148 (1991) 63, "This division between the Petrine and Pauline Christianity (between Jewish and Gentile Christians) is a fundamental presupposition of the Tübingen School with respect to Acts."

[2] R. Alan Cole, *Galatians,* Tyndale New Testament Commentaries (Grand Rapids: Eerdmans, 1989) 32; Merrill C. Tenney, *Galatians: The Charter of Christian Liberty* (Grand Rapids: Eerdmans, 1989) 99; Gundry, 259.

[3] Martin Hengel and Anna Marie Schemer, *Paul Between Damascus and Antioch: The Unknown Years,* trans. John Bowden (Louisville: Westminster John Knox) 133–34.

is to explore the relationship and interaction between the two apostles as perceived by Paul. How did he understand their relationship?

Galatians 1:18-21

The first contact that is mentioned between Peter and Paul is recorded by Paul in Galatians 1:18-21:

> Then after three years, I went up to Jerusalem to get acquainted with Peter and stayed with him for fifteen days. I saw none of the other apostles- only James, the Lord's brother. I assure you before God that what I am writing you is no lie. Later I went to Syria and Cilicia.

The related passage in Acts is found in 9:26-30:

> When he came to Jerusalem, he tried to join the disciples, but they were all afraid of him, not believing that he was really a disciple. But Barnabas took him and brought him to the apostles. He told them how Saul on his journey had seen the Lord and that the Lord had spoken to him, and how in Damascus he had preached fearlessly in the name of Jesus. So Saul stayed with them and moved about freely in Jerusalem, speaking boldly in the name of the Lord. He talked and debated with the Grecian Jews, but they tried to kill him. When the brothers learned of this, they took him down to Caesarea and sent him off to Tarsus.

While some would see these two passages as referring to different visits to Jerusalem,[4] many others see them as referring to the same visit.[5] In either case, they both describe Paul's early contact with some of the Jerusalem Christians and some of the apostles. While acknowledging the differences in the two passages, Hemer seems to make the most sense in his approach in saying that they both refer to the same visit.[6] The differences in the two passages lie in the fact that the intentions of the authors were different. Luke was only providing a generalized account of Paul's first visit to Jerusalem as a Christian. In Galatians, however, Paul was writing to clear the air in regard to his relationship with the original apostles. He was specific in who he had contact with and how long that contact lasted. "Luke says Paul had apostolic contact: Paul tells us whom he saw."[7] Tenney echoes

---

[4] Knox, 22–23; See also Gunther Bornkamm, *Paul* (Minneapolis: Fortress, 1995) 29–30.

[5] Hemer, 248–49; See also Marshall, 176.

[6] Hemer, ibid.

[7] Ibid., 249. Hemer goes on to say, "Paul first came to Jerusalem not to a welcome as a mighty evangelist of the future, but as a virtual outcast, rejected by both communities.

this when he says, "There is no essential conflict between Galatians 1:19 and Acts 9:27, since the latter does not specify which apostles were present and which were absent."[8]

Paul explains that the reason that he went to Jerusalem was, "to get acquainted with Peter." The fact that Paul wanted to meet and get to know Peter is important, in and of itself.[9] Peter was the acknowledged leader of the church in Jerusalem and was possibly known to Paul by reputation from his days as a persecutor of the church. This also seems to be an acknowledgement by Paul that at the time of this visit to Jerusalem, James had not moved into the primary position of authority in the church that he would later occupy. At this time Peter still occupied the central role of authority.[10] He was the logical choice from which to gain background information on Jesus' earthly life, as well as on the early days of the church. Both Paul's and Luke's accounts agree on the significance of Peter in the early church. For Paul, this significance only grows. While Peter drops out of sight from Acts after the Jerusalem Council in chapter 15, he still is mentioned in two of Paul's letters, Galatians and 1 Corinthians.[11]

It is also important to note that Paul emphasizes strongly the point that he waited "three years" before going to Jerusalem to meet Peter. He had already been engaged in three years of preaching and missionary work before he ever had contact with the other apostles.[12] Paul made this point so strongly because he wanted to emphasize, "the independence both of his gospel and his commission to preach it."[13] Paul said in verses 16 and 17, that after his conversion, "I did not consult any man, nor did I go up to Jerusalem to see those who were apostles before I was, but I went immediately into Arabia." These three years were the formative ones for Paul's

---

Barnabas broke the ice, and representatives of the apostles responded, perhaps fearfully. Paul declared Christ in the synagogues, but the bulk of the church shunned contact with him," 249.

[8] Tenney, 76.

[9] Bornkamm, *Paul*, 28.

[10] Cullman, 41.

[11] Hengel and Schwemer, 139.

[12] L. Ann Jervis, *Galatians,* New International Biblical Commentary (Peabody, Mass.: Hendrickson, 1999) 47, Paul, "was not a neophyte but a person of some Christian maturity."

[13] Ronald Y. K. Kung, *The Epistle to the Galatians,* The New International Commentary on the New Testament (Grand Rapids: Eerdmans, 1988) 73. See also R. E. Howard, *The Epistle to the Galatians through Philemon,* Beacon Bible Commentary (Kansas City: Beacon Hill, 1965) 38, "There is no suggestion that Paul's trip to Jerusalem was for the purpose of obtaining approval or sanction of his gospel. It was simply a visit to meet Peter, the recognized leader of the Church."

message and theology. By the time he did finally visit Jerusalem, his gospel was fully developed.[14]

The word that Paul uses here for his visit with Peter is *historeo*, which can be defined as, "to ascertain by inquiry and examination; to inquire of; to visit in order to become acquainted with."[15] The word also carries with it the idea of visiting someone to get information.[16] In his commentary on Galatians, Morris defines the verb in a similar way: "to visit and survey . . . a word which those, who seek to become acquainted with great and splendid cities, apply to themselves."[17] This is the only location in the New Testament where this word appears.[18] Paul chose this word very carefully to avoid any impression that he had received instruction or input from the apostles in Jerusalem in regards to the message that he had been preaching for the last three years.[19] Tenney understands that this visit was an opportunity for Paul to interview Peter and fill in the gaps of his knowledge concerning Jesus, the church, and the message that the apostles were preaching.[20] Dunn would be in agreement with Tenney. He defines *historeo* as, "to inquire into, or about, or from."[21] He understands this visit to be an opportunity for Paul, not to have his gospel validated, but to gain information from Peter, "other than the gospel itself."[22] This idea of Paul interviewing Peter, while attractive and partially correct, does not seem to fit the meaning of *historeo*. Boice understands it to be, "the telling of a story. Paul would have told his story, Peter his. So these two leading apostles became and acquainted and encouraged each other in their forthcoming work"[23]

---

[14] Cole, 93.

[15] Harold K. Moulton, ed., *The Analytical Greek Lexicon Revised 1978 Edition* (Grand Rapids: Zondervan, 1978) 204.

[16] Frederick W. Danker, ed., *A Greek-English Lexicon of the New Testament and Other Early Christian Literature* (Chicago: University of Chicago Press, 2000) 483.

[17] Leon Morris, *Galatians: Paul's Charter of Christian Freedom* (Downers Grove, Ill.: InterVarsity, 1996) 59, no. 79. See also W. E. Vine, *Vine's Expository Commentary on Galatians* (Nashville: Thomas Nelson, 1997) 33.

[18] Friedrich Buchsel, "ιστορεω (ιοτορια)," *Theological Dictionary of the New Testament*, Volume III, ed. Gerhard Kittel, trans. and ed. Geoffrey W. Bromiley (Grand Rapids: Eerdmans, 1965) 396. See also Jervis, 47.

[19] Kung, 75.

[20] Merrill C. Tenney, *New Testament Times* (Peabody, Mass.: Hendrickson, 1965) 243.

[21] James D. G. Dunn, *Jesus, Paul and the Law: Studies in Mark and Galatians* (Louisville: Westminster John Knox, 1990) 111ff.

[22] Ibid., 118.

[23] James Montgomery Boice, *Galatians*, Zondervan NIV Bible Commentary (Grand Rapids: Zondervan, 1994) 712.

It is also significant that Paul appeared to have been Peter's house-guest for the entire fifteen days that he was in Jerusalem. Hospitality was extremely important in the early church and, "was one of the basic pre-suppositions for the coherence of various Jesus communities and for the successful work of their itinerant missionaries."[24] The very fact that Peter opened his home to Paul for that long indicates Peter's own interest in becoming more acquainted with Paul. Just as Paul had heard of Peter and knew him by reputation, so Peter had probably heard of Paul, both before and after his conversion.[25]

In dealing with these passages in Galatians and Acts, most commentators focus on the aspect of Paul going to meet and get acquainted with Peter, to gain knowledge and background information from him. While this is obviously part of the story, there is another aspect that needs to be considered. The question, "What did Paul receive in the two weeks that he was with Peter and James?," is a valid one; however, it is also appropriate to ask, "What did Peter and James receive from Paul?"[26] Paul was a scribally trained Pharisee and had an extensive background in the prophetic promises and the Law.[27] Over the previous three years, Paul had, "received through a revelation of Jesus Christ,"[28] how all the promises in the Hebrew Scriptures had been fulfilled in Christ. Hengel makes the point that through Paul's interaction with Peter and James in this account in Galatians, it is possible that Paul actually imparted more to the Jerusalem Church than he received. This early positive encounter between Paul and Peter and James would have also carried over to the Apostolic Council that occurred some years later.[29]

Holmberg also sees the two apostles sharing on an equal level in this account. He points out that in the Jewish context, when two rabbis met for the first time, they would exchange "information about doctrinal statements from their own teachers and predecessors."[30] Thus, for two weeks, they each would have discussed their own understanding of the gospel. Peter would have answered Paul's questions about Jesus' earthly life and

---

24 Hengel and Schwemer, 144.

25 Ibid., 146.

26 Ibid., 147–48.

27 Ibid., 147.

28 Galatians 1:12.

29 Hengel and Schwemer, 149, "And could not this influence [Paul's] also have affected the decision at the Apostolic Council and the freer attitude of Peter which preceded it?"

30 Bengt Holmberg, *Paul and Power* (Philadelphia: Fortress, 1978) 17. See also Jervis, 47, "The impression given is of a visit between two statesmen of equal stature who meet primarily to learn from each other."

teaching and Paul would have shared his understanding of how his message tied in with the Hebrew Scriptures.[31]

Some scholars have questioned whether or not a fifteen day visit was long enough for Paul to receive anything of substance from Peter or James.[32] As was mentioned above, however, this may be asking the wrong question. Paul may have been imparting as much information, or even more than he was receiving. Hengel also makes the point that a two-week visit is not a short visit, "as all hosts know!"[33] He makes the point that, "The duration of the hospitality indicates the intensity of the exchange."[34]

It is possible that Paul intended to stay in Jerusalem longer than he did. In his account in Galatians, he does not give a reason why he left after only fifteen days. In Luke's account, however, we are told that Paul, "talked and debated with the Grecian Jews, but they tried to kill him."[35] Luke goes on to recount how after the plot on Paul's life was uncovered some of the brothers took him down to Caesarea and put him on a ship to Tarsus.[36] This ties in with Paul's account when he says that after visiting Jerusalem, he went to Syria and Cilicia.[37]

One of the results of this visit would have been to let Peter and the other apostles know that Paul was indeed a changed man. There would have naturally still been some apprehension regarding Paul among some of the Jerusalem believers;[38] however, a two-week encounter with Peter and James would serve notice to the church that Paul's conversion was real.[39] Paul says that after this visit, the report about him got around, "'The man who formerly persecuted us is now preaching the faith that he once tried to destroy.'" And they praised God because of me."[40]

The outcome of this meeting between Peter and Paul was the appearance of a friendship or at least a working relationship between the two men.

---

[31] Holmberg, 18.

[32] Howard, 38, "And it was a brief visit- only fifteen days in contrast to the three years that had passed since his conversion. Certainly such a short time would provide little opportunity for instruction or training." See also Frank J. Goodwin, *A Harmony of the Life of St. Paul* (Grand Rapids: Baker, 1951) 27.

[33] Hengel and Schwemer, 149.

[34] Ibid., 147.

[35] Acts 9:29.

[36] Acts 9:30.

[37] Galatians 1:21.

[38] Acts 9:26.

[39] Morris, 59. See also Holmberg, 14.

[40] Galatians 1:23-24.

There is no indication from this text that there was any type of quarrel or animosity between them. Indeed, on another occasion when there was a disagreement, Paul was quick to mention it in Galatians 2.[41] It was possibly because of the relationship that was established by the two men in this account that Paul was able to admonish Peter later on.[42] There is every reason to believe that this initial meeting between Peter and Paul ended on a cordial and respectful note.[43]

Galatians 2:1-10

> Fourteen years later I went up again to Jerusalem, this time with Barnabas. I took Titus along also. I went in response to a revelation and set before them the gospel that I preach among the Gentiles. But I did this privately to those who seemed to be leaders, for fear that I was running or had run my race in vain. (Gal 2:1-2)
>
> As for those who seemed to be important—whatever they were makes no difference to me; God does not judge by external appearance—those men added nothing to my message. On the contrary, they saw that I had been entrusted with the task of preaching the gospel to the Gentiles, just as Peter had been to the Jews. For God, who was at work in the ministry of Peter as an apostle to the Jews, was also at work in my ministry as an apostle to the Gentiles. James, Peter and John, those reputed to be pillars, gave me and Barnabas the right hand of fellowship when they recognized the grace given to me. They agreed that we should go to the Gentiles, and they to the Jews. (Gal 2:6-9)

This passage in Galatians deals with many different issues, most of which could easily distract from the focus on the relationship of Peter and Paul. This passage has been treated extensively by many scholars in exploring the relationship between Paul and his message, and the Jerusalem apostles and their message.[44] The passage that was looked at from Galatians 1 and this one have also been studied extensively in order to develop a chronology of Paul's life.[45] Our examination of this passage will concentrate on the

---

[41] Bornkamm, 28.

[42] Hengel and Schwemer, 149.

[43] Hengel, *Acts and the History of Earliest Christianity*, 95, "The fact that Paul could stay with Peter in Jerusalem for fourteen days indicates that there was a fundamental readiness for understanding between the two apostles."

[44] Dunn, 108–28; E. P Sanders, *Paul, the Law, and the Jewish People* (Philadelphia: Fortress, 1983) 171ff.; Munck, *Paul and the Salvation of Mankind*, 87–134.

[45] Knox, *Chapters in a Life of Paul*, and Riesner, *Paul's Early Period: Chronology, Mission*

interaction between Paul, Peter, and some of the other Jerusalem apostles. It will briefly discuss the aspect of chronology and look at a couple of the key elements involved.

First of all, it is important to note that Paul provides a specific time-frame for the reader to work with. He says that, "Fourteen years later I went up again to Jerusalem." He does not, however, make it clear as to whether he is referring to fourteen years from his conversion or his previous visit. Few scholars are dogmatic in taking one side or the other. Munck does make a strong case that the fourteen years that Paul is speaking of here are from his previous visit which he spoke of in Galatians 1:18-19.[46] This seems to make the most sense, but in either case, whether it was fourteen or seventeen years, it had been a long time since Paul had visited Jerusalem.

Another issue concerning the chronology of this passage in Galatians is the question of whether or not it is synonymous with the Jerusalem Council that is described in Acts 15. While many scholars believe that this is the case, there is still no clear consensus.[47] The two passages are very different and many scholars see them as referring to two different events.[48] Holmberg is one scholar who understands the two passages to be referring to the same conference. While he questions the historicity of Acts in many places, in this instance he feels that Luke and Paul were describing the same conference from different viewpoints.[49] Even though Paul's account in Galatians would be considered a primary source, Holmberg stresses the need for caution because Paul was an active participant in the events that took place and definitely not an objective observer.[50]

Marshall is representative of those who do not see the conference in Acts 15 and the one described by Paul here in Galatians 2 as referring to the same event. He understands that this visit by Paul to Jerusalem to

---

Strategy, Theology are two examples.

[46] Munck, 93, He makes his case based on the fact that Paul is talking about his two visits to Jerusalem. He is emphasizing the visits, not his conversion. See also Howard, 40; He follows the same line of reasoning that Munck does.

[47] Donald Guthrie, *Galatians,* The New Century Bible Commentary (Grand Rapids: Eerdmans, 1981) 29.

[48] Munck, 100; Morris, 64; Joseph N. Sanders, "Peter and Paul in Acts," *New Testament Studies* 2 (1955) 141, Sanders argues that Paul and Barnabas were not even present at the Jerusalem Council in Acts 15. "I am inclined to think that there was a meeting of Peter, Barnabas and James, which drew up the Apostolic decree, but that Luke was mistaken in including Paul among those present."

[49] Holmberg, 19.

[50] Ibid.

be synonymous with the one that Luke referred to in Acts 11:29-30.[51] Guthrie also adopts this view, thinking that it is easier to fit Paul's account of Galatians 2:1-10 into Luke's narrative in Acts 11:29-30.[52] If this view is correct, it is much easier to deal with the differences between the account of the Jerusalem Council in Acts 15 and the meeting between Paul, Barnabas, and some of the Jerusalem apostles here in Galatians 2:1-10. They are dealing with two completely different events.[53]

Our purpose here is not to write a history of the early church or a chronology of Paul's life, but to examine the relationship that existed between Peter and Paul.[54] It will focus attention on the passage at hand and treat Acts 15 later in the study. As has been mentioned, scholars are divided about where Galatians 2:1-10 fits in with Luke's chronology. That issue will not be resolved in this book. This passage will, however, tell us what Paul said about his trip to Jerusalem, as well as tell us what he says about his encounter with Peter while he was there.

One of the first things that can be seen about Paul's trip to Jerusalem in Galatians 2 is how different it was from his trip in Galatians 1. In Galatians 1, he went to Jerusalem, "to get acquainted with Peter." It appears that on his first trip Paul was traveling by himself. On this trip, however, Paul was traveling with Barnabas and Titus. Paul says that the reason for this second trip was, "in response to a revelation." Paul goes on to say that he, "set before them the gospel that I preach among the Gentiles. But I did this privately to those who seemed to be leaders . . ." So, while Paul's first trip was informal and involved just him and Peter and James, this trip appears to be much more formal.[55] Paul does not tell the reader what the revelation was that prompted this trip.[56] In verse 2, Paul only

---

[51] Marshall, 205.

[52] Guthrie, 32–33.

[53] Ibid., 245.

[54] W. M. Ramsay, *Historical Commentary on Galatians*, ed. Mark Wilson (Grand Rapids: Kregel, 1997) 48, "For a historian it would be necessary to add details that Paul did not need for his purpose, but which Luke thought necessary for his history. Each had to omit much from his brief account."

[55] Charles B. Cousar, *Galatians*, Interpretation: A Bible Commentary for Preaching and Teaching (Atlanta: John Knox, 1982) 14.

[56] Jervis, 51, She sees the idea of "revelation" here as having a two-fold meaning. First of all, Paul was aligning himself with the Galatian Christians. "Pagan people understand reference to revelation as an important part of the prophet's or religious person's credibility." Paul's reference to revelation also stresses his independence from the Jerusalem church. "Paul went up to Jerusalem in a position of strength, as one acting in response to divine instructions."

stated that he met with those, "who seemed to be leaders." In verse 9, he will identify these leaders as James, Peter, and John.

While this account in Galatians was not written by Paul to explain his relationship with Peter, he does provide a few clues as to how he perceived that relationship. One of the first clues that can be seen is in the tone of the passage. There is no evidence of animosity or conflict in Paul's writing. In fact, by the very act of going to Jerusalem to meet with some of the apostles regarding the gospel that he was preaching, two very important things about Paul can be seen. First of all, this visit showed a high level of respect for the Jerusalem apostles.[57] The phrase that Paul uses in referring to them, "those who seemed to be leaders," has been seen by some to be disrespectful and disparaging. According to Dunn, the phrase is neutral and can be interpreted in different ways. He says that, here, Paul is using it as an acknowledgement of, "the high standing in which the pillar apostles were held (by others), without constituting an endorsement by Paul himself."[58] Morris, however, understands that what Paul is saying is that he selected those apostles who appeared to be the most "significant leaders and laid his case before them."[59] Paul seems to be acknowledging the Jerusalem apostles in a respectful way, while at the same time, still maintaining his own independence from them. Paul is also careful not to establish any type of superiority over Peter, James, and John.[60]

Another phrase that Paul used in describing James, Peter, and John is in verse 9 where he refers to them as, "those reputed to be pillars." This is another place in which Paul could be interpreted as being sarcastic and disrespectful. Morris acknowledges that the phrase, "is not exactly cordial."[61] Guthrie, however, makes the point that what Paul is doing here is using the language of his opponents. "They were apparently drawing a distinction between Paul and the 'pillars.' The 'pillars' were held in repute, but by implication Paul was not."[62] Paul never attempts to downplay the authority of the Jerusalem apostles. What he does do, however, is to make the case that his own apostolic authority is just as valid as theirs is.

---

[57] Ibid., 52.

[58] Dunn, 114.

[59] Morris, 66. See also Vine, 40, "So, here; the apostle recognizes, alike by his actions and in his words, that James, Cephas, and John were what they were reputed in the church at Jerusalem to be, its responsible rulers and guides."

[60] Ramsay, *St. Paul the Traveller and the Roman Citizen*, 57.

[61] Morris, 74.

[62] Guthrie, 10.

Paul wants his readers to understand that it is not merely one's external appearance or one's background that makes someone an apostle. This is what he says in verse 6, "God does not judge by external appearance." The call of God and then the signs and deeds of an apostle must be present in someone's life if they are a true apostle.[63] In no way does Paul disparage the apostleship of the three that he meets with. At every point he seems to hold them in high esteem. His only concern is that his apostleship and equality with them also be acknowledged.

Paul makes it clear that this meeting with James, Peter, and John was a private one. The subject matter that Paul needed to discuss with them was very sensitive, as well as controversial, and it would not have been appropriate for this discussion to take place in a public forum.[64] This private meeting with some of the leading Jerusalem apostles shows that Paul regarded their opinions and input as valuable and also implies some measure of trust that they would be understanding and willing to listen to Paul with open minds. Ramsay understands that this was a formal visit that was very important for the future of the church. At the same time, however, it was a meeting of friends who shared a mutual respect for each other's calling and ministry.[65] This does not mean that there were never differences of opinion, as will be seen when Galatians 2:11-14 is examined. It does mean, however, that there could still be a basic unity and harmony between Paul and the Jerusalem apostles, even though they may not have agreed on every item of doctrine.[66]

The second thing that is observed in this visit of Paul to Jerusalem is his desire for unity in the church. It was never Paul's desire to see two churches coexisting, one for the Jews and another for the Gentiles.[67] This conviction that he had that there was only one church may have been one of the driving forces that brought him to Jerusalem for this meeting.[68] It appears that Paul was the one who made the effort to initiate this meeting with the Jerusalem apostles so that he could, "set before them the gospel

---

[63] Cousar, 40–41. See also André Lemaire, "The Ministries in the New Testament," *Biblical Theology Bulletin* 3 (1973) 143, ". . . an emphasis was placed on successful missionary activity, which was probably confirmed by 'signs of an apostle,' powerful preaching and proof of authority."

[64] Morris, 66.

[65] Ramsay, *Historical Commentary on Galatians*, 58.

[66] Munck, 102.

[67] This message of only one church is emphasized repeatedly by Paul in his other letters. See Eph 2:14-22 and Romans 9–11 for two examples.

[68] Cousar, 39, "This very conviction pushes him all the harder for understanding and solidarity with the Jerusalem leaders. He has no interest in starting a new cult."

that I preach among the Gentiles." Cousar believes that he would have gone to Jerusalem, "with a certain amount of apprehension about whether the leadership there is really subject to the gospel and whether the unity of the church can be maintained."[69]

As it turned out, Paul did not have anything to worry about. The unity of the church did not break down and agreements were reached that would have far-reaching consequences for the church.[70] The result of the meeting was that a division of labor was established. Paul would continue his ministry to the Gentile world while Peter and the Jerusalem apostles would continue their ministry to the Jewish world. In making this delineation among mission fields, the Jerusalem apostles acknowledged and validated both Paul's calling and his message.[71] He said that they, "added nothing to my message. On the contrary, they saw that I had been entrusted with the task of preaching the gospel to the Gentiles, just as Peter had been to the Jews."

Paul goes on to say that at the conclusion of the meeting James, Peter, and John gave him and Barnabas, "the right hand of fellowship." After an agreement was reached, all of the men shook hands on it. This was a pledge of friendship and agreement.[72] Guthrie points out that, "Then as now refusal to shake hands would have been regarded as an open testimony to disunity."[73] The shaking of hands by all of the apostles symbolized the unity of the fellowship that they shared.[74]

The conclusion that can be drawn from this passage is that the meeting described in Galatians 2:1-10 ends on a positive and friendly note. There is no indication of disunity or animosity between Paul and the Jerusalem leaders. On the contrary, Paul goes to great lengths to show that he and James, Peter, and John were all unified in the gospel that they preached as well as in the demarcations of their respective mission fields. They shook hands and parted as friends.

---

[69] Ibid., 39.

[70] Bornkamm, 31.

[71] Cousar, 44, This, "did not mean two gospels or even two separate territories of mission but rather a mutual recognition of the work of the other—a viable ecumenical endeavor."

[72] Howard, 44. See also Cole, 110, and Morris, 74.

[73] Guthrie, 83.

[74] Vine, 49–50.

Galatians 2:11-14

> When Peter came to Antioch, I opposed him to his face, because he
> was clearly in the wrong. Before certain men came from James, he
> used to eat with the Gentiles. But when they arrived, he began to
> draw back and separate himself from the Gentiles because he was
> afraid of those who belonged to the circumcision group. The other
> Jews joined him in his hypocrisy, so that by their hypocrisy even
> Barnabas was led astray. When I saw they were not acting in line
> with the truth of the gospel, I said to Peter in front of them all, "You
> are a Jew, yet you live like a Gentile and not like a Jew. How is it,
> then, that you force Gentiles to follow Jewish customs?"

The previous two meetings with Peter had ended on a positive note as far
as Paul was concerned.[75] This passage, however, details a confrontation between the two men in Antioch. The chronology poses a problem because
Paul does not tell us when this incident took place.[76] Scholars are divided
over where to place this encounter when developing a chronology of Paul's
life. For our purposes, it is not necessary to conduct an exhaustive study
to determine the timeframe for this passage. The most important elements
that concern the chronology will be briefly touched on.

One of the first issues that needs to be discussed is whether or not the
incident in Galatians 2:11-14 followed the meeting in Galatians 2:1-10 in
chronological order. According to Guthrie, there is no reason to assume
that the confrontation in Antioch followed the meeting in Jerusalem. He
believes that the incident took place at an earlier time. Paul recalls the
incident here to contrast Peter's previous behavior with the decision that
had been recently reached between him and the Jerusalem apostles. This
decision included Peter.[77] Guthrie makes the point that the reason that
Paul even mentioned this personal confrontation with Peter was not to
belittle or put him down in any way, but to establish the fact that Paul's
own apostolic authority was equal to that of even the most eminent of the
apostles.[78] Munck follows the same line of reasoning. Paul is not trying to
establish a chronology here. He places it, "last as the clearest proof of Paul's
independence."[79]

---

[75] David R. Catchpole, "Paul, James and the Apostolic Decree," *New Testament Studies* 23
(1977) 439.

[76] Cole, 114, "Unfortunately, we have no idea when or why Peter visited Antioch."

[77] Guthrie, 84.

[78] Ibid.

[79] Munck, 102.

Other scholars would place the encounter between Peter and Paul in Antioch after the Jerusalem Council in Acts 15.[80] Some think that the incident took place before the Jerusalem Council and may have even played some part in the conflict that led to the council.[81] While it may be difficult to establish exactly when this confrontation took place, the dynamics of it can be examined in the context of the relationship between Peter and Paul.

In describing the incident, Paul indicated that before the confrontation Peter had come to Antioch and participated in table-fellowship with the mixed church there. There is no reason provided for Peter's visit to Antioch. A contrast could be drawn here to Paul's visit to Jerusalem when he was Peter's guest for two weeks.[82] Could this have been a friendly visit in which Paul was repaying Peter's hospitality from those early years? The fact that Peter had gone to Antioch while Paul was presumably still ministering there with Barnabas indicates that the two apostles had maintained some type of a relationship over the years.

This visit by Peter to Antioch has also been speculated to be an official visit from a representative of the Jerusalem apostles. In the same way that he and John were sent to Samaria in Acts 8 to confirm the work of Philip and pray for the believers to be filled with the Holy Spirit, so Peter was sent to Antioch to confirm the work there.[83] There is no indication in Galatians or Acts, however, that this was the case. Paul does not provide any hint that Peter came to Antioch to confirm the work that he and Barnabas had been involved in for some time. In fact, according to Luke, Barnabas was the one who was originally sent to Antioch by the Jerusalem apostles.[84] Ramsay also refutes any hint that Peter went to Antioch to confirm or oversee the work there.[85]

It has also been speculated that this visit by Peter to Antioch corresponded with Acts 12:17 where, after being delivered from prison by an angel, "he left for another place." Luke gives no hint as to where this other

---

[80] Ibid., 74; See also Hiebert, *An Introduction to the New Testament,* Volume Two: *The Pauline Epistles* (Chicago: Moody, 1977) 86; F. F. Bruce, *Peter, Stephen, James and John: Studies in Non-Pauline Christianity* (Grand Rapids: Eerdmans, 1979) 34.

[81] Dunn, 153; Holmberg, 32; Ramsay, *St. Paul the Traveller and the Roman Citizen,* 162.

[82] Galatians 1:18.

[83] Cullman, 54.

[84] Acts 11:22.

[85] Ramsay, 166, "Peter's visit to Antioch was not of the same character as his visits to Samaria and other Churches at an earlier time, in which he was giving the Apostolic approval to the congregations established there."

place might have been and Antioch is as good a guess as any.[86] Packer believes that this would have been the logical opportunity for Peter to make a missionary tour through Asia Minor, including a visit to the church in Antioch.[87] Marshall also believes that Peter's leaving "for another place," was the time when he visited Antioch. For Luke, however, the detail of where Peter went was not important to his story, so he did not include it.[88]

Unlike Galatians 1:18 in which Paul told the reader how long he was with Peter in Jerusalem, there is no indication given here as to how long Peter stayed in Antioch. The only information that Paul provides about Peter's activities in Antioch was that he had participated in table-fellowship with some of the Gentile believers.[89] The word that Paul uses here for "to eat" is *synesthio*. This word implies a close fellowship and association.[90] It conveys the idea of table-fellowship, not just the eating of a meal together.[91] Jervis points out Paul uses the word in the progressive tense, suggesting that, "it was over a period of time that Peter joined Gentiles for meals."[92] Vine understands that this would have been Peter's practice since the incident with Cornelius in Acts 10.[93] Since that time, Peter had had no scruples about taking meals with Gentiles.

The type of meals that Paul is referring to here seems to be the common meal that the believers shared together as part of their fellowship.[94] While there is no indication that this meal included the Lord's Supper, that possibility also cannot be ruled out. A celebration of the Lord's Supper was an integral part of the early church and was probably included when the Galatian believers shared a meal together.[95]

The next thing that Paul relates about Peter's time in Antioch is the fact that after, "certain men came from James . . . he began to draw back and separate himself from the Gentiles." After some period of time in which

---

[86] Robert E. Osborne, "Where Did Peter Go?," *Canadian Journal of Theology* 14 (1968) 274; Charles F. Nesbitt, "What Did Become of Peter?," *Journal of Bible and Religion* 27 (1959) 12.

[87] J. W. Packer, *The Acts of the Apostles,* The Cambridge Bible Commentary (Cambridge: Cambridge University Press, 1966) 98.

[88] Marshall, 211.

[89] Galatians 2:12.

[90] Moulton, 388. This word is used in similar contexts in Luke 15:2 and 1 Corinthians 5:11.

[91] Johannes Behm, "εσθιω," *Theological Dictionary of the New Testament,* 2: 693.

[92] Jervis, 62.

[93] Vine, 55.

[94] Jervis, 62.

[95] Cole, 115.

Peter participated in table-fellowship with the Gentile Christians, he began to draw back and distance himself from them after the arrival of some Jewish Christians from Jerusalem. Peter's influence evidently caused the other Jewish Christians in the church in Antioch, including Barnabas, to also draw back from the Gentile Christians. It is easy to see how this would have torn at the foundation of the church in Antioch. Bruce understands the human aspect of the results of Peter's and the other Jewish Christians' behavior. It would have been a devastating blow to the Gentile Christians.[96] Guthrie adds to this thought when he says, "separation among brethren is not only lamentable but always causes embarrassment to the whole movement."[97] The message that Peter was sending to the Gentile Christians, whether it was intentional or not, was that they were not on the same level with the Jewish Christians and that something was lacking in their faith.[98]

It is commonly accepted that this incident took place a number of years after Peter's encounter with the Gentile Cornelius in Acts 10. In that incident Peter was given a vision from God to show him that he should not hesitate to go to Cornelius' house. After Peter preached and the Gentiles there received the gospel, Peter stayed with them for a few days.[99] Peter then had to defend his actions to the Jewish Christians in Jerusalem. Their criticism of him is contained in Acts 11:3, "You went into the house of uncircumcised men and ate with them." After Peter explained his actions in light of the vision he had received and the fact of the Holy Spirit coming on the Gentiles, the Jerusalem believers concluded, "So, then, God has granted even the Gentiles repentance unto life."[100]

The incident with Cornelius and the one at Antioch in Galatians 2:11-14 are both very similar. The question that naturally arises is why would Peter have felt a need to distance himself from the Gentile believers in Antioch after his experience with Cornelius? The most likely reason, according to Cousar, is that there was a wave of intense nationalism that was sweeping through the Jews in Palestine at this time.[101] Word

---

[96] Bruce, 34–35, "They must have felt themselves relegated to the status of second-class citizens in the church, with no hope of attaining first-class citizenship except by submitting to circumcision." See also Bruce, *Paul: Apostle of the Heart Set Free* (Grand Rapids: Eerdmans, 1977) 177–78.

[97] Guthrie, 85.

[98] Cole, 118–19.

[99] Acts 10:48.

[100] Acts 11:18.

[101] Cousar, 47. See also Cole, 116–17, Cole also feels that this incident might have been driven by an increase in the activity of the Zealots, who indirectly may have been putting pressure on the church in Jerusalem to avoid contact with Gentiles.

of Peter's willingness to embrace the Gentile believers had gotten back to Jerusalem and James was concerned enough to send some brothers, "to inform him of the possible repercussions for his Christian brothers and sisters in Jerusalem."[102] If this was the case, then Peter's abandonment of the common meals was, "based on a concern for the unity and peace of the church, at least the unity and peace of the Antioch and Jerusalem congregations."[103]

Whatever Peter's motives were for drawing back from fellowshipping with the Gentile Christians, Paul's analysis of the situation was that Peter, "was afraid of those who belonged to the circumcision group."[104] The question that should then be asked is, "Is this a fair assessment of Peter's personality?" Because Peter is mentioned in all four of the Gospels, as well as in Acts, we are better able to get a complete picture of his personality than many of the other figures found in the New Testament. In the Gospels, he is shown on occasion to be inconsistent in his behavior.[105] One example is found in Matthew 16:16-23, where right after Peter acknowledges Jesus as the Messiah, he rebukes Jesus for teaching about His coming death, and in turn gets rebuked by Jesus. It could be argued that the reason that Peter rebuked Jesus was out of his fear of losing Him. Peter also demonstrated the characteristic of fear after Jesus was arrested. Just prior to this he had boldly stated his devotion to Jesus, saying that he was willing to die for Him. Soon afterwards, however, he denied repeatedly that he even knew Jesus. Based on these two examples from earlier in Peter's life, it is likely that Paul's assessment of Peter is accurate and that he was afraid of the repercussions that would have occurred if he had continued to eat with the Gentile Christians.

The position that Peter occupied in the Jerusalem Church was in many ways a much more difficult position than the one Paul occupied in Antioch.[106] Peter possibly felt that if word got back to Jerusalem, "that he was eating with Gentiles it would compromise his position with the leading church."[107] There was probably also concern that Peter's behavior would leave the church in Jerusalem open to persecution by militant Jews. So, while Peter may have been operating out of fear, Cousar points out that he probably felt that he was doing the right thing. Paul understood this and,

---

[102] Ibid.

[103] Ibid.

[104] Galatians 2:12.

[105] Morris, 79. See also Cullman, 53.

[106] Ibid.

[107] Morris, 79.

"his concern is not that Peter is insincere but that he is *very* sincere and is blind to the full import of his actions."[108][author's italics] Paul understood the long-term ramifications of Peter's behavior. There is no indication that Peter was preaching a salvation by "works of the law" message in Antioch. Paul, however, understands that Peter's actions will lead to a theology of salvation by works, whether Peter intended it or not.[109]

It is important to note that when Paul confronted Peter about his actions, the confrontation was based on principle. This confrontation does not appear to be a personality conflict or a power-struggle in which Paul was trying to establish his own authority as an apostle. Paul does not appear to be attempting to downplay the authority of Peter.[110] In fact, Paul has already established his apostolic authority in Galatians 1 and 2:1-10, and he willingly acknowledged the authority of the Jerusalem apostles. When he challenged Peter, it was because Peter was in the wrong and needed to be challenged. Peter had violated a fundamental truth of the gospel that he and the Jerusalem apostles had agreed on. Peter's position as a leading apostle made his indiscretion even more serious because he influenced others to join him in separating from the Gentile believers.[111]

As Paul describes this incident, he lays all of the blame on Peter, saying, "he was clearly in the wrong." The NASB translates it as, "he stood condemned." While this sounds like a harsh judgment against Peter, Paul understood, much more clearly than Peter, the damage that he had done. As Cole says, Peter, "was acting not only against his conscience and against the clear revelation that he had received in Acts 10, but also against his past tradition and custom in Antioch."[112] Paul must have known of the vision that God had given to Peter and how it led him to Cornelius' house. Paul must have also known how Peter had defended his actions in Acts 11. Paul had seen, with his own eyes, Peter enjoying table-fellowship with the Gentile Christians in Antioch. There was no way that he was going to let Peter's hypocrisy go unchallenged.

It is significant that Paul states that he confronted Peter, "in front of them all," implying that the rebuke took place before the whole church.

---

[108] Cousar, 49.

[109] Ibid., 48.

[110] K. P. Donfried and J. A. Fitzmyer, "Peter in the Pauline Letters," in *Peter in the New Testament*, eds. Raymond E. Brown et al. (Minneapolis: Augsburg, 1973) 30. See also Cousar, 48, "The conflict with Peter, as far as Paul is concerned, is essentially a theological one. Paul gives no indication of a power-struggle between warring factions in the early church—Jerusalem on the one side and Paul and the Gentiles on the other."

[111] Ibid.

[112] Cole, 115.

Paul's understanding of the seriousness of Peter's sin precluded a private rebuke. His actions had presumably affected the entire church so the rebuke took place before the entire church.[113] This contrasts with the earlier contacts that Paul had with Peter. In Galatians 1:18-19, Paul had private meetings with Peter and James. In Galatians 2:1-10, Paul and Barnabas met privately with James, Peter, and John to lay the gospel that they were preaching before them. In this encounter in Antioch, however, Paul understood that there was too much at stake to try and rebuke Peter privately. It had to be done in a public meeting so that Paul could reemphasize to the entire church that the Gentiles did not have to obey the Law to become Christians.[114] In a very real sense, in rebuking Peter publicly, Paul was trying to undo some of the damage that he had done.

In examining the rebuke itself, Pheme Perkins has studied it in the light of the art of ancient rhetoric.[115] Paul occupied the place of the true philosopher, whose only regard was for the truth and not public opinion. In this instance in Antioch, "the philosopher is like a physician whose only concern is to heal the soul of his audience."[116] Peter's role was that of the, "honorable opponent who will be in danger of falling into vice without [Paul's] intervention."[117] In rebuking Peter, Paul was not attacking him but attempting to correct his behavior in front of all so that the entire community could be healed of the hurt that they had experienced.

The passage follows the rhetorical convention of showing that the speaker, Paul, "has demonstrated courage, integrity, and good will toward the audience by maintaining the truth against extraordinary odds."[118] Paul has made it clear that he was the one that stood up for the truth and stood against those who did not. He contrasts himself with Peter, who he shows to be weak, inconsistent, and hypocritical. "The picture of Peter is deliberately unflattering because Paul wishes to demonstrate the probity of his own character by contrast."[119]

---

[113] Vine, 56, "Peter's conduct had been seen by all, and by introducing a caste system into the church it was likely to have far-reaching and mischievous consequences. Hence, the public remonstrance."

[114] Galatians 2:15-21.

[115] Pheme Perkins, *Peter: Apostle for the Whole Church* (Minneapolis: Fortress, 2000) 115–18.

[116] Ibid., 115.

[117] Ibid.

[118] Ibid., 116.

[119] Ibid., 117–18.

The rhetorical argument that Paul has constructed here is designed to support the two actions he wishes his audience to take.[120] First of all, Paul wants the Galatians to understand that adopting the Jewish Law and the Jewish way of life is contrary to and incompatible with the gospel that he delivered to them. The second thing that Paul wants the Galatians to do is to expel those who are creating and stirring up conflict in their community by teaching and encouraging this type of lifestyle.

A final issue in regards to Paul's confrontation with Peter needs to be mentioned: the aftermath. A few questions still remain and need to be discussed. Was the rebuke successful? Did the confrontation affect Paul's relationship with the Antioch Church? Did the confrontation with Peter affect Paul's relationship with the Jerusalem Church? And finally, after the smoke had cleared, were Paul and Peter still friends?

First of all, in response to whether or not the rebuke was successful, scholars are divided in their opinions. Dunn states, "Our findings strengthen the probability that Paul's rebuke of Peter at Antioch was unsuccessful."[121] He gives three reasons to support his statement.[122] First of all, he thinks that it is likely that Paul would have mentioned it if Peter had given in and acknowledged that Paul was right. A second thing that Dunn points out is the idea that if Peter truly believed that he was doing the right thing by separating himself from the Gentile believers, the less likely he would have been to change his mind. The third reason that makes Dunn think that Paul was unsuccessful is that he believes that Peter would never have agreed with Paul that their common belief in justification by faith was in danger of being compromised. In Peter's mind, there were two separate issues here and Paul was blowing the one that involved table-fellowship between Jews and Gentiles out of proportion.

Dunn also understands that Paul's failure to change Peter's mind and correct the situation in Antioch had a negative impact on his relationship with the church there. "In short, as a result of the Antioch incident, Paul became an independent missionary."[123] He bases this on the fact that from here on out, the Acts account shows Paul spending very little time in Antioch, but settling for lengthy periods of time in Corinth and Ephesus. If Dunn is correct, then the incident with Peter did have a negative affect on Paul's relationship with the church in Antioch.[124]

---

[120] Ibid., 118.

[121] Dunn, 160.

[122] Ibid.

[123] Ibid., 161.

[124] Holmberg, 34, "The break with Barnabas and the Jewish Christian part of the

Another scholar who believes that Paul's rebuke of Peter was unsuccessful is Michael Goulder. He states that Paul, "lost the Antioch church to Peter and the others . . ."[125] Goulder believes that the Jewish influence in the Antioch Church was much more powerful than that of the Gentile Christians. Hence, when it came time to pick sides, Peter had more people that sided with him than with those that sided with Paul.[126]

On the other side of the debate, there are those who feel that Paul's rebuke of Peter was successful. Ramsay, for example, says, "Obviously, the rebuke which Paul gave must have been successful in the case of Peter and Barnabas."[127] Ramsay bases his belief on a study of the text itself in Galatians. The whole force of Paul's argument to the Galatians would have been nullified if he had not been successful. Ramsay also points out that Peter's behavior at the Jerusalem Conference is evidence that Paul's rebuke had worked. The words that Peter uses in Acts 15 to champion the cause of a Law-free gospel are very similar to the words that Paul shared with him in Galatians 2.[128] Peter seems to be reiterating the message that Paul preached to him.

Bruce also believes that Paul's rebuke of Peter was successful. He points out that Peter was much more conservative than Paul, yet he was still in basic agreement with him.[129] Bruce states that the fact that no more is heard of the incident is proof that Peter accepted the rebuke and did not continue that type of behavior.[130] If this is the case, there is no reason to assume that Paul's relationship with the church at Antioch was damaged. Even though Acts does show Paul spending more time away from Antioch, this probably has more to do with his own sense of calling than any type of tension in the church where he had spent so many years.

Another issue that needs to be raised is the question of how this incident affected Paul's relationship with the church at Jerusalem. This is not an issue that Paul deals with in any depth in his letters. Acts does give some hint of the tension between him and the Jerusalem Church in chapter 21 in describing an incident that took place several years later. Luke says in

Antiochene church effected a separation between the parties, at first theological, and then also geographical. After the Antioch Incident we see Paul emerging as an independent missionary and apostle, striking out far west into areas wholly his 'own.'"

125 Goulder, 9.

126 Ibid., 3.

127 Ramsay, 161.

128 Ibid., 162.

129 Bruce, 178.

130 F. F. Bruce, *The Spreading Flame: The Rise and Progress of Christ*ianity (Grand Rapids: Eerdmans, 1954) 122.

verse 17, "When we arrived at Jerusalem, the brothers received us warmly." However in verses 20-24 the tone changes somewhat as James speaks to Paul:

> You see, brother, how many thousands of Jews have believed, and all of them are zealous for the law. They have been informed that you teach all the Jews who live among the Gentiles to turn away from Moses, telling them not to circumcise their children or live according to our customs. What shall we do? They will certainly hear that you have come, so do what we tell you. There are four men with us who have made a vow. Take these men, join in their purification rites and pay their expenses, so that they can have their heads shaved. Then everybody will know there is no truth in these reports about you, but that you yourself are living in obedience to the law.

Chronologically, the incident described here in Acts takes place about ten years after the incident in Antioch.[131] While this passage does not show a serious conflict with the leaders of the Jerusalem Church, it does indicate that Paul has been misunderstood and misrepresented to the Jewish believers there. This passage shows the Jerusalem leaders going to great lengths to make Paul "presentable" to the Jewish community. Paul did not hesitate to do what James asked him to do to show his devotion to Judaism and keep the church unified. "He himself was happy to conform to Jewish customs when he found himself in Jewish society."[132] Paul said himself, "To the Jews I became like a Jew, to win the Jews. To those under the law I became as one under the law (though I myself am not under the law), so as to win those under the law."[133] It is interesting, however, in the name of wanting to appease the Jerusalem Church, that Paul should have to *do* something to prove his own zeal for the law.[134]

After Paul's arrest, there is no evidence that James or any of the other leaders attempted to intervene on Paul's behalf. There is no indication that they attempted to help Paul in any way when the mob attempted to kill him or while he was in Roman custody. If this is the case, it does not present a very flattering picture of James or the rest of the Jewish-Christian leadership.[135] The conclusions that could be drawn from this narrative are

---

[131] E. M. Blaiklock, *The Acts of the Apostles: An Historical Commentary*, Tyndale New Testament Commentaries (Grand Rapids: Eerdmans, 1976) 171.

[132] Bruce, *The Book of the Acts*, 406.

[133] 1 Corinthians 9:20.

[134] Packer, 177.

[135] Stagg, 222.

that the leadership of the church in Jerusalem was weak, scared, or glad that Paul was out of the picture.

The last issue that will be mentioned in regards to Galatians 2:11-14 is how the incident affected the relationship between Peter and Paul. There is no evidence from Paul to indicate that he maintained any animosity towards Peter after their confrontation. In fact, in the next section it will be seen that Paul mentions Peter again at a later time in his first letter to the Corinthians and has nothing bad to say about him. Munck concludes, "that in spite of the clash at Antioch there was no permanent discord between him and the Jerusalem leaders."[136] The Tübingen School was already mentioned in chapter 1. Their theory that there was, in fact, a permanent rift between Peter and Paul, as well as their followers was discussed.[137] Based on the text itself, however, there is nothing in Galatians to demonstrate a permanent break between Peter and Paul. As Hengel points out, it was probably because of the relationship that the two men had established early on that allowed Paul to correct Peter when he believed that he was in error.[138] True friendship will occasionally have these types of encounters.

1 Corinthians 1:10-12 and 3:21-23

> I appeal to you, brothers, in the name of our Lord Jesus Christ, that all of you agree with one another so that there may be no divisions among you and that you may be perfectly united in mind and thought. My brothers, some from Chloe's household have informed me that there are quarrels among you. What I mean is this: One of you says, "I follow Paul;" another, "I follow Apollos;" another, "I follow Cephas;" still another, "I follow Christ."

> So then, no more boasting about men! All things are yours, whether Paul or Apollos or Cephas or the world or life or death or the present or the future- all are yours, and you are of Christ, Christ is of God.

As Paul wrote this letter to the Corinthian Church, he was responding to problems that he had been made aware of and to questions from the Corinthian believers themselves. The first issue that he speaks to is that of factions or divisions that have arisen in the church. One of the main themes of 1 Corinthians is the importance of unity in the church. This

---

[136] Munck, 87.

[137] See chapter 1.

[138] Hengel and Schwemer, 149.

lack of unity was actually responsible for most of the problems that Paul addressed.[139]

Scholars are divided over how deep these divisions in the Corinthian Church went. Baur would be the most extreme in his understanding of this passage. In fact, he believed that the differences that are alluded to here could be narrowed down from Paul, Apollos, Peter, and Christ, to be just between Paul and Peter. As was mentioned in chapter 1, Baur thought that this passage hinted at a much deeper division in the early church than is commonly accepted.[140]

There are a number of others who do understand the problem that Paul was dealing with here to be competing parties within the church. This "party spirit" would create political turmoil within the church. Reed, for example, sees these parties that had aligned themselves with Paul, Peter, Apollos, or Christ to have different emphases in their doctrine.[141] This does not mean that the apostles themselves were divided. "Their differences actually formed a greater unity of the gospel beyond any one of them."[142] The people in Corinth, however, who identified themselves in one of these groups apparently made the differences in emphasis the basis for division and exclusion. Because each of these different groups believed that they were in the "right" group and that their opinions were the only correct ones there was little or no tolerance for those in any of the other groups.[143]

There is another approach to this problem in Corinth that does not place as much of an emphasis on organized divisions in the church there. In the text itself, Paul seems to be saying that they are acting as individuals when they are aligning themselves with a certain teacher. The NASB translates it, "each one of you is saying, 'I am of Paul,'" etc. According to this view, the members of the church were speaking only for themselves and not using "we" to indicate any type of formal group.[144] Munck does

---

[139] Craig Blomberg, *1 Corinthians,* The NIV Application Commentary, edited by Terry Muck (Grand Rapids: Zondervan, 1994) 42.

[140] Munck, 135–36.

[141] Oscar F. Reed, *Corinthians,* Beacon Bible Expositions, Volume 7 (Kansas City: Beacon Hill, 1976) 31.

[142] Ibid.

[143] French L. Arrington, *Divine Order in the Church: A Study of 1 Corinthians* (Grand Rapids: Baker, 1978) 24.

[144] Marion L. Soards, *1 Corinthians,* New International Biblical Commentary (Peabody, Mass.: Hendrickson, 1999) 33, "This shows us that, despite the suggestion of many scholars, there are not formal parties or fixed divisions in the church. Paul's report does not create the image of clusters or clear factions that are set over against one another. Rather, we see a congregation in which its members are in general turmoil."

not believe that Paul was combating organized factions in Corinth. He understands that it is simply, "divisions among church members for non-theological reasons."[145] His understanding is that the individual members aligned themselves with Peter, Paul, Apollo, or Christ. This was the reason that the Corinthian believers were divided. They all were attempting to follow a different leader.

As these verses are examined in an attempt to glean something of the relationship between Peter and Paul, the first thing that will be mentioned is Peter's relationship with the Corinthian Church. Acts informs the reader that Paul founded the church in Corinth and spent at least a year and a half there.[146] Acts 19:1 indicates that Apollos also spent some time in Corinth. There is no indication given in Acts as to whether or not Peter ever visited Corinth.[147] If he had been to Corinth at some point, the basis for some of the members' alliance to him would have been personal.[148] If Peter had not been to Corinth there were still sufficient reasons for his popularity there. First of all, Peter was an older Christian than Paul and had been the leader of the original Twelve Apostles.[149] This type of credential alone would carry much weight with both the Jewish and the Gentile Christians. Peter had actually been with Jesus while Paul had not.

A second reason for Peter's popularity in Corinth may also be because he would have appealed to the lower class members of the church.[150] Both Paul and Apollos were highly educated. Peter, however, had a background as a working man, being called to follow Jesus and leave his occupation of fishing behind. Peter had had no formal religious training (Acts 4:13) and would have appealed to those with a similar background in Corinth.

A third reason for Peter's popularity in Corinth may have had to do with the fact that he represented "Jewish Christianity" at its best. The Jewish Christians in Corinth may have felt the most comfortable with Peter's style of Christianity.[151] This seems to imply that there were a significant number

---

[145] Munck, 138–39, He goes on to say, "Paul therefore describes the conditions that he is combating not as factions but as bickerings, arising because the individual church members profess as their teacher Paul, Apollos, Cephas, or Christ, and exclude the others."

[146] Acts 18:1-19.

[147] Leon Morris, *1 Corinthians,* Tyndale New Testament Commentaries (Grand Rapids: Eerdmans, 1958) 40.

[148] Ibid. See also Asa Boyd Luter, Jr., "A New Testament Theology of Discipling," Th. D. diss., Dallas Theological Seminary, 1985, 156–57, Luter feels that Peter's evident popularity in Corinth would have been the result of a personal visit.

[149] Ibid.

[150] G. Coleman Luck, *First Corinthians* (Chicago: Moody, 1958) 17.

[151] Ibid.

of Jews in the church in Corinth who were eager to maintain their Jewish traditions.[152]

As these passages in 1 Corinthians 1 and 3 are examined, it is important to note that there is no hint of rebuke from Paul towards Apollos or Peter. If they had been responsible for developing or cultivating these divisions in any way Paul would have surely mentioned it. As Paul demonstrated in Galatians 2:11-14, he was not afraid to confront someone when he felt they were in the wrong. As it is, here in 1 Corinthians, Paul understands that the blame does not lie with Apollos or Peter, but with the Corinthian believers themselves. They are the ones that Paul holds responsible for these divisions.

Not only is there no word of rebuke from Paul to Apollos or Peter, Paul implies very strongly that they, unlike the Corinthian believers, are united. Paul says in 1 Corinthians 3:8-9, "The man who plants and the man who waters have one purpose, and each will be rewarded according to his own labor. For we are God's fellow workers . . ." As Blomberg says, "there is little evidence that Paul, Peter, and Apollos were themselves at odds with one another at this point."[153]

The safest conclusion that can be drawn from this passage is that Paul still maintained a respectful attitude towards Peter. Paul has no reservations about linking his own name with that of Peter and understood, as well as accepted, that Peter did occupy a very important place in the lives of many of the Corinthian believers. Peter's popularity in a church that was founded by Paul was not the issue that concerned Paul. It was the fact that Peter's name was being used to cause division.

1 Corinthians 9:5-6

> Don't we have the right to take a believing wife along with us, as do the other apostles and the Lord's brothers and Cephas? Or is it only I and Barnabas who must work for a living?

In these verses, Paul again links his name with that of Peter or Cephas. He is contrasting the way that he and Barnabas conduct their apostolic ministry with the way that Peter and the other apostles conduct theirs.[154] Again, Paul does not criticize any of the other apostles. In fact, he validates their

---

[152] Gundry, 277.

[153] Blomberg, 43. See also Munck, 150, "Paul's argument is directed, not against the persons whose names are invoked, nor against the factions that have gathered round them, but against the church as such."

[154] Soards, 187.

right to receive support from the churches and to take their wives along with them in their ministry. The point that Paul is trying to make, however, is that he has given up his own right to claim support from the churches and has chosen instead to support himself through his trade.[155] Reed observes that Paul was following the rabbinical pattern of maintaining a trade while he conducted his apostolic ministry.[156] In this way he would not be dependent on those he was trying to reach.

While these verses do not provide much information about the relationship between Peter and Paul, Paul can be seen here again acknowledging Peter's influence. Paul used Peter as an example because he was obviously already well known to the Corinthian believers. Paul in no way denigrates Peter's ministry or place in the church. Paul merely lists Peter here so that he can contrast their different approaches to the apostolic ministry. These different approaches to ministry will be examined much more closely in the following chapters.

1 Corinthians 15:3-5; 7-8

> For what I received I passed on to you as of first importance: that Christ died for our sins according to the Scriptures, that he was buried, that he was raised on the third day according to the Scriptures, and that he appeared to Peter, and then to the Twelve.
>
> Then he appeared to James, then to all the apostles, and last of all he appeared to me also, as one abnormally born.

While this passage is apologetic in its content and does not add much to the discussion about the relationship between Paul and Peter, there is one important point that needs to be made. Paul would not have had the first hand knowledge that is contained in this passage unless it was given to him. He alludes to this when he says, "what I received I passed on to you." Paul would have very likely gotten this information from his meeting with Peter and James described in Galatians 1:18-24.[157] This would appear to contradict what Paul said in Galatians 1 about not receiving his gospel from men but "by revelation from Jesus Christ." There is no contradiction, however, when it is understood that here in 1 Corinthians Paul is only talking about the traditions that he received from those who were apostles before him and

---

[155] Arrington, 88, "He deliberately refrained from using his rights lest people suspect his motives. He refused to take anything so that he could not be accused of using religion as a means of getting fat and of engaging in the work of an evangelist for easy money."

[156] Reed, 98.

[157] Blomberg, 295.

not his gospel.[158] So, even here, it is possible to see some further measure of Paul's respect for Peter and the Jerusalem apostles.

2 Peter 3:15-16

> Bear in mind that our Lord's patience means salvation, just as our dear brother Paul also wrote you with the wisdom that God gave him. He writes the same way in all his letters, speaking in them of these matters. His letters contain some things that are hard to understand, which ignorant and unstable people distort, as they do the other Scriptures, to their own destruction.

The letter of 2 Peter has had a controversial history and has left scholars divided over its authorship. Frederick Danker is representative of many scholars when he says, "That the Second Epistle of Peter is a relatively late document . . . and certainly not from the pen of Peter, the apostle, is almost universally recognized."[159] J. N. D. Kelly concludes that, "2 Peter belongs to the luxuriant crop of pseudo-Petrine literature which sprang up around the memory of the Prince of Apostles."[160] While this opinion is certainly prevalent, it has by no means been established to be the dominant one. Some of the critical issues that surround 2 Peter will be briefly highlighted, but for the purpose of this study, these arguments will not be fully developed.

There are a number of others that do accept 2 Peter as a genuine letter from the apostle. They base their view of 2 Peter on three key issues. First of all, this epistle was eventually accepted by the early Church, "as a genuine and canonical writing from the pen of Peter."[161] The early Church may have been late in accepting the letter into the canon, but in the end, 2 Peter was added to the New Testament. The early Church was especially conscious of the need to check carefully the authenticity of all writings that claimed to be apostolic.[162] The early Church's acceptance of 2 Peter as canonical is one of the strongest arguments for acknowledging its authenticity.

---

[158] Jack T. Sanders, "Paul's "Autobiographical" Statements in Galatians 1–2," *Journal of Biblical Literature* 85 (1966) 337–38.

[159] Frederick W. Danker, *2 Peter*, Proclamation Commentaries: The General Letters, ed. Gerhard Krodel (Minneapolis: Fortress, 1995) 84.

[160] J. N. D. Kelly, *A Commentary on the Epistles of Peter and Jude,* Thornapple Commentaries (Grand Rapids: Baker, 1969) 236.

[161] Gundry, 353.

[162] Norman Hillyer, *1 and 2 Peter, Jude,* New International Biblical Commentary (Peabody, Mass.: Hendrickson, 1992) 9.

The second argument for accepting 2 Peter as genuine has to do with the practice of pseudepigraphy. This practice involved an unknown person creating a document and using a well-known person's name to give it credibility. Green argues that pseudepigraphy was not an accepted practice in the early church.[163] Paul spoke against the practice in 2 Thessalonians 2:2 and 3:17. Serapion, the bishop of Antioch late in the second century, rejected the *Gospel of Peter* primarily because it was falsely attributed to Peter.[164] There were a number of other pseudepigraphic works that were also attributed to Peter. These included the *Gospel of Peter, Preaching of Peter, Acts of Peter,* and the *Apocalypse of Peter.* None of these were ever seriously considered to be genuine.[165] At the point in which it was discovered that 2 Peter was pseudepigraphic, it is very likely that it would have also been removed from circulation among the churches.

A last argument that will be mentioned regarding 2 Peter as actually being from the apostle himself has to do with the content of the letter. There is a large amount of autobiographical material in this letter. Hiebert says, "The claim to Petrine authorship is stronger in this epistle than in 1 Peter."[166] He refers to himself as, "Simon Peter, a servant and apostle of Jesus Christ," in verse one. He also makes reference to his upcoming martyrdom in 1:13-15. Another autobiographical section of the letter is 1:16-18 in which Peter recounts his time with Jesus on the Mount of Transfiguration. In 3:1, Peter also makes reference to a previous letter that he had written, possibly referring back to 1 Peter.

While the autobiographical information is not *prima facie* evidence that 2 Peter is genuine, it does strengthen the argument that it did come from Peter. A pseudigrapher would also have seen the value of inserting biographical material into the letter to try and build credibility.[167] However, the arguments for rejecting 2 Peter as genuine are not overwhelming and the autobiographical material relating to the transfiguration gives the appearance of coming from someone who was an eyewitness, which the author claims to be.

The passage in question now is the one in which Peter mentions Paul. If the letter of 2 Peter is actually from the pen of Peter, this passage is

---

[163] Michael Green, *2 Peter and Jude,* Tyndale New Testament Commentaries (Grand Rapids: Eerdmans, 1984) 32.

[164] Ibid.

[165] Hillyer, 11.

[166] D. Edmond Hiebert, *An Introduction to the Non-Pauline Epistles* (Chicago: Moody, 1962) 145.

[167] Kelly, 316.

extremely important in understanding the relationship between the two apostles. One of the first things that can be seen is the fact that Peter calls Paul a, "dear brother." The language that Peter uses here, "expresses the warm, harmonious apostleship that Peter and Paul share."[168] The incident in Antioch appears to have been long forgotten by Peter and he speaks of Paul in the friendly and loving terms of one Christian leader of another.[169]

A second observation that needs to be made concerning this passage is the fact that Peter refers to the God-given wisdom that Paul writes with. In this passage, Peter is personally endorsing the message that Paul preaches. In speaking of the wisdom that is present in Paul's letters, Peter elevates Paul's writings to the level of Scripture in verse 16.[170] This would have to be seen as an obvious endorsement of Paul's apostolic status.[171] Peter makes a reference to "all" of Paul's letters, possibly implying that a collection of these letters had already taken place. This is one of the arguments that some scholars use to demonstrate that 2 Peter is not genuine. The argument is that there is no way that there could have been a collection of Paul's letters at this early (mid-60's) date.[172] This argument makes the assumption that a collection of all of Paul's letters is what Peter is referring to. However, Peter only says that Paul, "writes the same way in all his letters." Peter would have very likely had some contact with some of Paul's letters in his own missionary travels in and is making reference to those letters, or "all" the ones that he had had the opportunity to read.[173]

A last observation that will be made has to do with Peter's reference to the way that Paul's letters are misused. "His letters contain some things that are hard to understand, which ignorant and unstable people distort . . ." If there was still animosity between the two apostles, this would have been an ideal opportunity for Peter to attack Paul for his "hard to understand" teaching. Instead, Peter expresses admiration for the wisdom with

---

[168] Hillyer, 223. See also Hiebert, 151, Peter, "regards Paul as a respected contemporary, not a venerated saint of a past age."

[169] Green, 145, "It is a gratuitous assumption, and one that runs counter to the whole Christian emphasis on brotherly love and forgiveness, to suppose that the split was permanent, and that Peter could never have spoken, therefore, in such warm terms of Paul as he is made to do here."

[170] Perkins, 124.

[171] Craig S. Keener, *New Testament*, The IVP Bible Background Commentary (Downers Grove, Ill.: InterVarsity, 1993) 733.

[172] Joseph B. Tyson, *The New Testament and Early Christianity* (New York: Macmillan, 1984) 412.

[173] Hiebert, 151, Hiebert says, "that it is very probable that the apostles kept in close touch with what each taught or wrote."

which Paul writes.[174] Peter does not take the opportunity to "get even" with Paul. Rather, he praises him for his insight and takes strong exception to those who do distort Paul's teaching.

To summarize, the passage in 2 Peter that was examined is a very important one in understanding the way that Peter felt about Paul. Peter refers to Paul as a "dear brother." Peter commends the wisdom that Paul writes with and demonstrates a familiarity with some of Paul's writings. Peter also very clearly elevates Paul's writings to the level of Scripture. This passage demonstrates that the Apostle Peter had no problem at all in associating himself with the Apostle Paul.

Conclusion

This chapter has examined the relationship between Peter and Paul as seen through their individual letters. Passages from Galatians, 1 Corinthians, and 2 Peter and were examined. Galatians 2:11-14 does indicate that there had been a conflict between the two apostles when Paul confronted Peter in Antioch about his hypocrisy. In each of the other passages regarding Peter, however, there does not appear to be any lingering animosity on Paul's part. Peter, for his part, refers to Paul as a "dear brother" in 2 Peter and speaks very highly of him and of his writings. The following chapters will examine the different aspects Peter and Paul's ministries. Their apostolic ministries will be compared and contrasted by discussing the different functions that they performed as apostles.

---

[174] Green, 146.

PART TWO

Introduction

THIS SECTION will examine the two apostles' ministries as recorded by Luke in Acts. Their apostolic ministries will be examined in the context of the following components: Leadership, Evangelism and Church Planting, Miracle Working and Healing, and Mystical or Supernatural Experiences.[1] These functions detail particular aspects of the two men's ministries. There are some situations in which these categories are shown to be overlapping. For example, in Acts 3 Peter functions in the role of a miracle worker and heals a lame man. This miracle then provides a setting for Peter to preach an evangelistic message to those who have witnessed the healing. An example of this overlap of the different categories from Paul's ministry is observed during his time in Troas. As he was leading a church service there in his role of a pastor, Eutychus fell out of the window and appears to have died. Paul, however, miraculously healed the boy and then continued the church service in his pastoral role. While the miracle and the pastoral ministry are part of the same event, they will be looked at separately in their respective categories.

---

[1] Krodel, "Peter in the Book of Acts," 40–42. See also Bernard T. Smyth, *Paul: Mystic and Missionary* (Maryknoll, N.Y.: Orbis, 1980) 149, and Jervell, 71.

3

The Leadership Roles of Peter and Paul in Acts

Peter the Leader

Peter and Paul provided significant leadership to the early church in their respective arenas. This chapter will examine the type of leadership that they provided. It will be seen that while Luke draws obvious parallels to the two apostles' ministries, he presents their leadership roles very differently. Peter is shown to occupy more of an administrative and governmental role in the early church in Jerusalem.[2] Luke clearly presents Peter, not only as the spokesman for the apostles, but also as their leader.[3] Paul's leadership, on the other hand, is shown to be more pastoral in nature to the churches that he is connected to. This is not to say that Peter did not function in a pastoral role. Luke, however, does not illustrate the pastoral side of Peter's ministry as strongly as he does in Paul's ministry. Pastoral ministry is emphasized much more strongly when Luke writes about Paul.

The first place that Peter's leadership is demonstrated is in Acts 1:15-26. There, he initiates and presides over the selection of an apostle to take Judas Iscariot's place. As Neil says, "Peter emerges right from the beginning as the undisputed head of the Christian community."[4] Luke makes it clear that it was Peter who initiated the proposal to select a replacement apostle. Peter stood and explained the Scriptural need for selecting another apostle. He understood that the core group of apostles that Jesus had selected could not fulfill their mission unless Judas' spot was filled.[5] He makes the case based on two verses from the Psalms, 69:25 and 109:8. What had happened with Judas was a fulfillment of prophecy and Peter interprets it as

---

[2] Brawley, 146, "Peter's functions in the administration of the early Christian community round out his actions."

[3] Joseph B. Tyson, "Authority in Acts," *The Bible Today* 30 (1992) 280.

[4] Neil, 68. See also Marshall, 63.

[5] Perkins, 89.

such. Their commission, as Peter understood it, was that the Twelve were going to become witnesses of the resurrection.[6]

After His resurrection, Jesus had spent forty days with His followers before the ascension, yet He had not picked out a replacement for Judas. It would have seemed proper and logical that Jesus would have dealt with this Himself since He was the one who appointed the original Twelve.[7] Instead, He left this responsibility to His followers.[8] When Peter took the initiative to appoint another apostle he was in a very real way, "taking over a major function of the departed Jesus."[9] Just before Jesus' arrest, He told Peter that he would deny Him three times, but that, "when you have turned back, strengthen your brothers."[10] As Peter began to exercise leadership in the group of disciples, he was strengthening them and helping them to see God's plan. After the ascension, there still may have been feelings of confusion and a lack of understanding among the apostles about what they were supposed to do. In dealing with the issues that surrounded Judas and the need to replace him, however, Peter was able to interpret the Scriptures to his fellow apostles and to show them where they fit into God's plan as the new Israel.[11] One of a Christian leader's primary responsibilities is to help people to see where they fit into the plan of God. Peter was able to articulate God's vision in such a way that the rest of the apostles could immediately fall in behind him.

The appointment of a new apostle also involved prayer. Luke seems to be drawing some parallel here to the way in which Jesus appointed the initial Twelve apostles. In his Gospel he writes, "One of those days Jesus went out to a mountainside to pray, and spent the night praying to God. When morning came, he called his disciples to him and chose twelve of them, whom he also designated apostles . . ."[12] The apostles here, under Peter's leadership, follow Jesus' example in praying before they cast lots to select a replacement apostle. So, in a very real way, Jesus is shown to be involved as the next apostle is selected.

The response of the others to Peter's leadership is indicative of their willingness to support and participate in the mission that Jesus had left for

---

[6] Acts 1:22.

[7] Haenchen, 164.

[8] Robert C. Tannehill, *The Narrative Unity of Luke-Acts A Literary Interpretation* Volume Two: *The Acts of the Apostles* (Minneapolis: Fortress, 1994) 21.

[9] Ibid., 20.

[10] Luke 22:32.

[11] Perkins, 89.

[12] Luke 6:12-13.

them. They immediately do what Peter recommends. "Peter's faith inspires the faith of the others."[13] It also demonstrates the reality of Peter's leadership in the early church. At this early point in the Jerusalem community Peter's leadership in the group seems to be an accepted fact. It might be noted here that Peter's leadership did not just extend to the Twelve. When Matthias was selected as the new apostle, it was out of a group of a hundred and twenty. These were the nucleus of the church in Jerusalem and it appears that they all looked to Peter for leadership. In these early days right before Pentecost, Luke makes a point of showing that Peter's strong leadership skills were exactly what the young community needed to stay focused.

A second place where Peter's leadership is clearly seen in Acts is in his confrontation with Ananias and Sapphira in Acts 5:1-11. There is much about this story that Luke does not tell. The fact that he includes the story at all, however, reveals a great deal about Luke. He is committed to providing an objective view of the young church and does not just present the victories and successes. This story illustrates the fact that the early church had its share of conflict but that strong leadership kept them on the right course.[14]

This narrative provides the first account of church discipline that is recorded in the New Testament. Peter is seen in his leadership capacity as the one who exercises this discipline.[15] Verse two states that after Ananias kept back some of the money, he "brought the rest and put it at the apostles' feet." The indication here is that Peter's encounter with Ananias took place publicly and in the presence of the other apostles.[16] Other apostles were present, yet it was Peter who initiated the confrontation with Ananias and Sapphira. Again, the leadership of Peter is evident in the fact that he was the one who took the initiative in dealing with the situation.

It seems clear that Luke, consciously or unconsciously, draws a parallel between Ananias and Achan in the book of Joshua.[17] The verb that Luke

---

[13] Tannehill, 21.

[14] Neil, 94, "It is a mark of his honesty as a Christian historian that he does not gloss over or omit the fact that there were black sheep in the fold, even in what he clearly regards as the Church's golden age."

[15] Cullman, 35.

[16] Ibid. See also, Brawley, 146–47, Here, Peter, "stands out individually in the administration of the funds to be distributed to the needy."

[17] Bruce, *The Book of the Acts*, 102, "The story of Ananias is to the book of Acts what the story of Achan is to the book of Joshua. In both narratives an act of deceit interrupts the victorious progress of the people of God." See also Arrington, 55, "Luke may be suggesting that just as sin entered into the nation of Israel through Achan's transgression, so had sin

uses to describe what Ananias had done, "has the negative connotation of embezzlement or misappropriation, and is the same verb used in the Septuagint translation of Joshua 7:1 to describe the sin of Achan."[18] In the same way that Achan's sin stopped the forward progress of Israel into the Promised Land, so Ananias' sin would stop the progress of the church if it was not dealt with appropriately. Peter, then, occupies the place of Joshua and, "holds court in the name of God."[19] Gundry also draws a comparison here between the judgment on Ananias and Sapphira and the judgment on Nadab and Abihu in Leviticus 10.[20] These disobedient priests were judged early in the history of Israel just as Ananias and Sapphira were judged early in the history of the church. The fact that those types of judgments did not continue in the life of Israel or in the life of the church are signs of God's grace, not an indication that He condones sin in His people.[21]

Arrington sees this passage in the context of spiritual warfare.[22] Ananias was an agent of Satan and was attempting to bring sin into the community. Peter occupies the role of the Holy Spirit's agent who must protect the integrity of the church. Peter's statement to Ananias indicates that he viewed this encounter in spiritual terms: "Ananias, how is it that Satan has so filled your heart that you have lied to the Holy Spirit . . . ?"[23] A parallel can also be seen here between Jesus and Peter. In Luke's gospel, Jesus was the one who was able to reveal what was hidden in people's hearts and minds. In Acts, as Peter has stepped into the leadership role of the early church, he also has become a prophet who, "exposes and rebukes the deceptive heart."[24]

Three hours after the confrontation with Ananias, Peter had to deal with his wife, Sapphira. Luke tells the reader that she did not know that her husband was dead. While Peter may have been surprised at Ananias' death, he had had three hours to think about it, "and to recognize in it the divine judgment for an attempt to deceive the church, and to deceive the Spirit

---

entered the community of believers through Annanias' deed."

[18] Richard P. Thompson, "Christian Community and Characterization in the Book of Acts: A Literary Study of the Lukan Concept of the Church," Ph.D. diss. (Dedman College Southern Methodist University, 1996) 218.

[19] Cullman, 35.

[20] Gundry, 223.

[21] Ibid.

[22] Arrington, 57.

[23] Acts 5:3.

[24] Tannehill, 79.

in the church."[25] It might seem strange that Peter did not immediately inform Sapphira of her husband's death. It is possible that this would have brought her to repentance and saved her life. Bruce even sees this as a lack of pastoral experience by Peter.[26] If Peter had informed her ahead of time about Ananias, however, it is likely that her repentance would not have been genuine. It would have been motivated by her husband's death rather than by genuine conviction. Peter was wise enough as a leader to understand this. At any rate, Peter did give Sapphira an opportunity to tell the truth and show signs of repentance.[27] Instead, she, like her husband, lied to Peter and clung to the story that she and Ananias had concocted. Calvin points out that the very fact that Peter was asking her about the price of the land should have brought her to repentance.[28] She and Ananias had devised their plan in secret. If Peter was asking about it, it was likely that the plot had become known. While Peter did not predict Ananias' death, he did predict Sapphira's: "The feet of the men who buried your husband are at the door, and they will carry you out also."[29] The result was that Sapphira, "fell down at his feet and died."

Not only does Peter function in the role of authority here, he also is the spokesperson for the author of Acts and the representative of all the Christians. As this representative, Thompson points out three ways in this passage that Peter contrasts Ananias' behavior with that of the other believers.[30] First, Peter stated that Satan had filled Ananias and not the Holy Spirit. The Christian community has been shown to be filled with the Spirit of God. Second, Peter informed Ananias that he had lied to the Christian community, as well as to God. This was not just a sin against God. He had also sinned against the church. Third, Peter draws attention to the fact that Ananias' problem was the fact that he had a dishonest heart. This is in contrast with the singleness of heart and honesty that the other believers in the community serve the Lord with.

While this example of Peter's leadership function is foreign to the modern reader, it served to protect the early church from spiritual attack.

---

[25] Bruce, 107.

[26] Ibid. "At this stage Peter had not had much experience in pastoral ministry; otherwise he would probably have broken the news of Ananias' death to her before he questioned her, and the results might have been happier."

[27] Marshall, 113.

[28] John Calvin, *The Acts of the Apostles 1–13*, Calvin's Commentaries, eds. David W. Torrance and Thomas F. Torrance, trans. John W. Fraser and W. J. G. McDonald (Grand Rapids: Erdmans, 1965) 136–37.

[29] Acts 5:9.

[30] Thompson, 219–20.

This would be a difficult encounter for any Christian leader to have to deal with. In Paul's farewell speech to the Ephesian elders, he reminded them of their duty to protect the people who were entrusted to them: "Keep watch over yourselves and all the flock of which the Holy Spirit has made you overseers. Be shepherds of the church of God . . ."[31] In exercising church discipline against Ananias and Sapphira, Peter was watching over the flock that had been entrusted to him.

Another example of Peter's leadership function is seen in Acts 8:14-17. In this passage, Peter and John are sent to Samaria, "to inspect the results of Philip's ministry."[32] This passage illustrates the fact that Peter's authority in the early church was not absolute. He is shown to be under the authority of the Christian community and he and John go to Samaria, "as emissaries of the apostles in Jerusalem."[33] In the same way, Paul and Barnabas will be sent out later by the church at Antioch on their first missionary journey, as well as on their trip to the Jerusalem Council.[34] In the early stages of the Christian mission, the Jerusalem church seemed to regard it as their duty to exercise some measure of supervision and control over the gospel as it progressed into new frontiers.[35] Apostolic control of the Christian mission was very important to the Jerusalem church during its early years.[36]

This apostolic visit to Samaria came after word of Philip's success in ministry had reached Jerusalem. Luke records that Philip was preaching to crowds of people and was seeing miraculous signs take place. Under Philip's ministry, people were being delivered from the power of evil spirits and many paralytics and cripples were being healed.[37] A genuine spiritual awakening was taking place in Samaria. While Philip is never designated as an *apostle*, the work that he was performing in Samaria was apostolic in nature. His preaching of the gospel, his healing of the sick, and his exorcism of evil spirits from people was exactly the same type of ministry that

---

[31] Acts 20: 28

[32] Blaiklock, 80.

[33] Brawley, 147, Brawley states that Peter was, "prominent but not preeminent."

[34] Acts 13:1-4 and 15:3.

[35] Bruce, 168. The Jerusalem church's sending Barnabas to Antioch (Acts 11:22-24) is another example of their attempt to supervise the missionary work. See also Munck, *The Acts of the Apostles*, 75.

[36] Talbert, 86, "It is a way of saying that the expanding religious experience of messianic Judaism is under the control of the true tradition about Jesus, embodied in the apostles."

[37] Acts 8:6-7.

Jesus and the apostles had performed.[38] Philip was following the pattern of apostolic ministry that was common in the early church.

There continues to be debate over why Peter and John went to Samaria. Even though Philip was enjoying a successful ministry there Luke makes it clear that the Samaritan believers did not receive the Holy Spirit until Peter and John came and laid their hands on them and prayed for them.[39] The theological implications of this passage are beyond the scope of this study. In addressing the leadership function of Peter, however, it can be noted that the apostolic presence in Samaria served to validate what God was doing there and to show solidarity between the Christians in Jerusalem and the new Samaritan believers.[40] Because of the tension that existed between the Jews and the Samaritans, it was important that steps be taken to show the Samaritan Christians, "that they were fully incorporated into the Christian community."[41] By having two of the most eminent apostles visit Samaria, the Jerusalem church seemed to be extending the right hand of fellowship to the Samaritan believers, thus taking positive steps to acknowledge the relationship between the two groups.

Another incident from this time in Samaria also serves to highlight Peter's leadership capacity as an apostle. This was his confrontation with Simon Magus. Simon was well known as a sorcerer and he evidently had quite a following. According to Luke, Simon was known as, "the divine power known as the Great Power."[42] Simon had a large following in Samaria that he amazed with his magic.[43] When Philip came through Samaria, however, many of Simon's followers were converted under Philip's ministry. Then, even, "Simon himself believed and was baptized. And he followed Philip everywhere, astonished by the great signs and miracles he saw."[44] It

---

[38] Bruce, 165.

[39] Acts 8:15-16.

[40] Neil, 122.

[41] Williams, 157, Williams goes on to say, "Without a clear connecting link between the church in Samaria and that in Jerusalem, the schism that had for so long plagued Jewish-Samaritan relations might well have been carried over into the church."

[42] Acts 8:10. See Hans-Josef Klauck, *Magic and Paganism in Early Christianity: The World of the Acts of the Apostles*, trans. Brian Mcneil (Minneapolis: Fortress, 2003) 15, "'The great power' is a designation which, taken in isolation, can serve as a euphemism for the divine name itself, e.g. in Samaritan sources and in magical texts."

[43] Gerd Ludemann, "The Acts of the Apostles and the Beginnings of Simonian Gnosis," *New Testament Studies* 33 (1987) 422. Ludemann quotes a document by Justin Martyr a century later that states that Simon was confessed as the "first god" and worshipped by many of the Samaritans.

[44] Acts 8:13.

appears that Simon experienced a conversion of sorts and began to follow Philip.

When Peter and John came to Samaria, Simon saw that the Holy Spirit was given to people when the apostles laid their hands on them. He offered them money and said, "Give me this ability so that everyone on whom I lay my hands may receive the Holy Spirit."[45] Peter's rebuke was swift:

> May your money perish with you, because you thought you could buy the gift of God with money! You have no part or share in this ministry, because your heart is not right before God. Repent of this wickedness and pray to the Lord. Perhaps he will forgive you for having such a thought in your heart. For I see that you are full of bitterness and captive to sin.[46]

Simon then asked Peter to pray for him so that nothing Peter had prophesied would come to pass. The story ends without any type of resolution.[47]

Simon's issue here seems to be that he wanted to add the ability to bestow the Holy Spirit to his repertoire of magical services that he provided. His offer to buy the authority to confer the Holy Spirit is stereotypical of the ancient magician.[48] If he could give the Holy Spirit to others, for a price, his prestige and wealth would increase.[49] With this ability, Simon would also be the equal of the apostles. As Krodel says, "Religious magic is man's attempt to manipulate God and usually profit by it."[50] This attempt to buy spiritual authority from Peter also demonstrates his misunderstanding of the role of the apostles. By offering them money for the Holy Spirit, he seems to regard them as magicians like himself.[51]

This story provides another example of church discipline at the hands of Peter.[52] It is not clear exactly what Simon's role was as he followed Philip. Luke seems to imply that Simon had some authority in the evolving Christian group in Samaria. When Peter rebuked Simon he told him he had, "no part or share in this ministry." If Simon was evolving as

---

[45] Acts 8:19.

[46] Acts 8:20-23.

[47] Ludemann, 424.

[48] Garrett, 70.

[49] Gerhard Krodel, *Acts*, Augsburg Commentary on the New Testament (Minneapolis: Augsburg, 1986) 165.

[50] Ibid.

[51] Garrett, 70.

[52] Neil, 123, "Peter as chief Apostle exercises the authority of the Church to discipline sinners."

a Christian leader, Peter's rebuke is even more poignant. Spiritual authority is a weighty responsibility. Those who possess it must constantly guard their motives and beware of using their position for their own ends.[53] Peter would later write that pastors should not be, "greedy for money."[54] Simon's desire to purchase the ability to bestow the Holy Spirit had to be dealt with strongly. God's gifts are always given freely.

One final example of Peter's leadership function will be examined. Peter is the only one of the Twelve mentioned by name at the Jerusalem Council in Acts 15. The "apostles" are mentioned several times as being present, but it appears that Peter was the designated representative of the Twelve at the conference. In his speech, he appears to be speaking on behalf of the apostles. This has been his pattern throughout Acts. His closing statement is inclusive of the other apostles, "*We* believe it is through the grace of our Lord Jesus that *we* are saved, just as they are."[55] (my italics)

Peter's speech in Acts 15 reminds the council delegates that God had chosen to use him as the first apostle to take the gospel to the Gentiles. Bruce makes the point that Peter represents two different groups of people as he speaks here.[56] First of all, he is speaking as the leader of the apostles in favor of a law-free gospel. As the leader of the apostles he had been led by the Holy Spirit several years earlier to take the gospel into a Gentile's home. God had responded by saving and filling Cornelius and the members of his household with the Holy Spirit in the same manner that He had filled the Jewish believers on the Day of Pentecost. Peter's point was that God did not show any distinction between the Gentiles and the Jews when they believed and gave them both the same gift of the Holy Spirit.

The second group that Peter represented when he spoke were "the rank and file of Galilean Jews."[57] They knew enough of the Law to know what foods were acceptable or unacceptable, as well as that fraternization with Gentiles was forbidden. At the same time, however, it was unrealistic to assume that every Jew, "could be expected to know or practise all the details of legal tradition."[58] If they as "good Jews" could not hope to keep all of the Law, how could the Gentiles with no background at all in the Jewish Law hope to keep it?

---

[53] Marshall, 158.

[54] 1 Peter 5:3.

[55] Acts 15:11.

[56] Bruce, 290–91.

[57] Ibid., 291.

[58] Ibid.

The language that Peter uses in his speech is very Pauline sounding. In fact, it sounds much like what Paul said to Peter when he rebuked him in Galatians 2:14ff. This has led many commentators to assume that Luke put this speech in Peter's mouth. If this is the case, Luke's Peter then becomes the chief spokesman for the Pauline position.[59] Peter, then, is the one in Acts who most clearly, "articulates Paul's vision of the Gentile mission."[60] While this view might be acceptable if Acts is understood to be written much later, as the Tübingen School insisted, it is not acceptable if Acts is understood to be written at an earlier date, as most conservative scholars insist. What seems more likely is that the Jerusalem Council took place some time after Paul had rebuked Peter in Antioch. As mentioned previously, Peter evidently took this rebuke to heart, and here, is echoing a similar message to what Paul had spoken to him.

While there is no doubt that Peter does echo some of Paul's ideas in his speech, there is also no reason to believe that he could not have made this speech himself. It is possible that Peter was even unconscious of the fact that he was preaching some of the same thoughts that Paul had preached to him in Antioch.[61] As mentioned in the discussion on Paul's visit with Peter from Galatians 1:18-19, it is very likely that Paul occupied an influential place in Peter's life. Peter took heed to Paul's rebuke and was in effect, molded through Paul's words.[62] In Peter's closing statement, he sums up the gospel as he understands it, "We believe it is through the grace of our Lord Jesus that we are saved, just as they are." Peter makes it clear here that he is not speaking just for himself. He is speaking on behalf of all the apostles and the elders, as well as Barnabas and Paul.[63] This statement of unity by Peter quieted the assembly and prepared the way for Barnabas and Paul to speak.[64]

It is also clear that by the time of the Jerusalem Council, James has taken over the primary leadership role in the Jerusalem church. Peter, however, still occupies an influential role, as will be seen. Cullman sees Peter at the Jerusalem Council in the capacity of a missionary leader, and no longer

---

[59] William O. Walker, Jr., "Acts and the Pauline Corpus Revisited: Peter's Speech at the Jerusalem Conference," in *Literary Studies in Luke-Acts: Essays in Honor of Joseph B. Tyson,* eds. Richard P. Thompson and Thomas E. Phillips (Macon: Mercer University Press, 1998) 85.

[60] Ibid.

[61] Stott, 245.

[62] Hengel and Schwemer, 209.

[63] Gooding, 232–33.

[64] Packer, 126.

as *the* leader of the church.[65] The leadership of the Jerusalem church has passed to James and he clearly presides over the meeting. Cullman believes that Peter, Paul, and Barnabas interrupted their missionary activities to go to the council in Jerusalem.[66] Whether or not this is the case, Peter was clearly the leading missionary present. His speech recounted how God used him to be the first to take the gospel to the Gentiles when he preached at Cornelius' house.[67] It was Peter's speech that calmed the crowd. They had been arguing over whether or not the Gentiles should be required to be circumcised and obey the Law. After Peter's speech, "The whole assembly became silent . . ."[68] Peter had used his influence and dealt with the issue at hand by appealing to the teaching of the gospel and his own experience.[69] It appears that James also gives a lot of weight to Peter's speech in the decision that he made in regards to the Gentile believers.[70]

Teruo Kobayashi takes a different view from most scholars in regards to the role that Peter played at the Jerusalem Council and in his continuing role of leadership in the early church. He sees two separate groups, the apostles and the elders, that work together to bring leadership to the church. According to Kobayashi, Peter was the leader of the apostles and James was the leader of the elders.[71] In his view, Peter's ministry did not evolve to one that was primarily that of a traveling evangelist. Rather, he traveled as a representative of the apostles to the places where churches had already been established.[72]

This view, while interesting, does not seem to take into account the fact that Peter disappears from Acts after the Jerusalem Council. If Luke wanted to show that Peter had a continuing leadership role in Jerusalem,

---

[65] Cullman, 51.

[66] Ibid. See also Bruce, 289, "Peter probably came back from his ministry among Jews of the dispersion in order to be present."

[67] John Nollant, "A Fresh Look at Acts 15:10." *New Testament Studies* 27 (1980–1981), Peter used the Cornelius episode to show how God had supernaturally led him to a Gentile audience. This prepared the assembly for Barnabas and Saul to describe their ministry among the Gentile world.

[68] Acts 15:12.

[69] John Calvin, *Acts 14–28*, Calvin's New Testament Commentaries, eds. David W. Torrance and Thomas F. Torrance, trans. John W. Fraser (Grand Rapids: Eerdmans, 1966) 43.

[70] Krodel, "Peter in the Book of Acts," 50, "Peter provides the decisive witness; James provides the decisive judgment or decision; the apostles and elders provide the sentence or the enforcement of the decision."

[71] Teruo Kobayashi, "The Role of Peter According to the Theological Understanding of Paul, Mark, and Luke-Acts," Ph.D. diss, Drew University, 1963, 280.

[72] Ibid., 278.

it is unlikely that he would have written him out of the story after chapter 15. There also is no indication in Acts that the apostles and the elders are operating independently of each other. They seem to work together as a corporate leadership body. Kobayashi's view also does not take into account the fact that James' authority continues to grow throughout Acts. As James role has grown, Peter's has not become stronger but more ambiguous.[73] The clearest indication that Kobayashi's view of Peter is flawed is the fact that at the Jerusalem Council it is James who makes the final decision after hearing from everyone who needed to speak. He acknowledges Peter's influence, yet James decides what the course of action is going to be. "It is my judgment, therefore, that we should not make it difficult for the Gentiles who are turning to God."[74] This is the statement of a man who appears comfortable making decisions. James' decision then appears to have been accepted by everyone that was present without question. After James speaks, there is no more discussion or debate among the delegates. There is also no suggestion, "that acceptance by the apostles and elders is required to validate James' decision."[75] The apostles and elders appear to be submitted to James' authority.

Having asserted James' leadership at the Jerusalem Council in no way diminishes the influence and authority that Peter still operated in. His influence was felt throughout the conference. Without Peter's speech, it is doubtful that James would have been able to accomplish what he did in only requiring the Gentiles to abstain from sexual immorality and observe a few basic dietary laws. It is also very likely that without Peter's speech, Barnabas and Paul would not have been given a fair hearing when they got up to speak. Even though the official leadership of the church had passed to James, Peter's influence was still strong. He was able to use his influence in a positive way to produce a positive result at the Jerusalem Council.

One final aspect of the Jerusalem Council that should be noted is the fact that this is the only place in Acts where Peter and Paul are listed as being together at the same location at the same time. These verses in Acts 15 show Peter and Paul standing together before the Jerusalem Council in unity of doctrine and unity of spirit. There is no hint of disagreement or conflict between the two apostles, and Peter goes to great lengths to demonstrate that they are preaching the same Gospel message. James then

---

[73] Tyson, 281, "The change in patterns of authority is illustrated in the changing role of Peter himself. Although he was first presented as the speaker for the apostles, in later incidents he occupies an ambiguous position."

[74] Acts 15:19.

[75] Tyson, 282.

adds the weight of the Scriptures to the occasion and quotes a passage from Amos that strengthened the case of Peter, Barnabas, and Paul for the inclusion of the Gentiles into the church.[76] While this passage in Acts 15 does not provide any interaction between Peter and Paul, the unity between the two apostles is clearly demonstrated. Luke uses the Jerusalem Council to highlight the fact that Peter (representing the apostles and the Jerusalem church) and Paul (representing the mission to the Gentiles) are both in essential continuity in the message that they are preaching.

Peter's leadership role in the early church started off as a governmental role. He provided direction for the church and helped to guide it during its early years. In the early days, Peter was the one that the other apostles looked to for leadership. Over time, however, Peter's role in the church changed from that of governmental leadership to more of an itinerant evangelist. He still occupied a place influence in the church, as was seen at the Jerusalem Council, but the primary leadership role of the Jerusalem church had been passed on to James.

Paul the Pastor

In examining Paul's role as a leader in the early church, it will be seen that Luke primarily portrays Paul's leadership in the context of him as a pastor. Pastoral ministry was as much a part of Paul's apostleship as was his evangelistic ministry.[77] Paul and Barnabas' first missionary trip ended on a pastoral note: "Then they returned to Lystra, Iconium and Antioch, strengthening the disciples and encouraging them to remain true to the faith."[78] These churches had been started by the apostles. They did not want to go back to Antioch until they had done everything that they could to equip them for the coming persecution. Paul's second missionary journey was initiated out of a pastoral concern: "Let us go back and visit the brothers in all the towns where we preached the word of the Lord and see how they are doing."[79] This trip began with Paul and Silas traveling, "through Syria and Cilicia, strengthening the churches."[80] Even though there were numerous evangelistic opportunities on this trip, it started off as a pastoral visit to the churches that he and Barnabas had founded.[81] The third missionary jour-

---

[76] Williams, 264.

[77] P. Beasley-Murray, "Paul as Pastor," in *Dictionary of Paul and His Letters*, ed. Gerald F. Hawthorne et al. (Downers Grove, Ill.: InterVarsity, 1993) 654.

[78] Acts 14:21-22.

[79] Acts 15:36.

[80] Acts 15:41.

[81] Peter Back, "Exegesis on Some Key Passages Relating to Mission: Part 2—Acts 14:21-28,

ney also began with pastoral visits to the churches in Galatia and Phrygia where Paul was, "strengthening all the disciples."[82] Luke shows over and over again that Paul's constant focus was on the building of the church.[83] This pastoral aspect of Paul's apostolic ministry is seen throughout his missionary journeys.

The first example of Paul in a pastoral role is seen in Antioch. Luke explains that the church in Antioch was started when, "a great number of people believed and turned to the Lord." This took place after many of the believers in Jerusalem had been scattered in the aftermath of Stephen's martyrdom. Barnabas was sent from Jerusalem to evaluate and then oversee the work.[84] As discussed previously, the Jerusalem church kept a close watch on new works outside of Jerusalem. Barnabas represented the apostles in evaluating what was going on at Antioch.[85] When he arrived, Barnabas, "was glad and encouraged them all to remain true to the Lord with all their hearts."[86] At some point, Barnabas saw the need to bring Paul (still called Saul at that point) to Antioch to help him. Luke does not record the reasoning behind Barnabas' decision to bring Paul to Antioch.[87] Perhaps he felt that Paul's background uniquely suited him for this type of ministry in a predominantly Gentile environment. With both men in Antioch, the result was that, "for a whole year Barnabas and Saul met with the church and taught great numbers of people."[88] It seems clear that during this time in Antioch, Paul occupied a subordinate role to Barnabas.[89] Paul did not help found the church but was brought on to assist Barnabas in a pastoral role and in teaching the new congregation. Barnabas and Paul already had a relationship from the time of Paul's first post-conversion trip to Jerusalem. Barnabas knew Paul well enough that he felt comfortable in asking him to

---

Acts 15:36-41 and Acts 16:2," *Evangel* 20 (2002) 21.

[82] Acts 18:23.

[83] Richard B. Cook, "Paul, the Organizer," *Missiology: An International Review* 9 (1981) 485–86.

[84] Bruce, 226, Bruce thinks that it is very likely, considering Barnabas' background, "that he took the initiative in offering his services for this mission, and his offer was eagerly accepted."

[85] Ibid., 227.

[86] Acts 11:23.

[87] Ramsay, 45–46, "It lies in Luke's style to give no reason why Barnabas summoned Saul to Antioch. The historian records essential facts as they occurred; but he does not obtrude on the reader his own private conception as to causes or motives."

[88] Acts 11:26.

[89] Riesner, 271.

become a part of the leadership team in the Antioch church.[90] The year that the two men spent working together in Antioch would have solidified and strengthened that relationship.[91] As a subordinate of Barnabas' Paul would have also gained valuable training for future ministry.[92]

It appears that the primary role of Barnabas and Paul was in teaching and instructing the church in Antioch after the apostolic pattern.[93] Even though Paul did not have strong ties to the Jerusalem church, Barnabas did. He would have conveyed the apostolic teaching as he had received it from the apostles and Paul would have taught the Gospel as he had received it by special revelation from the Lord.[94] This time of ministry in Antioch have allowed the two men to get comfortable in working together. It would have also have given them the opportunity to get acquainted with each other's theology and understanding of the gospel.

The time that Barnabas and Paul worked together in Antioch was also significant for another reason. They were actively working together in a mixed environment of both Jewish and Gentile believers.[95] This mixed church in Antioch was the first of its kind and Barnabas and Paul were two of the key leaders there. They were both able to see first hand the direction that the Holy Spirit seemed to be taking His church. Paul would later duplicate this concept of the mixed congregation throughout the Roman Empire as he planted churches.

While Luke does not provide a lot of specific information about Barnabas and Paul's time in Antioch, he does convey the sense that this was a foundational time for the church, as well as for the two men. The role that Barnabas had occupied in the Jerusalem church is unclear, other than providing financial support. Acts does indicate, however, that Barnabas was an active member of the church there. It appears that Paul was engaged in missionary work before Barnabas recruited him. This was very likely the

---

[90] Talbert, 116, Talbert points out that Barnabas is shown vouching for the authenticity of Paul's salvation, as well as the authenticity of his ministry.

[91] George W. Murray, "Paul's Corporate Evangelism in the Book of Acts," *Bibliotheca Sacra* 155 (1998) 191.

[92] Edmond Hiebert, *In Paul's Shadow: Friends and Foes of the Great Apostle* (Greenville: Bob Jones University Press, 1992) 44.

[93] Williams, 205.

[94] Galatians 1:12.

[95] Thompson, 319. Thompson goes on to say, "For the first time in the Acts narrative, Luke characterizes the Christian community as a group of believers in which the gospel message transcended the social and ethnic distinctions between Jews and Gentiles—a group of believers distinguished primarily by the presence of God and by the communal bonds that joined it together," 324.

first local church that Paul had been a part of and it would prove to be a determining factor for the rest of his ministry.

The next example of Paul's pastoral ministry that will be examined is seen in Acts 14:21-23:

> Then they returned to Lystra, Iconium, and Antioch, strengthening the disciples and encouraging them to remain true to the faith. "'We must go through many hardships to enter the kingdom of God,'" they said. Paul and Barnabas appointed elders for them in each church and, with prayer and fasting, committed them to the Lord, in whom they had put their trust.

Paul's pastoral nature is seen clearly in this example.[96] He and Barnabas return to the cities where the persecution had been the heaviest on their first missionary journey. Luke does not indicate how much time Paul and Barnabas spent in these three cities on their return trip. The implication, however, is that they spent enough time with the churches to solidify them, strengthen them, and identify those among them who had leadership ability. The churches had to have capable leaders if they were to survive. This passage provides a clear illustration of Paul's pattern of discipleship.[97] It was never his goal to just see people converted. He wanted to see them integrated into a Christian community. Paul took every opportunity to equip these young churches for what lay ahead. He strengthened the disciples through his teaching. He then organized them into congregations and appointed capable leaders for them.[98] Paul then maintained contact through personal visits or those of one of his co-workers, as well as through his letters.

Paul's pastoral care is shown in two ways in this passage. First of all, Paul prepared the congregations for the coming persecution. The statement, "We must go through many hardships to enter the kingdom of God," appears representative of the manner in which Paul exhorted the believers to remain true to the faith.[99] Up until this point, most of the persecution had been directed at Barnabas and Paul. They were preparing to leave, however, and it was very likely that the persecutors would now turn their attention

---

[96] Tannehill, 180.

[97] Luter, 103.

[98] Robert Banks, *Paul's Idea of Community* (Peabody, Mass.: Hendrickson, 1994) 67, Paul's intent was not only, "the fashioning of merely of mature individuals but of mature communities as well."

[99] David F. Detwiler, "Paul's Approach to the Great Commission in Acts 14:21-23," *Bibliotheca Sacra* 152 (1995) 37, Detwiler sees Paul's statement about hardships as a summary of the teaching that he used to prepare them for persecution.

from them to the communities that were being left behind.[100] Paul wanted to let these new believers know what they could expect so that when it came, they would not be surprised and overcome by it.[101] Paul was not preaching a message of purification through trials and tribulations. Rather, it was understood that those who followed Jesus would be persecuted and it was through perseverance that their salvation was assured.[102] Tribulation was going to come to these young converts. That was the reality of the situation. As a pastor, Paul wanted to make sure that these new believers had been prepared as much as possible for the hardships that awaited them. This passage corresponds to what Paul told the Thessalonian believers in a similar situation, "For indeed when we were with you, we kept telling you in advance that we were going to suffer affliction; and so it came to pass, as you know."[103]

The second way that Paul's pastoral care is demonstrated in this passage is in the appointment of elders in each of the congregations. With Barnabas and Paul leaving, there needed to be qualified people left in charge. The elders that Luke describes here would correspond to the leaders of the local synagogue. They would be responsible for worship, teaching, administration, and church discipline.[104] Stott draws attention to the fact that the appointment of elders is both local and plural.[105] It was local in the sense that the elders came from within each individual group. It was not outsiders that were placed in charge. It was people from within the congregation. It was plural in the sense that there appeared to be a team of elders appointed for each congregation. Then, as now, looking after a congregation requires a team of committed leaders. Ramsay sees this story to be indicative of the way that Paul went about establishing churches.[106] If these new groups of believers were to survive the persecution that would surely come, they needed strong leaders that would guide them through the difficult times ahead. "Spiritual leadership is the key to effective local church ministry and Paul and Barnabas provided for this need as they es-

---

[100] Ibid., 181.

[101] Marshall, 241.

[102] Krodel, *Acts*, Augsburg Commentary on the New Testament, 261.

[103] 1 Thessalonians 3:4.

[104] Arrington, 147.

[105] Stott, 236.

[106] Ramsay, 121, "It is clear, therefore, that Paul everywhere instituted Elders in his new Churches; and on our hypothesis as to the accurate and methodical expression of the historian, we are bound to infer that this first case is intended to be typical of the way of appointment followed in all later cases."

tablished churches in Lystra, Iconium, and Antioch."[107] It appears that Paul was not content to leave these cities until he and Barnabas had put local leaders in charge. Leaving them without adequate leadership was not an option for Paul. He had to know that his converts were going to be taken care of.

The next place that Paul's pastoral ministry is mentioned is in Acts 18, which discusses his ministry in Corinth. Luke provides some details on how the church in Corinth was started. Paul, as was his practice, had started off preaching in the synagogue. The Jews, however, became abusive and Paul left them stating, "From now on I will go to the Gentiles."[108] Paul then moved his ministry next door to the synagogue and began meeting in the house of Titius Justus, a god-fearer.[109] Luke also records that Crispus, the ruler of the synagogue and, "his entire household believed in the Lord; and many of the Corinthians who heard him believed and were baptized."[110] Tannehill points out that Paul's move from the synagogue did not involve giving up much ground.[111] Being that close to the synagogue would still allow Paul to have some influence there. Titius Justus was a god-fearing Gentile with a home large enough to accommodate the group meeting there and it was adjacent to the synagogue. "People who had been accustomed to attend the synagogue did not have to leave their habitual route if they wished to go on hearing Paul: they made their way toward the synagogue, as usual, but turned in next door."[112] There was an additional prestige bestowed on the young church by having the former ruler of the synagogue, Crispus, as one of the foundational members.

While in Corinth, Paul received a vision encouraging him not to fear and to keep on speaking. This vision will be discussed in detail in the chapter devoted to discussing Mystical Experiences. The result of the vision, however, was that Paul stayed in Corinth for a year and a half, "teach-

---

[107] Detwiler, 38.

[108] Acts 18:6.

[109] Thompson, 400–401, This narrative marks the first time in the accounts of the Pauline missions that the Christian community separated from the Jewish synagogue, "suggesting that the Jewish rejection of the gospel message created that scenario."

[110] Acts 18:8. Paul referred to Cripus in 1 Corinthians 1:14 as one of the few families that he himself baptized in Corinth. It is also very likely that Titius Justus is "Gaius" that Paul refers to in 1 Corinthians 1:14 and Romans 16:23. According to Bruce, *Paul: Apostle of the Heart Set Free*, 251, his full name would have been Gaius Titius Justus, marking him as a Roman citizen.

[111] Tannehill, 222.

[112] Bruce, 350.

ing them the word of God."[113] There were many other situations in Paul's ministry where he was forced by persecution to leave before he had had a chance to fully develop the church and its leaders. This eighteen-month period of ministry in Corinth, however, allowed Paul to establish the church in the way that he saw fit. He was able to build the community without fear or distraction. This extensive period of ministry that Paul spent in Corinth also allowed him to develop the leaders that he would leave in charge when he left. Paul alluded to this process of building the church in 1 Corinthians 3:10, "By the grace God has given me, I laid a foundation as an expert builder, and someone else is building on it."[114]

It is not insignificant that Paul wrote to the Corinthians as he did after spending a year and a half with them. He was their pastor and would have gotten to know them well and vice versa. This period of time was evidently very significant for the church as well as for Paul. There is more information about the inner workings of the Corinthian church than about any other church in the New Testament except the Jerusalem church. Not only does Luke go into some detail about the church in Corinth which he does not do in other places, two of Paul's longer letters to the church there also survived to become a part of the New Testament.[115]

Another city in which Paul's pastoral ministry was clearly seen was in Ephesus. Luke describes Paul's work there in Acts 19. This was another city in which Paul spent a significant amount of time. Luke records that Paul spent two years teaching at the hall of Tyrannus. Paul said later that he spent a total of three years in Ephesus.[116] The first part of the chapter, in which Paul met twelve disciples in Ephesus who had not received the Holy Spirit, will be dealt with under the section dealing with Mystical Experiences. Luke records that Paul again started his ministry in the synagogue. He taught there for three months before unspecified opposition forced him out. Luke does not state in this case that it was the synagogue authorities that forced Paul out.[117] In any case, this was the longest period of time that Paul had been able to preach in a synagogue.[118] When he did decide to leave the synagogue Paul, "took the disciples with him and

---

[113] Acts 18:11.

[114] Calvin, 136, "We also gather how difficult and laborious the building of the Church is, when the most distinguished master-builder spent so much time in laying the foundation of one."

[115] Blaiklock, 149

[116] Acts 20:31.

[117] Bruce, 290.

[118] Krodel, 360.

had discussions daily in the lecture hall of Tyrannus."[119] Luke does not record how many disciples Paul took with him when he left the synagogue. Luke did, however, recount the story of the twelve disciples in the first part of the chapter. These twelve were likely the foundational members of the Ephesian church.[120] It is probably safe to conclude that when Paul left the synagogue to begin holding his own meetings he started with at least this core of twelve believers, and probably more.

These meetings at the hall of Tyrannus went on daily for two years. When Paul was preaching regularly at the synagogue, his public influence would have been limited to once a week. Now freed from the confines of the synagogue Paul spoke daily in the rented hall, multiplying his influence in Ephesus.[121] The way that Luke describes these meetings in the hall of Tyrannus does not sound like gatherings that were limited to only believers. They sound more like open lectures in which Paul taught and discussed Christianity with all those who were interested. According to Luke, the results of these meetings was that, "all the Jews and Greeks who lived in the province of Asia heard the word of the Lord."[122] Paul's pastoral ministry among the Ephesian believers would also be enhanced as he made himself available daily to those who came to the hall of Tyrannus.

While these meetings in the hall of Tyrannus sound more evangelistic than pastoral, there can be little doubt that Paul's pastoral nature influenced the growth of the church in Ephesus. Later in Acts, Paul met with the elders of the Ephesian church at Miletus to tell them good-bye. Paul sensed that his end was near and he did not think that he would see them again. He wanted to meet with them one final time and address them. That speech is recorded in Acts 20:18-35. This is a very significant speech and contains Paul's perception of his time of ministry while in Ephesus. This is the only message in Acts where Paul specifically addresses a Christian audience and it is the only place in Acts where Paul describes the manner in which he conducted his ministry. This passage sounds the closest to the Paul that is revealed through his letters.[123] The message here also provides the clearest picture in Acts of the type of leadership that existed in the Gentile churches.[124]

---

[119] Acts 19:9.

[120] Thompson, 407, "What Luke clearly depicts in this initial scene of Paul's Ephesian ministry is the establishment of the Christian community . . . ."

[121] Krodel, 360–61.

[122] Acts 19:10.

[123] Stott, 323.

[124] Joseph B. Tyson, "The Emerging Church and the Problem of Authority in Acts,"

Paul's sermon to the Ephesian elders provides a number of insights into the way that he conducted his apostolic ministry and specifically the area of pastoral ministry. First of all, Paul reminds them of his attitude. He said that he, "served the Lord with great humility." Paul's humble attitude is reminiscent of Jesus' attitude. He never forced His agenda or His message on people. Jesus said that He, "did not come to be served, but to serve and to give his life as a ransom for many." [125] It is apparent that Paul followed this pattern of service in Ephesus. One of the ways that Paul's humility was shown was in the fact that he did not accept financial help from the church. He stated, "You yourselves know that these hands of mine have supplied my own needs and the needs of my companions." [126] Paul evidently worked at his occupation in the morning and then taught and fulfilled his pastoral duties in the afternoon. [127] Paul's example of humility and service provided a model for the Ephesian elders to emulate. [128] Paul concludes his sermon by reminding them in verse 35, "In everything I did, I showed you that by this kind of hard work we must help the weak, remembering the words the Lord Jesus himself said: 'It is more blessed to give than to receive.'" Paul had set a personal example before them and now he was reminding them of Jesus' own words and example. Paul never hesitated to use himself as an example.

A second insight that this sermon provides is in the sphere of Paul's ministry. Paul tells them that he did not hesitate, "to preach anything that would be helpful to you but have taught you publicly and from house to house." Paul established the Ephesian church on the preaching of the gospel. Paul had preached and taught in the synagogue, the hall of Tyrannus, and in people's homes. As a pastor, Paul was always in the public eye and never attempted to hide what he was teaching. [129] His message was straightforward and clear and he never hid the fact that his goal was to make converts and establish churches. He states in verse 21, "I have declared to both Jews and Greeks that they must turn to God in repentance and have faith in our Lord Jesus." His pastoral ministry was not confined to just the

---

Interpretation 42 (1988) 143.

[125] Matthew 20:28.

[126] Acts 20:34.

[127] Neil, 204, "The picture we get is of Paul working at his trade daily from daybreak to 11 AM (20:34; 1 C. 4:12), and then engaging in teaching and discussion for the next five hours with any who were prepared to listen, when Tyrannus had finished his lectures and the room was available."

[128] Arrington, 210.

[129] Marshall, 330.

house churches. Paul was a pastor in the synagogue, his workshop, and in the hall of Tyrannus.

The last insight that this sermon gives into Paul's pastoral ministry is that of the passion that he feels for the Ephesian church. While Paul was present, he was able to protect the church from false teaching and the "savage wolves" that would want to harm the people of God in Ephesus. Now that he is leaving, however, his concern is evident that the believers be protected from attack. Paul encourages the elders to, "Keep watch over yourselves and all the flock of which the Holy Spirit has made you over-seers."[130] Paul is encouraging the elders to do what he did by caring for the flock that God has given them responsibility for. Paul reminds them here of the weighty responsibility that they have been given to guard the sheep. The cost of the sheep was high; they were purchased with the blood of Christ.[131] The elders are responsible to make sure that the flock is fed with the proper spiritual nourishment.[132] The context here indicates that the spiritual nourishment the elders are to provide is found in the preaching and teaching of the Word of God. This ministry of the Word would be one of the main weapons that the pastors would have to protect their flock.[133] Again, Paul reminds them of his own example, "So be on your guard! Remember that for three years I never stopped warning each of you night and day with tears."[134]

One final passage regarding "Paul the Pastor" will be examined. This one concerns Paul's visit with the believers in Troas during his final journey to Jerusalem in Acts 20:7-12. Luke records in verse 6 that Paul stayed there for seven days. Luke writes in verse 7, that, "On the first day of the week we came together to break bread. Paul spoke to the people and, because he intended to leave the next day, kept on talking until midnight." The raising of Eutychus from the dead will be dealt with in the section on "Paul the Miracle Worker." In this passage, "Luke allows us a glimpse of what was probably a typical meeting of Christians in these early days of the church."[135] In fact, this is one of the very few first century church services in which the modern reader is allowed to get some glimpse of what went

---

[130] Acts 20:28.

[131] John Ernest Best, "Paul's Theology of the Corporate Life of the Local Church," Th. D. diss., Dallas Theological Seminary, 1984, 54.

[132] Arrington, 209, "They had been appointed by the Spirit, and he had given them spiritual gifts equipping them for their ministry as shepherds of the church of God."

[133] Beasley-Murray, 654.

[134] Acts 20:31.

[135] Williams, 347.

on. It should be noted that this passage in Acts is one of the "we" passages indicating that Luke was present at this meeting and providing an eyewitness account.

Paul appears to lead this meeting. The central elements of the worship are the breaking of bread together and Paul's preaching. Most scholars accept that the breaking of bread is referring to a celebration of the Lord's Supper.[136] This was likely the regular weekly meeting of the believers in Troas, and Paul, as the honored special guest led the meeting. Luke does not specify what time the meeting started. He does, however, record the fact that Paul spoke until midnight. After the incident with Eutychus, they "broke bread and ate." Paul then continued his message until daybreak. Bruce comments on the length of Paul's message, "Church meetings were not regulated by the clock in those days, and the opportunity of listening to Paul was not one to be cut short; what did it matter if his conversation went on until midnight?"[137]

This is the last picture that Luke provides of Paul in a pastoral role. This view of Paul in Acts corresponds with the pastoral view of Paul that is seen in his letters. Here in Troas, Paul seems to enjoy the atmosphere of fellowship that is present in the church. He takes great pleasure in spending this time with one of his churches. He makes no effort to close the meeting early, even though he was leaving the next morning. Luke's portrayal of Paul as a pastor seems to capture the essence of the type of leadership that Paul provided for the communities that he founded.

In comparing the leadership styles of Peter and Paul, it was noted that Luke portrays Peter as having more of a governmental type of authority in the early days of the Jerusalem church. He provided direction, as in the case of selecting Matthias to take Judas' place. Peter was involved in church discipline, as in the case of Ananias and Sapphira. He provided approval and oversight for the Samaritan mission that Philip was involved in. As one of the inner circle (Peter, James, and John) of the original Twelve, Peter's authority to lead and speak for Jesus to His followers was unquestioned. Peter's strong leadership in the tumultuous days after Jesus' ascension provided the stability that the early church needed. His strong leadership was also needed as the community was being formed in Jerusalem and as they attempted to understand what their role and mission was.

It could be argued that Peter was functioning as a pastor in the church at Jerusalem. Luke, however, does not emphasize this aspect of Peter's leadership. If anything, the Twelve possibly worked together to provide

---

[136] Marshall, 325; Stott, 321; Bruce, 384.

[137] Bruce, 384–85.

pastoral oversight for the church in Jerusalem. Over time, Peter's role shifted outward to more of that of a traveling missionary and evangelist. In Acts, Luke shows Peter working throughout Palestine in that role. While Luke makes some allusions to Peter being involved in pastoral ministry, it is not nearly as pronounced as it is in Paul's ministry.

Luke's presentation of the leadership aspect of Paul's ministry clearly highlights his role as a pastor, first in Antioch, and then in the churches that he started. On at least three different occasions Paul spent significant amounts of time in particular cities operating in the role of a pastor. This took place in Antioch, Corinth, and Ephesus. He worked with Barnabas in Antioch for a year. He was in Corinth for at least a year and a half, and he was in Ephesus for three years.

Luke shows that Paul's authority and leadership come from the fact that he was the spiritual father to his group of churches that looked to him for leadership. It was natural for them to look to Paul in this way because he was the one who was responsible for their conversion. He was also the one who discipled them and trained their leaders. In many ways Paul was still a pastor to them, even though he had entrusted the leadership of the particular church to others.

Paul's message to the Ephesian elders was discussed. In this sermon Paul discusses at some length, his pastoral ministry in Ephesus. He reminded them that he had served among them, "with great humility," and that he had proclaimed to them, "the whole will of God." Paul makes no mention in this message of miracles but seems to be purposely highlighting his example as a servant among them. Luke appears to use this message by Paul to present him as the consummate pastor, passionately concerned with passing on some last instructions to the Ephesian elders before he continues on in his fateful trip to Jerusalem.

Even though Paul is not portrayed as a governmental leader in the same way that Peter is, Luke still shows that Paul occupied a very important leadership role in the early church. He was the one, who more than anyone else, brought the first organization and church government to those early Christian communities that he founded. In a very real sense, he was able to take that which Peter and the Twelve started and translate it to the Greek world.

While Luke presents the leadership aspects of the two apostles' ministries differently, he still makes it very clear that they had much in common. Both men attempted to follow Jesus' example in the way that they exercised their authority. Peter and Paul both provided key leadership at crucial stages of the church's growth. As one of the original Twelve apostles, Peter helped the church to grow in its early days in Jerusalem. He helped that church, in particular, to stay on track during times of intense persecution. Peter lived up to his nickname of "the Rock." Paul's ministry of evangelism and church planting will be discussed later. As a pastor, however, he nurtured the churches that he had started so that they would be able to withstand persecution. He saw himself as a shepherd of the flock of God that had been purchased with the blood of Christ.

Evangelism and Church Planting

THE next aspect of Peter and Paul's apostolic ministries that will be examined is that of evangelism and church planting. Both men were heavily involved in evangelism and missionary work. It was discussed in the previous section how Peter's role evolved from one of a leadership position in the Jerusalem church into that of a missionary. Cullman says, "Peter is not the archetype of the church official but of the missionary."[1] The two functions of church administration and missionary work were eventually separated. From the evidence that is presented in Acts, these two functions were divided between James and Peter.[2] Cullman sees this division of church administration and missionary work to be the result of a, "gradual and natural development."[3] As both men saw the type of work that they were suited and gifted for, they were able over a period of time, to make a smooth transition into those roles. In the long run, Peter seemed to be much more effective in an evangelistic role, and from what is seen of James at the Jerusalem Council, he seemed to flourish in his leadership role. On the other hand, from the very beginning of Paul's ministry, he was involved in evangelistic activity. Schmithals believes that all of the apostles were called to be missionaries.[4] In his understanding, the nature of the apostolic office was an evangelistic one. Schmithals believes that all of the apostles were involved in the same type of evangelistic work that is exemplified in the ministries of Peter and Paul. They were just the two that Luke focused on. This section will examine how each man sought to spread the Gospel message and also examine the sphere that each man felt called to.

---

[1] Cullman, 41.

[2] Ibid., 41–42.

[3] Ibid, 42.

[4] Walter Schmithals, *The Office of Apostle in the Early Church*, trans. John E. Steely, (Nashville: Abingdon, 1969) 23.

Peter the Evangelist

The first place in Acts that Peter is seen in an evangelistic role is on the day of Pentecost in 2:14-41. Peter's leadership role is also seen in this passage as he steps forward with the rest of the Twelve and speaks on their behalf. It is Peter's message here that shows his evangelistic ability. The Holy Spirit had fallen on the 120 people in the house with accompanying physical manifestations. This experience will be discussed in the chapter dealing with "Mystical and Supernatural Experiences." The noise of the group praying and speaking in other languages caused a crowd to assemble. Peter then addressed the crowd.

Before engaging Peter's sermon, this is an appropriate place to discuss some of the critical issues that are associated with the various speeches and sermons in Acts. Many scholars believe that the speeches in Acts are Lukan creations that he put into the mouths of his characters. Krodel, for example, in referring to Peter's message here in Acts 2 says, "Like all speeches in Acts this keynote address is a Lukan composition."[5] Haenchen provides another example of this point of view when he says that the speeches in Acts, "are literary compositions thought out to the last detail."[6] These scholars believe that Luke followed the culturally accepted norm in inventing speeches for the people that he was writing about. Many historians of Luke's day were not very concerned with the accuracy of the account that they were writing.[7] Luke has often been placed in this category.

One of the arguments that is often used is that Luke was not present for most of the speeches in Acts so there was no way he could have known, for example, what Peter preached on Pentecost or at Cornelius' house.[8] While it does appear to be a fact that Luke was not present for a number of the speeches in Acts, there is no reason that he could not have spoken with someone who was there and gotten a summary of the sermon. Even the most conservative New Testament scholar acknowledges that Luke did not record the speeches or sermons verbatim. It is possible that the author of Acts summarized what he heard himself or what one of his sources told him.

Hemer understands the primary issue here to be the question of whether or not the speeches are Lukan creations or Lukan summaries.[9] There is a

---

[5] Krodel, *Acts*, Proclamation Commentaries, 19.

[6] Haenchen, 82.

[7] Marshall, *Luke: Historian and Theologian*, 56.

[8] Krodel, *Acts*, Augsburg Commentary on the New Testament, 34–35.

[9] Hemer, 418.

big difference between the two. If the speeches are in fact Lukan creations and not actual speeches or sermons from Peter, Paul, etc., it changes the way that Luke is perceived as a historian.[10] In chapter 1 of this study, the idea was put forth that Luke was both a reliable historian and a theologian. The idea that Luke put speeches and sermons into his character's mouths to advance his own theological positions serves to weaken his position as a historian. It is inconsistent to argue that on the one hand, Luke is reliable as a historian, yet at the same time to accept the premise that he created sermons and speeches that historical characters in his book supposedly spoke. He prefaced his gospel by saying that he, "carefully investigated everything from the beginning."[11] Luke appears to be committed to providing an accurate account of the things that he wrote about. Even Krodel acknowledges that, "Luke was a better historian than anyone else among his contemporaries."[12] Luke's reliability as a historian, then, "must in the end be judged by the detailed assessment of his performance."[13]

Other scholars have attempted to find some middle ground between the idea Lukan summaries versus Lukan creations. Keathley, for example, argues that the speeches in Acts are literary compositions because they, "reflect the same Lukan style and vocabulary that are found in the narrative sections of the book."[14] While arguing that they are Lukan creations, however, he also believes that the central theme of the particular speech or sermon had been preserved in the oral traditions of the church. Luke took this as his starting point and then used his literary ability to craft a speech that fit with his particular theological views.[15]

While this is an interesting theory, the problem comes when an interpreter attempts to determine what part of the speech is genuine and which part is literary composition. At this point, the interpreter is back where they started in not knowing if the speeches are historically accurate or not. If Luke is a reliable historian, would he invent material for the sake of his readers? He claimed that he investigated everything carefully before he wrote his gospel. He has given no reason to doubt that he did any less when he wrote Acts.

---

[10] Ibid., 42, "The question whether the content of a reported speech represents what was actually said is in its way a question of historical reliability."

[11] Luke 1:3.

[12] Krodel, 41.

[13] Hemer, 43.

[14] Naymond H. Keathley, *The Church's Mission to the Gentiles: Acts of the Apostles, Epistles of Paul* (Macon, Ga.: Smyth & Helwys, 1999) 27–28.

[15] Ibid.

Haenchen, however, argues that only the naïve believe that Luke went about writing Acts in the same way that he wrote his gospel.[16] There simply were not the same kinds of written sources available to him as there had been for the gospel. The only written source that Haenchen acknowledges is that of a travel diary from one of Paul's companions. While conceding Haenchen's point about written sources being limited, it must be noted that he does not appear to consider the possibility that the author of Acts had living sources that he was able to draw from. Luke, to some degree, may have had personal access to the Twelve and others that would have been able to provide him with much information about the early days of the church. If the author of Acts was in fact Luke, the companion of Paul, he obviously would have drawn much material and information from him as well.

Another argument Krodel makes for the speeches in Acts being Lukan creations is the fact that they are so short.[17] He believes that Luke deliberately wrote them short for his readers. The length of the speeches should not provide a basis for rejecting them as historically accurate, however. It has been argued already that the messages that Luke includes in Acts are summaries or abstracts of the whole message. They are not meant to be entire sermons. By including portions and summaries of the speeches, Luke is able to provide the reader with the essence of the particular message that one of his characters made.

While in no way resolving the debate about whether or not the speeches in Acts are Lukan creations or summaries, the case has been made that Luke did, in fact, make the attempt to provide an accurate synopsis of the different messages that he records. He is selective in the material that he presents and he edited what he did include. This selectivity by Luke should come as no surprise and it was discussed in chapter 1 of this study. The speeches and sermons that he includes in Acts appear to be genuine abstracts of real messages rather than literary creations of the author.[18]

In turning now to Peter's message on Pentecost, the first thing that he addresses is the charge of drunkenness: "They have had too much wine."[19] It is easy to see why a charge of drunkenness was made. Pentecost was one

---

[16] Haenchen, 82.

[17] Krodel, 35.

[18] Hemer, 427, "In Luke's writing the spoken word is not a thing apart, a set-piece embodying a distinct literary technique of commentary. It is embedded in the narrative, in a degree which forces the question whether the sources which can be traced in some parts point to the use of respectable sources elsewhere."

[19] Acts 2:13.

of the three great festivals of Israel and there were thousands of pilgrims in Jerusalem that had come from all over the world to be part of the festivities.[20] Luke emphasizes the fact by stating that, "God-fearing Jews from every nation under heaven" had come to Jerusalem.[21] Pentecost was a harvest festival in which the people celebrated and gave thanks to God for the harvest. It was also a celebration that commemorated God's giving of the Law to Moses at Sinai.[22] In the context of a national holiday with thousands of pilgrims visiting friends and family in Jerusalem, the idea of people drinking too much wine is not that far fetched. Peter's argument against drunkenness is simple, however: "It's only nine in the morning!"[23] While they might feel a hangover from the previous night's drinking, it is unlikely that they would have started drinking this early.[24] Peter's answer that it is too early in the morning to have started drinking injects humor into the situation and possibly helps prepare the crowd to listen to what he says.[25]

Peter then begins to explain what has happened. In his message he quotes three different passages of Scripture: Joel 2:28-32, Psalm 16:8-11, and Psalm 110:1. He anchors his message firmly in Scriptures that would have been familiar to his audience. While Peter quotes the passage in Joel, he does not provide any commentary for it. He lets the Scripture speak for itself. It was being fulfilled before the onlooker's eyes. God was starting to pour his Spirit out, "on all people." Both men and women, young and old were experiencing the fulfillment of the prophecy. This was only the beginning but this visible outpouring on the disciples was the evidence that the "last days" had begun.[26] The passage from Joel also expresses the fact that the promise of the outpouring of God's Spirit, "will be progressively realized through the course of the mission."[27] The last verse that Peter quotes from Joel says, "And everyone who calls on the name of the Lord will be saved." This verse previews the inclusion of the Samaritans and the Gentiles in the promise of God. At this point, however, Peter was probably

---

[20] Charles F. Pfeiffer, Howard F. Vos, John Rea, eds., *Wycliffe Bible Encyclopedia Volume 2: K–Z* (Chicago: Moody, 1975) 1306.

[21] Acts 2:5.

[22] Ibid., 1307.

[23] Acts 2:15.

[24] Talbert, 44, "In the Mediterranean world, even the worst debauchery did not begin until nine in the morning."

[25] Bruce, 60.

[26] Bruce, "The Significance of the Speeches for Interpreting Acts," 21.

[27] Tannehill, "The Functions of Peter's Mission Speeches in the Narrative of Acts," 404.

only thinking of the Jewish people who lived in distant lands.[28] Many of these would have made up Peter's audience, having made the long trip to Jerusalem for the festival.

Peter then provides an overview of Jesus' ministry, crucifixion, and resurrection. Many in the crowd would have been familiar with Jesus, especially those who were residents of Jerusalem. If those in the crowd who were residents of Jerusalem had supported their leaders in rejecting and killing their Messiah, they must now face the fact that they have opposed God's purpose for their nation.[29] This is why Peter's message is very pointed and direct. God did miracles through Jesus openly and in public. Many that Peter was speaking to had probably had the opportunity to see Jesus in action. These mighty works that Jesus performed were evidence that God had been working through Him.[30] However, many in the crowd were responsible for helping to hand over Jesus to the Romans. As Peter said, "and you, with the help of wicked men, put him to death by nailing him on the cross."[31] Peter's essential message in emphasizing that Jesus had fulfilled the Old Testament prophecies would have still been valid, even without making this point as strongly as he did.[32] It was important to Peter, however, that his audience be confronted with their guilt in the death of Christ so that they could receive forgiveness. Even though Peter laid the responsibility for Jesus' death at the feet of many in his audience, it is also clear that the God's ultimate purpose was fulfilled through Christ's death.[33]

Peter then discusses the fact that God raised Jesus from the dead and uses a second passage of Scripture to establish a basis for the resurrection. He quotes from Psalm 16:8-11. Peter does provide some commentary for these verses. He points out that David was a prophet and was speaking prophetically that one of his descendants would be placed on his throne in fulfillment of the covenant that God had established with him. "Seeing what was ahead, he spoke of the resurrection of the Christ, that he was not abandoned to the grave, nor did his body see decay."[34] David could

---

[28] Bruce, *The Book of the Acts*, 61, "Luke sees in these words an adumbration of the worldwide Gentile mission, even if Peter could not have realized their full import when he quoted them on the day of Pentecost." See also Blaiklock, 59.

[29] Tannehill, 402.

[30] Neil, 76.

[31] Acts 2:23.

[32] Morris, 115.

[33] John T. Carroll and Joel B. Green, *The Death of Jesus in Early Christianity* (Peabody, Mass.: Hendrickson, 1995) 68–69. See also Morris, 123.

[34] Acts 2:31.

not have been speaking of himself in these verses because he had died and his tomb was a well-known landmark. David further predicted that God would raise this descendant from the dead.[35] By using this Scripture to establish the resurrection, Peter then goes a step farther and proclaims Jesus as Lord.[36] Being raised from the dead, Jesus was, "Exalted to the right hand of God,"[37] and established as the Messiah of God.

The third passage of Scripture that Peter uses is Psalm 110:1. This verse builds on the idea of the Lordship of Christ. This verse is not addressed to David personally. This invitation here to sit at God's right hand is not given to him. It is another prophetic passage addressed to the son of David, and has found its fulfillment in Christ.[38] Peter's use of this passage from the Psalms serves to highlight the Lordship of Christ.[39] Peter concludes his message, "Therefore, let all Israel be assured of this: God has made this Jesus, whom you crucified, both Lord and Christ."[40]

The results of Peter's evangelistic sermon were immediately seen. "When the people heard this, they were cut to the heart and said to Peter and the other apostles, "'Brothers, what shall we do?'""[41] Peter's response took them to a place of decision for Christ: "Repent and be baptized, every one of you, in the name of Jesus Christ for the forgiveness of your sins."[42] Bruce notes, "Peter's preaching proved effective, not only persuading his hearers' minds but convicting their consciences."[43] Tannehill points out the fact that Peter emphasized the recent crime of many in his audience of handing an innocent man over to be crucified. His words have the desired effect and many in the crowd, "are shocked to recognize what they have done and immediately cry out for some remedy."[44] Peter links the death of Jesus with a call for repentance.[45] He also understood that conviction and feelings of guilt were not enough. The people needed to repent of their sins

---

[35] Jacques Dupont, *The Salvation of the Gentiles: Studies in the Acts of the Apostles*, trans. John R. Keating (New York: Paulist, 1979) 108–109.

[36] Williams, 53.

[37] Acts 2:33.

[38] Bruce, 67

[39] Dupont, 112–13.

[40] Acts 2: 36.

[41] Acts 2:37.

[42] Acts 2:38.

[43] Bruce, 69.

[44] Tannehill, 404.

[45] Carroll and Green, 78–79.

and be baptized. Repentance had to do with a change of heart and baptism was an outward symbol of that change.[46]

Luke records that "about three thousand" people accepted Peter's invitation and were added to the church. The new community went from having around 120 members to over 3,000 members after Peter's first evangelistic sermon. It is only here and in 4:4 that Luke provides the reader with specific numerical results of evangelistic activity. In a number of other passages, he refers to growth and expansion in the church in general terms, without providing any specific numbers.[47] Luke only gives specific figures in regards to Jewish Christianity.[48] While he discusses the growth of the Gentile church and shows Paul planting church after church in the Greek world, he does not see a need to provide any numbers.

Some scholars would argue that the "three thousand" that Luke mentions is an unrealistic number.[49] In reality, however, there is no reason to doubt Luke's narrative. The city was full of pilgrims because of Pentecost and a large crowd would gather quickly in response to seeing and hearing something unusual. If Peter had a strong voice, he could have easily preached to a crowd of multiple thousands. An example of this type of open air preaching is seen in early American history. Benjamin Franklin describes an outdoor meeting in which he heard evangelist George Whitfield preach. Ever the scientist and thinker, Franklin computed the crowd at 30,000, all who would have been able to hear Whitefield's sermon clearly.[50]

In further dealing with the issue of three thousand people being added to the church, it is important to remember that many of these were pilgrims and would be returning to their homelands taking the Gospel with them and forming Christian communities there.[51] It is also likely that the bap-

---

[46] Arrington, 31–32.

[47] Acts 6:1; 8:6; and 9:31 are three examples.

[48] Krodel, 91.

[49] Ibid., 72. Krodel, for example, believes that Luke exaggerated the number of converts. His argument is a weak one, however. He asks the question, "For instance, where in Jerusalem could such a mass of people have gathered?" Krodel also questions how Peter could have spoken to such a large group without amplification. These questions are dealt with above.

[50] Benjamin Franklin, *Autobiography and Selected Writings*, ed. Larzer Ziff (New York: Holt, Rinehart and Winston, 1965) 110, Franklin says of Whitefield, "He had a loud and clear voice, and articulated his words and sentences so perfectly, that he might be heard and understood at a great distance, especially as his auditories, however numerous, observed the most exact silence."

[51] Williams, 55. See also Neil, 80, "Such a large number would have involved massive organizational problems not suggested in verses 44–7. What is more likely is that many overseas Jews who were in Jerusalem for Pentecost returned to their own countries as baptized Christians, thus furthering the anonymous spread of the Gospel which is so

tisms did not all take place that day. There was probably further instruction and teaching provided for these new believers.[52] This is implied in verse 40 where, "With many other words he warned them; and he pleaded with them," and also in verse 42 which states that, "They devoted themselves to the apostles' teaching."

The next place in which Peter is seen in an evangelistic setting is in Acts 3. After healing the crippled man at the temple, Peter takes advantage of the crowd that gathers to preach an evangelistic message. The miracle will be dealt with separately in the next chapter. The attention here will be on the message that Peter preached and what resulted from it. It can be noted here that Peter's evangelistic ministry is almost exclusively based on interpreting an act of God.[53] On Pentecost, his sermon was based on interpreting the outpouring of the Holy Spirit to the crowd that gathered. Here, he will interpret the healing of the lame man to those who gather and let them know that God is the One responsible. Even his message to Cornelius' household is given after both he and Cornelius had had visions. Peter again interprets what God is saying.

From a literary point of view, the situation in Acts 3 is very similar to what happened in chapter 2. A supernatural event took place and Peter used it as a platform to preach to the curious and amazed onlookers. Those who had seen the miracle, "were filled with wonder and amazement at what had happened to him."[54] As word spread through the crowd about the miracle, "all the people were astonished and came running to them in the place called Solomon's Colonnade."[55]

When Peter saw what was happening, he realized that the miracle had provided him with an opportunity to address those who were there. The first thing that he did was to deflect any credit for the healing from John or himself. Peter then appealed to the nationalism of the crowd by referring to the "God of Abraham, Isaac and Jacob, the God of our fathers," and associating Jesus with Him. Like the Pentecost speech, Peter again preaches a message of repentance for the specific act of handing Jesus over to be crucified. In this message, however, Peter expands the call to repentance and gives both the positive and the negative possibilities that the audience

---

frequently attested in Acts."

[52] Williams, 55.

[53] David W. Gill, *Peter the Rock: Extraordinary Insights from an Ordinary Man* (Downers Grove, Ill.: InterVarsity, 1986.) 142.

[54] Acts 3:10.

[55] Acts 3:11.

must choose.[56] On the positive side, repentance would bring a forgiveness of their sins, times of refreshing, and a relationship with Christ. On the negative side, failure to repent would result in being cut off from God and the community.

In this message, Peter presents Jesus as the new Moses who must be obeyed. In so doing, he makes it clear that only those who accept Jesus and His message can be regarded as the people of God.[57] Peter quotes from Deuteronomy 18:15, 18-19 and also makes mention of, "all the prophets from Samuel on," who had also, "foretold these days," and reminding the audience that they were, "heirs of the prophets and of the covenant God made with your fathers." After referring to Moses and the prophets, Peter then makes reference to Abraham and quotes Genesis 22:18, "Through your offspring all peoples on earth will be blessed." As Jews, Peter's audience occupied a privileged position as children of Abraham. However, under the new covenant that God was establishing in Christ, the only way that they could take advantage of this privilege was through repentance.[58]

Peter's message starts off being pointed and direct. In strong terms, he accuses his hearers of handing Jesus over to be crucified. "You handed him over to be killed, and you disowned him before Pilate . . . You disowned the Holy and Righteous One . . . You killed the author of life."[59] After speaking so strongly, Peter then changes his tone and speaks in conciliatory terms. "Now, brothers, I know that you acted in ignorance, as did your leaders."[60] Peter's aim was to win these Jews over, not to condemn them. They were responsible for an innocent man's death, yet pardon and forgiveness were available to all that would receive it. He wanted his audience to feel convicted but he also wanted them to be able to respond to his message of repentance.

The result of Peter's message was spectacular. Luke does not say specifically how many were converted through this message. He does, however, say that after this sermon, the total number of men who had believed had grown to, "about five thousand." Williams points out that the word Luke uses for "men" is generally used to show men as being distinct from women.[61] Luke may only be officially counting men, yet still be inferring

---

[56] Tannehill, 406.

[57] Neil, 86.

[58] Talbert, 56. See also Tannehill, *The Narrative Unity of Luke-Acts A Literary Interpretation, Volume Two: The Acts of the Apostles*, 56.

[59] Acts 3:13-15.

[60] Acts 3:17.

[61] Williams, 79.

that women were responding to the message also. If women were included, the number of converts may well have been over 5,000. Peter's success as an evangelist can be clearly seen in this figure. The implication that Luke gives is that two of Peter's sermons have accounted for over 5,000 people being added to the church. This rapid growth also appeared to be one of the factors that lead to the persecution of the early church. A small movement is easy to ignore. Several thousand converts over a short period of time are much more difficult to ignore.[62]

Another example of Peter as an evangelist is seen in Acts 8:25. After Peter and John went to Samaria and assisted Philip, they worked their way back to Jerusalem, "preaching the gospel in many Samaritan villages." Once Peter and John had seen the Samaritans accepting the gospel and receiving the Holy Spirit, they took every opportunity to share the message in the villages that they went through. In their minds, at least, the wall of separation between the Jews and the Samaritans had come down. The Samaritan mission continued through two of the most eminent of the Jerusalem apostles and showed that, "The reception of the Samaritans into the church was thus firmly endorsed."[63] This verse is merely a summary statement by Luke and he does not provide any specific details about Peter and John's evangelistic work. It does show, however, the direction that Peter's ministry seemed to be going in. Peter has progressed from only preaching to a Jewish audience to a Samaritan audience. In the next picture that Luke provides of Peter as an evangelist, he will be seen progressing even farther, taking the gospel message into the house of a Gentile.

The last example of Peter's evangelistic ministry that will be discussed is that of his encounter with Cornelius in Acts 10. This story also involves Peter having a vision. This vision will be discussed later in the chapter on Supernatural and Mystical Experiences. The vision was instrumental in shifting the way that he thought. The focus here will be on Peter's actual time of ministry in Cornelius' house and the results of that ministry. This entire episode is very important to Luke. This can be seen by the fact that it is repeated in one form or other three times. The amount of space that he devotes to the story of Cornelius indicates how important it was to Luke.[64] This narrative, "stands as a pivotal event in the narrative sequence."[65]

---

[62] Neil, 88.

[63] Marshall, *The Acts of the Apostles*, 160.

[64] Joseph B. Tyson, "The Gentile Mission and the Authority of Scripture in Acts," *New Testament Studies* 33 (1987) 624, "The centerpiece of Luke's treatment of the Gentile mission is in the story of Cornelius."

[65] Thompson, 295.

The type of message that Peter preached in Cornelius' house was both similar and different from that he had preached to Jewish audiences.[66] It was similar in that it contained the four basic elements that were present in all apostolic preaching: the fulfillment of prophecy, a recounting of Jesus' ministry, death, and resurrection, the apostles' personal witness, and the assurance of forgiveness to all who believe in Jesus.[67] This sermon is the first recorded preaching of the gospel to the Gentile world.[68] Peter's sermon is also different from those he has preached to Jewish audiences in several ways. First of all, there is no accusation of the Gentiles for complicity in the death of Jesus. He lays the blame for Jesus' death squarely on the Jews, "They killed him by hanging him on a tree."[69] Secondly, Peter does not assume that his audience has as much firsthand knowledge as the Jews do about Jesus' ministry. He provides them with more background information about Jesus' life and ministry and explains what His mission was.[70] A third way that this message is different from those preached to the Jews is in its tone. Peter begins his message by building a bridge to his audience, "I now realize how true it is that God does not show favoritism but accepts men from every nation who fear him and do what is right."[71] Because Peter is not accusing the Gentiles of being a part of Jesus' murder, his sermon is much less pointed. Peter emphasizes a message of peace that is available through the forgiveness of sins.

This entire episode has expanded Peter's theology. He is beginning to see the gospel as universal. His message shows a progression and development of thought. Peter points out that Jesus' ministry was limited to, "the people of Israel." However, he makes it clear that forgiveness is for, "everyone who believes in him." Even though Peter does not level any charges against this Gentile audience like he has against the Jewish audiences that he has preached to, he still emphasizes their need for repentance and the forgiveness of sins.[72]

---

[66] Tannehill, "The Functions of Peter's Mission Speeches in the Narrative of Acts," 414.

[67] Bruce, "The Significance of the Speeches for Interpreting Acts," 22.

[68] Williams, 191.

[69] Acts 10:39.

[70] A. T. Robertson, *Epochs in the Life of Simon Peter* (Grand Rapids: Baker, 1974) 230, "Peter could assume little or no knowledge on the part of his hearers."

[71] Acts 10:34-35. See Bruce, *The Book of the Acts*, 211, "The first words that Peter spoke were words of the weightiest import, sweeping away the racial and religious prejudices of centuries."

[72] Marion L. Soards, *The Speeches in Acts: Their Content, Context, and Concerns* (Louisville: Westminster John Knox, 1994) 76.

The results of Peter's message in Cornelius' house produced a different type of result than what was seen in his previous sermons. The two sermons that are recorded in Acts 2 and 4 produced several thousands of converts. Luke did not record the Holy Spirit falling on Peter's Jewish audience in the temple after the healing of the lame man. While Peter was still speaking in Cornelius' home, however, the Holy Spirit came upon his audience and they began, "speaking in tongues and praising God."

The order of events is actually reversed here. The Gentiles' reception of the Holy Spirit is mentioned before they are baptized and there is no explicit mention of their saving faith. Arrington takes this to mean that Peter's preaching did not lead to the conversion of the Gentiles. According to him, they were already saved, "for before Peter arrived in Caesarea God had granted to them repentance that leads to life."[73] Peter's ministry among them lead to their being baptized with the Holy Spirit.[74] When Peter defended his actions in Acts 11, he equated what happened at Cornelius' house with what had happened to the Jewish believers at Pentecost. Peter uses this same argument in his speech at the Jerusalem Council when he says that God gave, "the Holy Spirit to them, just as he did to us."[75] In Arrington's mind, the Gentiles in Cornelius' house had somehow already come to faith and Peter's ministry among them was so that they might receive the gift of the Holy Spirit and be confirmed as being a part of the people of God.

Arrington's argument, while interesting, does not hold up under close scrutiny. Luke does not give any indication that Peter was addressing an audience of believers. He does imply that they were God-fearers and were obviously very receptive to Peter's message. While there is no explicit mention of saving faith in this account, it is certainly implied.[76] Peter does imply that the Gentiles came to faith when he presented his defense of the incident in Acts 11:17: "So if God gave them the same gift as he gave us, who believed in the Lord Jesus Christ, who was I to think that I could oppose God?" The understanding here by Peter seems to be that the Gentiles received the Holy Spirit at the same time that they believed. As Peter was speaking to them, faith was birthed in their hearts. They were converted and they received the gift of the Spirit at the same time.

After Peter observed the manifestation of the Holy Spirit on those at Cornelius' house, he gave instructions to those who had accompanied him

---

[73] Arrington, 113.

[74] Ibid.

[75] Acts 15:8. See also Stronstad, 67.

[76] Bruce, 217.

to baptize them. Luke then records that Peter stayed with them for a few days. Instead of withdrawing immediately, as most Jewish people would have done, Peter was willing to continue in the hospitality of Cornelius. This time was likely spent in fellowship and absorbing the apostle's teaching. This was also an opportunity to create a friendship between the Jewish and the Gentile believers.[77]

In examining Peter's ministry as an evangelist, it should be noted that while Luke shows Peter to be very successful in that role, there is no indication that he ever planted any churches. He was one of the founding apostles of the church in Jerusalem and it could be argued that a Christian community was founded in Cornelius' home. Other than these two possible examples, however, there is nothing to show that Peter made a habit of establishing churches in the areas that he evangelized. Even in those two examples there is nothing to demonstrate Peter taking an active role in establishing those communities. Luke clearly presents Peter as an evangelist but never portrays him as a church planter. Rather, Peter seemed comfortable working where others had laid the groundwork. In Samaria, for example, Philip had already been working there for some time, and had possibly already established Christian communities when Peter and John came down from Jerusalem. Another example of Peter building on someone else's foundation would be the church in Corinth. There is no indication in Acts that Peter visited that city. It was pointed out, however, in the study that Paul seemed to indicate that Peter had spent some time in Corinth and refers to him in 1 Corinthians in a familiar way to the church there. Acts clearly indicates that the church in Corinth was started by Paul. If Peter did spend time there, this is another indication that he felt more comfortable building on someone else's foundation.

Paul the Evangelist and Church Planter

Evangelism is one of the primary activities that Luke shows Paul to be involved in. Evangelism could be said to be the primary thrust of Paul's apostolic ministry.[78] Paul's evangelistic sermons can be divided into two groups, those that he preached in the synagogue to Jews and God-fearers, and those that he preached outside the synagogue to Gentiles. Paul understood that the commission that he received from Jesus on the Damascus road involved him carrying the message of the gospel to those who had not heard it. Paul's

---

[77] Marshall, 195.

[78] Hengel and Schwemer, 298. See also Schmithals, 22–23, "The commission of the apostle consists in the fact that the mission is entrusted to him . . . Apostles are indeed always missionaries, but not all missionaries are also apostles."

evangelistic sermons will be examined and discussed. The results of Paul's evangelistic efforts will also be examined.

A natural outgrowth of Paul's evangelistic ministry was the founding of churches in the towns where he had preached. Planting churches can be seen in Acts as Paul's ultimate goal. By establishing a strong, indigenous church in a location, he could be sure that the gospel would continue to be proclaimed after he left.[79] As Bowers says, "The planting of churches is so integral a feature of the Pauline mission that one may rightly conclude that Paul experienced his mission in principal part as an ecclesiological undertaking."[80] This appears to fall right into line with Luke's own purpose for Acts. His narrative provides an overview of the first thirty years of the church and shows how it became a viable entity.[81] By the end of Acts, Christian communities dot the landscape of the Roman Empire. Evangelism and church planting will be examined together in this section.

In examining the way that Paul evangelized and planted churches, this section will also look at the way that Paul used other people to reach his apostolic goals. This becomes more visible beginning with Paul's second missionary journey. He is seen as leading a team of "missionary-organizers."[82] It will be seen that Paul's team members were active participants in helping him to plant and nurture churches.

Paul's Evangelistic Outreach in the Synagogue

Paul's evangelistic ministry in the synagogue will be discussed first. While Paul referred to himself as the "apostle to the Gentiles," in Galatians 2:8, Luke's presentation of his evangelistic activity shows that the majority of his missionary endeavors started in the synagogue. By starting in the synagogue of the city that he was in, Paul had access to an audience with a background and understanding of the Jewish Scriptures. Ironically, it was also the synagogue that allowed Paul to connect with the greatest number of receptive Gentiles.[83] Paul's normal pattern was to preach in the synagogue until the Jewish leaders began opposing him. At that time, he would

---

[79] Jonkman, 3.

[80] Paul Bowers, "Church and Mission in Paul," *Journal for the Study of the New Testament* 44 (1991) 89.

[81] Joseph B. Tyson, "The Emerging Church and the Problem of Authority in Acts," *Interpretation* 42 (1988) 132.

[82] Cook, 487.

[83] Richard Oster, *The Acts of the Apostles, Part II: 13:1—28:31,* The Living Word Commentary (Abilene: Abilene Christian University Press, 1984) 21.

withdraw to another location with whatever disciples he had made, both Jews and Gentiles alike.

Paul's first evangelistic sermon was preached just days after his conversion at the synagogue in Damascus. Luke records, "At once he began to preach in the synagogues that Jesus is the Son of God."[84] Paul's theology was not fully developed yet but even at this stage as a new believer, he, "grew more and more powerful and baffled the Jews living in Damascus by proving that Jesus is the Christ."[85] Tannehill points out the importance of the fact that Paul immediately started evangelizing. He did not receive extensive instruction in theology or of the church's tradition before he became a missionary.[86] Paul immediately began preaching what he knew so far, with that being "Jesus is the Son of God." This theme became a very important one for Paul and he is the only one who refers to Jesus as the Son of God in Acts.[87]

The next place in Acts where Paul is seen preaching in the synagogue is in 13:5 at the beginning of the first missionary journey with Barnabas. Luke only writes that, "they proclaimed the word of God in the Jewish synagogues" in Salamis, on Cyprus. Luke appears to be illustrating the way that Paul and Barnabas conducted their evangelistic work. He confirms this a chapter later when he says, "At Iconium Paul and Barnabas *went as usual* into the Jewish synagogue."[88] Luke goes on to say that, "They traveled through the whole island until they came to Paphos."[89] The implication is that they preached in all the synagogues as they traveled across the island.[90]

In Acts 13:16-41, Luke records the most complete summary of one of Paul's synagogue messages.[91] This sermon was preached on the first Sabbath that he and Barnabas were in Pisidian Antioch. Luke apparently regarded this as a significant event based on how much space he devoted to it and the way he treated the sermon in Acts.[92] Luke probably meant for this sermon to be representative of the way that Paul preached to a mixed Jewish and

---

[84] Acts 9:20.

[85] Acts 9:22.

[86] Tannehill, *The Narrative Unity of Luke-Acts A Literary Interpretation,* Volume Two: *The Acts of the Apostles,* 122.

[87] Williams, 174.

[88] Acts 14:1.

[89] Acts 13:6.

[90] Ramsay, 73.

[91] Stott, 222.

[92] Thompson, 344.

Gentile audience. There are similarities in content and style between this message and Peter's Pentecost message in Acts 2 as well as his temple speech in Acts 3.[93] This has led many scholars to conclude that all three speeches are Lukan compositions. While this is a possibility, there is also no reason why this message could not be an accurate summary of what Paul actually preached. Kilgallen points out,

> Even if one imagine the speech to be a creation of Luke and an idealized expression of Pauline preaching in the Diaspora, one cannot fail to see how at so many points the speech has been particularized to the needs and hopes of the Antiochans.[94]

Bruce makes the point that the messages were similar because there was "little difference in substance between the Petrine and Pauline presentations of the gospel to Jewish audiences."[95] In actuality, this speech of Paul's comes closer in style and content to Stephen's speech in Acts 7 than it does to Peter's Pentecost or Temple speeches. In any event, it is not unreasonable to assume that Peter and Paul would both emphasize the same things in their preaching. Both would have preached the same essential *kerygma* that was developing in the early church.[96]

The main similarities between Peter's messages and Paul's is that they all show Jesus as the fulfillment of the prophecies that are found in the Hebrew Scriptures.[97] Both his death and resurrection were foretold and the Jews became unwitting accomplices in helping to fulfill the Scriptures: "The people of Jerusalem and their rulers did not recognize Jesus, yet in

---

[93] Tannehill, "The Functions of Peter's Mission Speeches in the Narrative of Acts," 403.

[94] John J. Kilgallen, "Acts 13:38-39: Culmination of Paul's Speech in Pisidia," *Biblica* 69 (1988) 484–85. See also Foakes-Jackson, 117, "If the speech is a composition put into the mouth of Paul, there is no small skill displayed in the deft employment of Pauline phrases and ideas."

[95] Bruce, *Paul: Apostle of the Heart Set Free*, 165.

[96] C. H. Dodd, *The Apostolic Preaching and its Developments*, http://www.religion-online. org/cgi-bin/relsearchd.dll 1964 (October 15, 2001) 7–8, Dodd identifies five elements that composed the *kerygma*. First, the age of fulfillment has come. God had fulfilled what the prophets had foretold. Secondly, this fulfillment had taken place through the ministry, death, and resurrection of Jesus. Thirdly, by virtue of His resurrection, Jesus has been exalted to the right hand of God. Fourthly, the Holy Spirit Who had been poured out on Pentecost and was present in the church is the sign of Christ's present power and glory. The fifth aspect of the *kerygma* that Dodd identifies is the fact that the Messianic Age will reach its consummation at the return of Christ. The sixth and final aspect of the *kerygma* that was preached in the early church was an appeal to repentance so that the hearers could also become a part of the community of believers.

[97] Stott, 224.

condemning him they fulfilled the words of the prophets that are read every Sabbath."[98]

Aside from the similarities, there are also notable differences between Peter and Paul's messages. First of all, Paul does not hold his audience in Pisidian Antioch responsible for the death of Jesus. Like Peter, he places the blame squarely on the Jews of Jerusalem when he says, "they asked Pilate to have him executed."[99] Paul, unlike Peter, is unable to use the death of Jesus as a basis for calling his audience to repentance.[100] Paul does still call his audience to faith so that they can receive forgiveness for their sins (13:38). Paul also mentions that the result of their faith is justification, "from everything you could not be justified from by the Law of Moses."[101] This is also the only mention of the Law in Paul's message. He does not mention it at all in his brief recounting of Israel's history. This early sermon by Paul showed that he already understood that the Law was unable to bring about anyone's salvation and that no one could keep it completely.

Another difference between the two sermons is Paul's perspective. When he mentions the resurrection in verses 30-31, he refers to those who were apostles before him when he says, "They are now his witnesses to our people." Paul then shifts from "they" to "we" when he says in verse 32, "We tell you the good news."[102] While Paul's letters make it clear that he sees himself as an apostle on the same level as the Twelve, it is also clear from his message here that he understands the unique role that the Twelve had. Even though Paul was not a witness of the resurrection in the same way that Peter and the other apostles were, he is nevertheless, a witness of the life-changing power of Christ. Paul had not been a witness to Jesus' earthly ministry as the Twelve had, but he had seen the resurrected Christ on the Damascus road and had received his commission from Him.[103]

Paul's sermon can be divided into four sections.[104] First of all he presents a brief recounting of two of the most significant events in Israel's history: the Exodus from Egypt and the ascension of David to the throne of Israel. The second section of the message briefly summarizes the ministry of John the Baptist and Jesus. Paul also discusses the crucifixion and resur-

---

[98] Acts 13:27.

[99] Acts 13:28.

[100] Tannehill, 403.

[101] Acts 13:39.

[102] Stott, 24.

[103] Tannehill, *The Narrative Unity of Luke-Acts A Literary Interpretation,* Volume Two: *The Acts of the Apostles,* 169.

[104] Kilgallen, 485–86.

rection of Jesus. The third section of this sermon then provides a scriptural basis by mentioning three Old Testament passages that support what Paul is talking about. Foakes-Jackson makes the suggestion that Paul used the Scriptures that had been read earlier in the service as his text.[105] The final section of Paul's sermon is a warning to not reject Jesus and provides an Old Testament prophecy of what will happen if they do.

There can be no mistake that the purpose of this message is evangelistic.[106] Paul culminates his sermon with verses 38-39:

> Therefore, my brothers, I want you to know that through Jesus the forgiveness of sins is proclaimed to you. Through him everyone who believes is justified from everything you could not be justified from by the law of Moses.

He clearly is trying to influence and change the minds of his audience. He wants the audience to experience the gift of God's salvation.[107] As Paul concludes his sermon to this audience in Galatia by talking about justification by faith, it is important to remember that this will be the theme of his letter to these same Galatians just a few years later.[108] Paul will later remind them,

> We who are Jews by birth and not 'Gentile sinners' know that a man is not justified by observing the law, but by faith in Jesus Christ. So we, too, have put our faith in Christ Jesus that we may be justified by faith in Christ and not by observing the law, because by observing the law no one will be justified.[109]

Evidently these Gentile God-fearers had been thoroughly indoctrinated as to the idea that salvation was found in the law. Paul introduced the idea of justification by faith during his synagogue sermon but really developed his thoughts later on in his letter to the Galatian believers. He likely spent time in the days following this message explaining his views to those who were interested in hearing more.

In discussing the results of Paul's evangelistic endeavors, it bears pointing out that Luke records the results of Paul's evangelistic success in a different way than he did for Peter. On two different occasions, Luke recorded

---

[105] Foakes-Jackson, 115. See also Bruce, 162, "The preaching of the gospel in synagogues would be largely a matter of expounding the scripture lessons in terms of their Christian fulfillment."

[106] Kilgallen, 481.

[107] Ibid., 495.

[108] Stott, 225.

[109] Galatians 2:15-16.

the actual number of people who responded to Peter's messages. These are in Acts 2:41 and 4:4. During Paul's ministry, however, Luke never provides any definite numbers of converts. He indicates whether or not Paul was successful in a particular city without getting specific. For instance, after Paul's synagogue message in Pisidian Antioch, Luke makes it clear that many believed and accepted his message. "When the congregation was dismissed, many of the Jews and devout converts to Judaism followed Paul and Barnabas, who talked with them and urged them to continue in the grace of God."[110] Luke then records that when Paul made it clear he was turning to the Gentiles, "all that were appointed for eternal life believed. The word of the Lord spread through the whole region."[111] While Luke does not tell how many converts this sermon produced, it seems obvious that it produced quite a few. The converts would have been the ones that Paul and Barnabas urged, "to continue in the grace of God."[112] While Luke does not record that Paul and Barnabas organized the new believers into a church until they came back through on their return trip these would have been the core group that the apostles would have built on later.[113] It is likely that they continued meeting together after the apostles left.

Paul's evangelistic activity continued after he and Barnabas left Pisidian Antioch. They traveled to Iconium and spoke in the synagogue there. Luke records that "they spoke so effectively that a great number of Jews and Gentiles believed."[114]Again, Luke makes it clear that the evangelistic ministry was successful but he does not provide any specific numbers. Krodel believes that when Luke says that, "a great number of Jews and Gentiles believed," that it is his way of saying that a new Christian community was formed.[115] While this is possible, it is not until the apostles come back on the return leg of their trip that anything is said about organizing the believers into communities. It could be that they were already meeting together on a regular basis after the apostles were forced to leave. When Paul and Barnabas came back through, they appointed leaders for them. Paul and Barnabas were successful enough in Iconium that they attracted the attention of Jews who were opposed to the gospel. This is itself an indication of how effective Paul and Barnabas were in their missionary work. It is unlikely that there would have been opposition if so many people were not

---

[110] Acts 13:43.

[111] Acts 13:48-49.

[112] Stott, 226

[113] Krodel, 245.

[114] Acts 14:1.

[115] Krodel, 252.

responding to the message. Calvin makes the point that it was the fruit of their ministry that would have helped Paul and Barnabas endure the persecution.[116] Because they had seen so many people respond to the gospel, they knew that they were in the will of God and were more willing to put up with the opposition and endure the hardships.

The apostles "spent considerable time" in Iconium. Luke does not specify how long they were there but he does say that they performed "miraculous signs and wonders." This will be more fully developed in the next chapter under the section of "Paul the Miracle Worker," however, it is important to note that this was an important part of Paul's evangelistic ministry just as it had been with Peter. The miracles that they performed often provided them with a platform from which to evangelize. The final result in Iconium was that, "The people of the city were divided; some sided with the Jews, others with the apostles."[117]

The next instance of synagogue ministry that Luke writes about was on the second missionary journey in the city of Thessalonica. Luke says, "As his custom was, Paul went into the synagogue, and on three Sabbath days he reasoned with them from the Scriptures, explaining and proving that the Christ had to suffer and rise from the dead."[118] The results of this synagogue ministry were, "Some of the Jews were persuaded and joined Paul and Silas, as did a large number of God-fearing Greeks and not a few prominent women."[119]

Persecution from the Jews eventually forced Paul to leave Thessalonica. While Luke does not provide any specifics about the church that was left there, Paul's two letters to the Thessalonians do. In his first letter to the Thessalonians, Paul mentions the fact that while he was in Athens, he sent Timothy to check on the believers in Thessalonica. When Paul receives the good report from Timothy that the young church is doing well, he is clearly relieved:

> But Timothy has just come to us from you and has brought good news about your faith and love. He has told us that you always have pleasant memories of us and that you long to see us, just as we also long to see you. Therefore, brothers, in all of our distress and persecution we were encouraged about you because of your faith. For now we really live, since you are standing firm in the Lord.[120]

---

[116] Calvin, 1–2.

[117] Acts 14:4.

[118] Acts 17:2-3.

[119] Acts 17:4.

[120] 1 Thessalonians 3:6-8.

In Acts, Luke does not provide many details about the founding of the Thessalonian church. Those kinds of specific details were not important for Luke's purposes. Paul's two letters to them fill in some of the blank spaces that were left by Luke. While Acts covers the evangelistic aspects of Paul's synagogue ministry in Thessalonica, the letters emphasize his pastoral ministry among the believers. Paul was encouraged by what Timothy told him of the Thessalonians steadfastness. At the same time, he felt a need to write them a letter of instruction so that they might continue to grow into spiritual maturity.[121]

Ernest Best is representative of those scholars who raise questions concerning the validity of Luke's account of Paul's Thessalonian ministry versus Paul's own account in his letters. The biggest question seems to be Luke's record of Paul only being there for three Sabbaths.[122] At first glance, it seems that Luke appears to be saying that Paul and his team were only in Thessalonica for a minimum of three or four weeks. Paul's letters clearly indicate that he was there longer than that. An example of this is found in Philippians 4:16 where Paul refers to financial help that he received from the Philippians on more than one occasion while he was in Thessalonica. The letters to the Thessalonians also seem to demonstrate that Paul had taught them many things about the Christian faith that could not have been compressed into three synagogue meetings. Rather than discounting Luke's account as inaccurate, however, it is probably better to understand that the three Sabbaths that Luke refers to are only speaking of Paul's ministry to the Jews.[123] After being forced out of the synagogue, he and his associates were probably in Thessalonica for several months, focusing their ministry on the Gentiles, before the persecution forced them to leave. Rather than being inaccurate as Best suggests, this appears to be another instance in which Luke omitted the details that he did not consider important. What appears to be a problem with Luke's chronology is most likely another example of his brevity in describing certain events.

While Acts does not say much about the church that Paul left behind in Thessalonica, his letters make it clear that it was a church of some influence: "And so you became a model to all the believers in Macedonia

---

[121] F. F. Bruce, *1 & 2 Thessalonians,* Word Biblical Commentary (Waco, Tex.: Word, 1982) 69.

[122] Ernest Best, *A Commentary on the First and Second Epistles to the Thessalonians,* Harper's New Testament Commentaries (New York: Harper & Row, 1972) 5.

[123] Stott, 271. See also Neil, 187, "His letters to the Thessalonians indicate that he stayed long enough to receive financial help from the Philippian church on at least two occasions (Phil 4:16), although he was also supporting himself by working at his own trade- which itself suggests a longer stay than three weeks (1 Thess 2:9; 2 Thess 3:7-12)."

and Achaia . . . your faith in God has become known everywhere."[124] This becomes even more significant in light of the fact that Paul and his team were forced to leave Thessalonica before he felt that the church was strong enough to stand on its on.

From Thessalonica, Paul went to Berea and preached in the synagogue there. Paul's message was well received. Luke records that the Bereans, "received the message with great eagerness and examined the Scriptures everyday to see if what Paul said was true."[125] The result of Paul's synagogue ministry in Berea was that, "Many of the Jews believed, as did also a number of prominent Greek women and many Greek men."[126] It is interesting to note that in Berea, Paul preached or taught daily in the synagogue, as opposed to just on the Sabbath. The Berean Jews received Paul without bias or prejudice. They had an "unprejudiced openness in studying the Scriptures."[127] The Bereans seemed to have an openness and a hunger for spiritual things like no other Jewish audience that Paul had encountered. Their daily discussions with Paul resulted in many of them receiving Paul's message and becoming believers. Once again, without giving any further details about the new believers in Berea, Luke seems to indicate that a church is formed there. Persecution from Thessalonian Jews soon forced Paul and his team to leave the city.

The founding of the Thessalonian and the Berean churches provide an interesting picture of the way that Paul relied on his associates. When the persecution became severe in Thessalonica, "the brothers sent Paul and Silas away to Berea."[128] There is no mention of Timothy leaving with Paul and Silas, although he is with them later in Berea. It seems likely that Timothy stayed for a short while in Thessalonica, continuing what Paul had started. He would not have been as well known as Paul and could have quietly taught and strengthened the believers. Pillette points out that Timothy had been working with Paul for less than a year and his own Christian experience was not that much longer than the Thessalonian's.[129] Paul, nevertheless, felt confident that Timothy was up to the task. After working for some time in Thessalonica, Timothy rejoined Paul and Silas in Berea. When the persecution became heated later on in Berea, Paul again was forced to leave

---

[124] 1 Thessalonians 1:7-8.

[125] Acts 17:11.

[126] Acts 17:12.

[127] Stott, 274.

[128] Acts 17:10.

[129] Bard M. Pillette, "Paul and His Fellow Workers: A Study of the Use of Authority," Ph. D. diss., Dallas Theological Seminary, 1992, 196–97.

but Silas and Timothy stayed behind, presumably to help solidify the work there.

Paul indicates in 1 Thessalonians that he sent Timothy back to Thessalonica while he was in Athens, after he was forced to leave Berea. "We sent Timothy, who is our brother and God's fellow worker in spreading the gospel of Christ, to strengthen and encourage you in your faith, so that no one would be unsettled by these trials."[130] It seems likely that Paul sent a message to Timothy in Berea instructing him to go back to Thessalonica.[131] Paul's letter makes it clear that Timothy was sent "to strengthen and encourage" the Thessalonian believers and to remind them of the things that Paul had taught them. *Strengthening* and *encouraging* are the technical terms used by Paul in his description of the pastoral ministry.[132] It is probably safe to assume that Timothy was performing the same type of tasks that Paul would have performed had he been there: preaching, teaching, pastoral care, and leadership training.[133]

In both letters to the Thessalonians, Paul lists Timothy's name in the salutation along with his and Silas', reminding the believers of his involvement with the church there. Maness points out that Timothy was the only one of Paul's fellow-workers who was present for the entirety of both the Second and Third Missionary journeys. During both of those time periods, he was either working directly with Paul or serving as his envoy in Macedonia and Corinth.[134] Paul evidently had great faith in Timothy's abilities. He was a valuable member of Paul's team and was able to handle difficult and delicate tasks in Paul's name.

After Paul was forced to leave Berea, Luke records that he went to Athens. There, "he reasoned in the synagogue with the Jews and the God-fearing Greeks, as well as in the marketplace day by day with those who happened to be there."[135] Luke provides no further details about Paul's synagogue ministry in Athens, but he does go into great detail covering Paul's speech at the Aeropagus. This will be discussed in the next subsection.

---

[130] 1 Thessalonians 3:2.

[131] Best, 131.

[132] Ibid., 134, These terms, "represent what a good pastor does to build up his people in the face of persecution, trouble, lack of resolution and imperfect knowledge of the Christian way."

[133] Stephen Maness, "The Pauline Congregations, Paul, and His Co-Workers: Determinative Trajectories for the Ministries of Paul's Partners in the Gospel," Ph.D. diss., Southwestern Baptist Theological Seminary, 1998, 25.

[134] Ibid., 85–86.

[135] Acts 17:17.

Luke provides two more examples of Paul's synagogue ministry in the cities of Corinth and Ephesus. Both of these were discussed to some degree under the heading of "Paul the Pastor." A couple of points need to be highlighted. In Corinth, Luke states that Paul went to the synagogue every Sabbath, "trying to persuade Jews and Greeks."[136] In the next verse it says that, "Paul devoted himself exclusively to preaching, testifying to the Jews that Jesus was the Christ." Once again the apostle is seen in an evangelistic role in a synagogue setting. He attempted to persuade his hearers that Jesus was the Christ. There is no indication of how long Paul was able to preach in the synagogue, but eventually, persecution forced him to withdraw.

As was mentioned in the previous chapter, Luke gives us more detail about how the Corinthian church was started than he does about any other church in Acts. After preaching in the synagogue for some length of time, Paul eventually withdrew to the house next door to the synagogue and continued holding meetings. It was in Corinth that Paul developed a lifelong relationship with Aquila and Priscilla.[137] They worked at the same trade and Paul, "stayed and worked with them."[138] While Luke does not specify what role they played in the Corinthian church, it is probable that they assisted Paul in the work of the ministry. It also bears noting that Paul did not devote himself exclusively to preaching in Corinth until Silas and Timothy joined him. Their help and support was obviously very important to Paul.[139] It is also likely that when Silas and Timothy returned from Macedonia that they brought with them the financial gift from the Philippian church (Phil. 4:15) which allowed Paul to concentrate on preaching and teaching full-time.[140] While Luke only emphasizes what Paul himself did, it is apparent that Paul's team of co-workers were active participants in helping him to plant and then nurture the churches. Luke focuses his attention on Paul and his apostolic ministry in the second half of acts, but it is impossible to miss the fact that Paul was not alone in his ministry. His team played a large part in what Paul accomplished.

---

[136] 1 Corinthians 18:4.

[137] Mario Barbero, "A First-Century Couple, Priscilla and Aquila: Their House Churches and Missionary Activity," Ph.D. diss., The Catholic University of America, 2001, 73, "Paul's association with them is probably an important factor in the success of the Corinthian mission since they provide him with lodging and with work." See also p. 95, "The workshop of Aquila and Priscilla offers Paul not only an opportunity to work and earn his living, but also provides a ready audience for his preaching."

[138] Acts 18:2.

[139] Hiebert, 6, "He worked most efficiently when he had some coworkers with him, and he was uneasy without any attendants."

[140] Arrington, 184.

Paul stopped in Ephesus very briefly at the end of his second mission-ary journey. He spoke in the synagogue, "and reasoned with the Jews."[141] When they asked him to stay longer he declined, but promised to return if he could. What is very significant, however, is the fact that Paul left Priscilla and Aquila in Ephesus after he left. Barbero believes that this was part of Paul's strategy. The couple would be establishing their business in Ephesus, but they would also be laying the groundwork for Paul's mission in the city when he returned.[142] While Luke does not say much about their time in Ephesus, he does mention the account with Apollos. When he came to preach in the synagogue in Ephesus, it became clear to Priscilla and Aquila that he needed more instruction in the faith. After they heard him speak, "they invited him to their home and explained to him the way of God more adequately."[143] This short narrative provides important informa-tion about Priscilla and Aquila. First of all, they themselves had sufficient Scriptural background that they could complete Apollos where he was lacking.[144] Apollos was also probably, "instructed in the distinctive Pauline doctrines."[145] A second interesting point is that they brought him into their home to instruct him. This implies more than just a casual encounter. They took the time to get to know Apollos and build a relationship with him. Later, in 1 Corinthians 16:19, Paul refers to the church that meets in Priscilla and Aquila's house in Ephesus. This couple's house was evidently a center for Christian activity in Ephesus and it is understandable that they would bring Apollos to their home to meet other believers and to receive spiritual encouragement himself.[146] Priscilla and Aquila's wisdom in dealing with Apollos provides a very clear example of the type of people that Paul surrounded himself with. This account of their encounter with Apollos also provides an excellent representation of the quality of ministry that Priscilla and Aquila provided.

When Paul returned to Ephesus on his third missionary journey, Luke does not say anything about his reunion with Priscilla and Aquila. Paul went back to the synagogue and preached there for three months, "arguing persuasively about the kingdom of God."[147] After he withdrew to the hall

---

[141] Acts 18:19.

[142] Barbero, 88.

[143] Acts 18:26.

[144] Barbero, 92, "It is not so much to correct what Apollos teaches, but rather to complete the information he imparts."

[145] Marshall, 304.

[146] Barbero, 305–6.

[147] Acts 19:8.

of Tyrannus, he continued his ministry for two years. Luke says very little about how the church in Ephesus was formed and organized. From the little that is recorded about Priscilla and Aquila, however, it is very likely that they occupied a significant role in the church's formation, as well as providing ongoing leadership after Paul left. Priscilla and Aquila provide another example of Paul's ability to use other people to reach his apostolic goals.

Paul's Evangelistic Activity Outside the Synagogue

There are fewer accounts of Paul's ministry outside the synagogue than might be expected from the "apostle to the Gentiles." Luke, in fact, only includes two evangelistic addresses from Paul to pagan audiences. One was preached in Lystra, the other in Athens. Like much of Acts, Luke seems to include these two messages as representative of the way in which Paul attempted to evangelize those who had no knowledge or understanding of the Jewish Law. This section will also contain a discussion of Paul's ministry in Philippi.

After persecution forced Paul and Barnabas to leave Iconium, they, "continued to preach the good news" in Lystra, Derbe, and the surrounding countryside. In Lystra, Paul healed a lame man. This healing will also be discussed in detail in the next chapter. This miracle caused the people who witnessed it to want to offer sacrifices to Paul and Barnabas mistaking them for the Greek gods, Zeus and Hermes. When the apostles realized what was going on, they shared a brief message to get the people to stop the sacrifices. Luke does not record if Paul, Barnabas, or both of them spoke to the crowd. Krodel believes that this speech should be credited to Paul since Luke has just stated that he was the chief speaker.[148] More than likely, it took both of them to get the crowd calmed down and to keep them from offering sacrifices to the apostles. This message recorded in Acts 14:14-18 could be another summary by Luke. Considering the circumstances at the time it was spoken, however, it is more likely an accurate recording of the entire message. This was not the time for a lengthy discourse!

The apostles start off by quickly denying any divinity and appeal to the Lystrans' common humanity. "Men, why are you doing this? We too are only men, human like you are."[149] This message contains no appeal to the Jewish Scriptures since it is very unlikely that the audience would have had any knowledge of them. When speaking to Jews or Gentile God-

---

[148] Krodel, 258.
[149] Acts 14:15.

fearers, the Scriptures became a common link between the apostles and their audience. Here, the common link that they appeal to is their humanity and the fact that they were all created by the one true God, "who made heaven and earth and sea and everything in them."[150] Instead of discussing the fulfillment of prophecies, the apostles talk about God the creator.[151] His power is demonstrated in His creation: "he has not left himself without testimony."[152] God has demonstrated His kindness to His creation by providing rain for their crops and plenty of food for them to enjoy.

In making their speech to the Lystrans, Paul and Barnabas also appeal to them, "to turn from these worthless things to the living God," a clear reference to their worship of idols. At the same time, Paul does not harshly condemn their idolatrous past.[153] He understands that they were acting out of ignorance and moves on to the positive aspects of discussing the living God rather than dwelling on their idolatry. Not many years later, Paul would write to the Christians in Thessalonica reminding them that they too, "turned to God from idols to serve the living and true God."[154] Paul and Barnabas' goal was to see these Lystrans turn to the true God from their idols, also.

The apostle's words restrained the crowd from offering sacrifices to them. There is no other indication given by Luke as to what results were gained by Paul and Barnabas' evangelistic attempts in Lystra. Later on in chapter 16, however, Luke will introduce a young believer from Lystra named Timothy. Luke will also mention the "brothers at Lystra and Iconium" in 16:2 so there evidently was some fruit that was borne from that missionary trip. On the whole, however, the apostles did not appear to have very much success in Lystra.[155]

The next city that Paul and Barnabas preached in was Derbe and things seemed to go better there than they had in Lystra. Luke does not give any details of their ministry. He only says, "They preached the good news in that city and won a large number of disciples."[156] Derbe is the

---

[150] Acts 14:15.

[151] Bruce, *The Book of the Acts*, 276–77, Bruce makes the point that the apostles use the language of the Old Testament as they make their appeal to the Lystrans. "The providence of God in giving human beings rainfall and harvest is an Old Testament theme (cf. Gen 8:22), and the conjunction of "'food and rejoicing'" (cf. 2:46) is a feature of Old Testament language."

[152] Acts 14:17.

[153] Tannehill, 179.

[154] 1 Thessalonians 1:9.

[155] Bruce, "The Significance of the Speeches for Interpreting Acts," 23.

[156] Acts 14:21.

only town in Galatia that Paul preached in which Luke does not mention persecution.[157] It would appear that this ministry in Derbe was unrelated to the synagogue since Luke does not continue his habit of mentioning it whenever Paul preached there. Bruce understands Luke to mean that a church was formed in Derbe, so even though he does not provide numbers of converts and only provides a summary of the ministry there, it is clear that this was a successful missionary campaign.[158]

The next instance of Paul evangelizing outside of the synagogue that will be discussed is found on his second missionary trip in the city of Philippi. One of Paul's most beloved churches was established here. In Acts 16, Luke provides several different glimpses of Paul's ministry time in Philippi. As is his pattern, he provides very little in the way of a chronological framework. This narrative contains one of the "we" passages, indicating that the author was an eyewitness for much of what he described. Even though this account took place outside of a synagogue, it is evident that even in a city without much of a Jewish influence, Paul was still counting on being able to locate some God-fearing Gentiles. This did happen when he and his team went outside the city gate on the Sabbath looking for a place of prayer. Paul found a group of women gathered for prayer by the river. Luke records the beginnings of Christianity in Philippi:

> We sat down and began to speak to the women gathered there. One of those listening was a woman named Lydia, a dealer in purple cloth from the city of Thyatira, who was a worshiper of God. The Lord opened her heart to respond to Paul's message. When she and the members of her household were baptized, she invited us to her home. "If you consider me a believer in the Lord," she said, "come and stay at my house." And she persuaded us.[159]

In examining this account, it appears that Lydia was the leader of this group of women.[160] She probably already had some understanding of the Jewish Scriptures. Bruce points out that there was a Jewish colony in her hometown of Thyatira, and that it was probably there that she became a God-fearer.[161] Luke does not mention the presence of any Jewish men or male God-fearers in Philippi, so it is likely that Lydia took it upon herself to gather around her those women who were interested in learning about

---

[157] Williams, 253.

[158] Bruce, *The Book of the Acts*, 279.

[159] Acts 16:13-15.

[160] Bruce, *Paul: Apostle of the Heart Set Free*, 220. See also, Guthrie, 139.

[161] Ibid.

the God of Israel. By responding in faith to Paul's message, Lydia was again leading the way for the other women.

It has already been noted how Luke makes a point of showing the important place that women occupied in the early church. He builds on that in this narrative by showing that a woman was the first convert in Europe and that her home became the first meeting place for the church in Philippi. Lydia became the hostess for the first church in Europe.[162] There is no indication of whether or not Lydia was married.[163] It does seem clear, however, that she occupied the leadership role in her home. She was responsible for those in her household turning to God and being baptized. It can be surmised, based on what Luke has shown of Lydia leading the group of women in prayers and in leading her own household, that she also became an influential leader in the Philippian church. Her ability to gather and then lead other people would have been ideal traits for a Christian leader to have.

The account of the demon possessed girl that Paul healed will be examined in the next chapter. The account of the earthquake that took place while Paul and Silas were in jail will also be examined later in the chapter discussing mystical and supernatural experiences under the section of, "Paul the Mystic." After the earthquake took place, however, Luke presents another example of Paul's evangelistic ministry.

After the earthquake occurred, the jailer thought that all the prisoners had escaped and prepared to commit suicide. Paul intervened and told him not to harm himself.

> The jailer called for lights, rushed in and fell trembling before Paul and Silas. He then brought them out and asked, "Sirs, what must I do to be saved?" They replied, "Believe in the Lord Jesus, and you will be saved- you and your household." Then they spoke the word of the Lord to him and all the others in his house. At that hour of the night the jailer took them and washed their wounds; them immediately he and all his family were baptized.[164]

---

[162] Tannehill, 197, From this point on in the narrative of Acts, Luke, "acknowledges the important role that local sponsors played in the establishment of the church and demonstrates the necessary partnership between traveling missionaries and local supporters."

[163] Keener, 369, Keener says that the way that Luke speaks of Lydia seems to indicate that she was unmarried and was in charge of her household, or at the very least her husband was completely uninvolved and allowed his wife considerable freedom. See also Neil, 182. Neil believes that Lydia was a widow.

[164] Acts 16:29-33.

Luke goes on to record that the jailer, "was filled with joy because he had come to believe in God- he and his whole family."[165] Luke's account of Paul's evangelistic outreach in Philippi has shown the conversion of two whole families, as well as the slave girl that was delivered from demons. It is probable that others had been converted, however, as is his style, Luke provides these as representatives of Paul and Silas' ministry.

When the jailer asked Paul and Silas, "What must I do to be saved?," it is not clear exactly what he meant. He had possibly heard the apostles singing and praying in the jail before the earthquake. He may have also heard them preach in town. Krodel believes that the earthquake would have been seen as a sign of divine judgment and the jailer was desirous that the apostles show him how to avoid it.[166] The jailer may have seen Paul and Silas as representatives of the gods after the earthquake and was asking them to intervene on his behalf.[167] Another possibility was that the jailer saw them as powerful magicians that he had mistreated and was now asking that his life be spared.[168] In any event, he realized that Paul and Silas had the answer to his question and he threw himself at their feet in humility. He took them into his home and they explained the message of salvation to him and his entire household. As they spoke and answered questions, faith was birthed in their hearts.[169] This account provides a clear example of Paul teaching the gospel and making sure that his hearers have some understanding of it before they are baptized.[170] Lydia and the members of her household were the first Philippians that Paul baptized. As it turned out, the jailer and his family were the last ones that the apostles baptized.[171]

Luke does not give any indication how long Paul and his team stayed in Philippi. The only hint that they were there for some time is found in Acts 16:18, in reference to the demon-possessed slave girl, "She kept this up for many days." It is possible that Paul was in Philippi for several weeks, possibly even a few months before they were forced to leave. This would have been enough time to establish a congregation, especially if one of the

---

[165] Acts 16:34.

[166] Krodel, 312.

[167] Keener, 370. This is also reminiscent of what happened in Lystra in Acts 14. After the healing of the lame man, the crowd believed that Zeus and Hermes had come down to earth.

[168] Neil, 185. Neil rewords the jailer's question to say, "How can I be saved from the consequences of having ill-treated two obviously powerful magicians?"

[169] Arrington, 171–72.

[170] Neil, 185, "We may be sure that baptism would not take place until Paul had been satisfied that what had begun as superstitious fear ended as genuine Christian faith."

[171] Bruce, 221.

126

team members was left behind to assist. When Paul and Silas were released from jail and asked to leave the city, they first went to Lydia's house, "where they met with the brothers and encouraged them."[172] Williams notes, "Evidently the work had gone ahead in Philippi, and there were now a number of Christians."[173]

While Luke does not provide any details about the organizational structure of the Philippian church, it must be noted that his narrative changed back to a third person account when the apostles left Philippi. The "we" narrative does not start again until chapter 20. This shift seems to indicate that Luke stayed behind in Philippi. Bruce believes that Luke stayed and is later identified by Paul as the, "loyal yokefellow" of Philippians 4:3.[174] The second missionary journey saw Paul begin to use his co-workers in an ever increasing capacity. As discussed previously, both Timothy and Silas were used in Thessalonica and Berea after persecution forced Paul to leave. Priscilla and Aquila helped Paul plant churches in Corinth and Ephesus. In this context, it appears that Luke was left behind in Philippi to help establish the church. As mentioned in chapter 1 of this study, Luke writes as a pastor so it is no surprise that he would occupy a pastoral role in Philippi until local leaders could be developed. While opposition forced Paul and Silas to leave, Luke was able to stay behind and carry on the work that they had started in Philippi. Paul again is shown relying on one of his teammates to help him expand the Gospel.

The last account of Paul's evangelistic ministry outside of the synagogue that will be examined took place in Athens. This story is recorded in Acts 17. As mentioned previously, Luke does mention Paul reasoning in the synagogue in Athens, but the focal point for him seemed to be Paul's ministry in the marketplace which then led to him speaking at the Areopagus.

While Paul was in Athens waiting for Silas and Timothy to rejoin him, "he was greatly distressed to see that the city was full of idols."[175] Paul was no stranger to the idolatry of the Greeks; however, in Athens, he saw it on a scale that roused him to anger. Rather than being impressed by the culture and artistic beauty of Athens, Paul was offended, as any good Jew would be.[176] Williams does not think that Paul originally planned on preaching in Athens. The level of idolatry that he saw, however, compelled him to do

---

[172] Acts 16:40.

[173] Williams, 292.

[174] Bruce, 221–22. See also Bruce, *Philippians,* New International Biblical Commentary (Peabody, Mass.: Hendrickson, 1989) 138.

[175] Acts 17:16.

[176] Marshall, 283.

so.[177] Luke does not say how long Paul was in Athens but he does say that Paul reasoned, "day by day," with those in the market. This new "philosopher" eventually got the attention of the Epicurean and Stoic philosophers and they began to dispute with him. The perception of Paul that they had was that he was proclaiming foreign deities because he, "was preaching the good news about Jesus and the resurrection."[178]

The Greek philosophers then took Paul to a meeting of the Areopagus and asked him to explain the new teaching that he was proclaiming, "May we know what this new teaching is that you are presenting? You are bringing some strange ideas to our ears."[179] Luke points out in a narrative aside that the Athenians and others who lived there spent their time in listening to and discussing the latest ideas. Paul's speech to them provides a clear example of the way that Paul preached to Gentile audiences who had no background in the Jewish Law. As with the other speeches in Acts, it appears to be representative of the way that Paul preached. This sermon is the last recorded missionary sermon in Acts and could be seen as the climax of Paul's ministry to the Gentiles.[180]

Paul begins his message by commenting on how religious the Athenians are. He has observed their many grand temples and altars set up throughout the city. The word that Paul uses here for *religious* is *deisidaimonesterous,* which can also be translated to mean *superstitious.*[181] It can have a positive or negative connotation, depending on how it was used.[182] It is a comparative and Paul probably picked this word to say that the Athenians were more religious than most people. This would have been a true statement, yet it did not carry a judgmental tone with it. In this way, Paul could express his own feelings for their religion without giving offense to his audience.[183] As an evangelist, Paul wanted to reach his hearers, not alienate them.

---

[177] C. S. C. Williams, 200–201.

[178] Acts 17:18.

[179] Acts 17:19-20.

[180] Krodel, 327.

[181] Danker, 216. According to Danker, the word is usually used in a denigrating sense. Here, however, Paul seems to use it to mean "devout" or "religious." See also Werner Foerster, "δεισιδαιμονεστερους," *Theological Dictionary of the New Testament* 2: 20. Forester says that *deisidaimonesterous* is used as a general expression of piety. It can be used to describe a pious attitude towards the gods, but on the other hand, can also be used to refer to an excessive fear of them, and carries the idea of a fear of evil spirits. In Paul's use of *deisidaimonesterous*, he seems to be emphasizing the positive rather the negative aspects of the word.

[182] Williams, 304.

[183] Ibid. See also Bruce, *The Book of the Acts*, 335, This, "was a vague term in Greek as

The basis for Paul's opening statement is the fact that as he walked around the city looking at their objects of worship, he came across an altar that was inscribed: "TO AN UNKNOWN GOD."[184] It is possible that the influence of the Jews throughout the Greek world inspired this altar. This unknown god could actually be the God of Israel, whose name was never used.[185] It is much more likely, however, that the Athenians had altars to unknown gods and goddesses throughout the city in an effort to appease any that they did not specifically have altars or temples set up for. Since the Athenians did not have a background in the Hebrew Scriptures, this inscription becomes the text that Paul builds his sermon on.[186]

Paul then declares his intentions to his audience: "Now what you worship as something unknown I am going to proclaim to you."[187] He begins by describing the Unknown God as the One who created the heavens and the earth. Paul tells them that He does not live in man-made temples and human hands do not serve Him. Even though Paul does not refer to the Scriptures, his language is nevertheless steeped in Old Testament imagery as he speaks. One example of this is the clear reference he makes to Isaiah 42:5:

> Thus says the God the Lord, Who created the heavens and stretched them out, Who spread out the earth and its offspring, Who gives breath to the people on it, And spirit to those who walk in it . . .

In describing God as the Creator, Paul is clearly showing the difference between Him and the idolatry of the Greeks. The God that Paul is preaching is completely separate from His creation, "and the attempt to make God visible in images, temples, and cults constitutes idolatry, the ultimate sin."[188]

After describing God as the Creator, Paul then refers to Him as the Sustainer of life.[189] He, "gives all men life and everything else."[190] Since God is the giver of life to all men, it becomes obvious that there is nothing that man can supply God with. This seems to make allusion to Psalm

---

"'religion'" is in English, and what was piety to Greeks was superstition to Jews (and *vice versa*)."

[184] Acts 17:23.

[185] Foakes-Jackson, 165.

[186] Bruce, *Paul: Apostle of the Heart Set Free*, 239.

[187] Acts 17:23.

[188] Krodel, 331.

[189] Stott, 285.

[190] Acts 17:25.

50:10-12. Verse 10 says, "For every beast of the forest is Mine, the cattle on a thousand hills." Paul may have also been making another point here. The Greeks often saw Zeus as the source of life.[191] Paul could be subtly making the point that the true and living God was the source of life, not Zeus.

The next point that Paul made was that God, "made every nation of men, that they should inhabit the whole earth."[192] Because all mankind is related through the creation, Paul is able to lay the foundation here that his message excludes no one.[193] The Gospel is universal in its scope. God's desire was, "that men would seek him and perhaps reach out for him and find him, though he is not far from each one of us."[194] The picture that Paul paints here is that of a blind person groping in the darkness for what they are trying to find.[195] Without the ability to see, all they can do is feel around for what they want. God is not far from His creatures, however, but because of their blindness, they are unable to locate Him.

Paul then uses material from two different Greek writers to emphasize his points. He is attempting, "to present his message in a way that critically engages the cultural world that he has entered."[196] Paul firsts quotes Epimenides of Crete when he says in verse 28, "For in him we live and move and have our being."[197] The apostle then cites the Cilician poet, Aratus, in the same verse when he says, "We are his offspring."[198] Even though Aratus was referring to Zeus as the source of off-spring, Paul is still building on his original point of explaining the "unknown God" to his audience. Quoting the Scriptures to an audience that does not acknowledge their authority would have been a waste of time. What Paul did instead was use familiar Greek works that conveyed the Scriptural principles that he wanted to emphasize. Paul's goal was to communicate with his audience at a level that they could understand and relate to.

Paul's next point builds on Aratus' quote. Since we are God's offspring, we should not think that we can build any image that adequately represents Him. This may not seem like a very strong rebuke against idolatry but Paul's goal is not to judge or rebuke his listeners. Instead, he wants them to respond to the message of salvation that he is preaching. As Paul concludes

---

[191] Williams, 306.

[192] Acts 17:26.

[193] Tannehill, 211.

[194] Acts 17:27.

[195] Krodel, 335.

[196] Tannehill, 214.

[197] Arrington, 180.

[198] Ibid.

his message, he does so by emphasizing the need for repentance and pointing out that there will be a Day of Judgment. If Paul's hearers genuinely repent and turn to the true God, the issue of idolatry should become a non-issue. True repentance would involve not only turning to the living God, but also turning away from their idols.[199]

When Paul told the Athenians that there was going to be a Day of Judgment, he said that it would be, "by the man he has appointed. He has given proof of this to all men by raising him from the dead."[200] The statement about the resurrection produced a division in his audience. Some sneered but others told Paul that they wanted to hear him again on the subject. Paul's preaching of the resurrection was what got the Athenian philosopher's attention in the first place when he, "was preaching the good news about Jesus and the resurrection," in the marketplace. The Greeks already saw their souls as immortal. The idea of a physical resurrection was nonsensical to them.[201]

Luke records the results of Paul's evangelistic ministry in Athens in 17:34: "A few men became followers of Paul and believed. Among them was Dionysius, a member of the Areopagus, also a woman named Damaris, and a number of others." Krodel again understands Luke's language here to mean that a church was formed in Athens.[202] Marshall, on the other hand, feels that it is doubtful that a church was formed at this time.[203] This would appear to be the stronger view. Luke's language indicates that there were few converts and there is no mention of anyone being baptized in Athens. There is also no other mention in the New Testament of a church in Athens. It is likely that a church was eventually formed there, it is just not clear as to whether or not it took place on Paul's first visit to the city. One of the converts that Luke mentions by name, Dionysius, is later said to have become the bishop of Athens.[204] If this is an accurate tradition, perhaps he formed a congregation there sometime later.

In comparing and contrasting the evangelistic ministries of Peter and Paul, it is clear that both men were very effective in this particular role. They both had the ability to preach messages that impacted people and caused them to want to repent. In looking at the similarities in their evan-

---

[199] Krodel, 338.

[200] Acts 17:31.

[201] Neil, 193.

[202] Krodel, 339.

[203] Marshall, 291.

[204] Foakes-Jackson, 167. See also Packer, 149, "Dionysius, bishop of Corinth (*c.* AD 170) calls Dionysius the Areopgite the first bishop of the church at Athens."

gelistic styles, it is first observed that both apostles relied heavily on the Hebrew Scriptures in their preaching to Jewish audiences. In both of Peter's sermons to the Jews in Acts 2 and Acts 3, he clearly articulates the fact that Jesus was the fulfillment of the Old Testament prophecies. He quotes from the Hebrew Scriptures and interprets them in the light of the Lord Jesus. In a similar fashion, in Paul's message to the synagogue audience at Pisidian Anticoh, he also quoted extensively from the Scriptures to demonstrate that Jesus was the Messiah.

Peter and Paul both also had the ability to adapt their message when speaking with non-Jewish audiences. When Peter spoke to those assembled at Cornelius' house, he did not quote any passages of Scripture or rely on a specific text. Rather, he recounted the life and ministry of Jesus and used that as the basis for his message. Peter also explained the meaning of the death and resurrection of Jesus. This was an audience that probably had some knowledge of Jesus but a limited knowledge of the Hebrew Scriptures. In keeping his message centered on the Person of the Lord Jesus, Peter took his audience to a place of faith.

When Paul spoke to the Greek audience at the Areopagus in Athens, instead of using Scriptures that they would not be familiar with, he used an inscription from one of their pagan altars as a text. He also quoted two Greek writers to make his points. It was pointed out in the study that even though Paul did not quote from the Scriptures specifically, his language was steeped in the language of the Old Testament. His audience was hearing the Scripture without realizing it.

In relating the evangelistic aspects of Peter and Paul's apostolic ministries, Luke also illustrates their successes. Peter's initial success among the Jews was impressive. Luke records that 3,000 people were added to the church after listening to Peter's Pentecost sermon. At least another 2,000 responded to his message in the temple after the lame man was healed. While Luke does not provide any specific numbers of converts for Paul's evangelistic messages, he still makes it clear that Paul was very successful. After Paul preached in the synagogue at Iconium, for example, "a great number of Jews and Gentiles believed."[205] In Acts 17:4 Luke writes, "Some of the Jews were persuaded and joined Paul and Silas, as did a large number of God-fearing Greeks and not a few prominent women."

Even though Luke does not give any numbers for Paul's evangelistic work, he shows his success in another way. The churches that Paul founded are the primary manner in which Luke illustrates his success. In Acts Paul is seen planting churches in Pisidian Antioch, Iconium, Lystra, Derbe,

---

[205] Acts 14:1.

Philippi, Thessalonica, Berea, Corinth, and Ephesus. It is also very likely that he started churches in other cities as well that Luke did not see fit to write about. The congregation in Troas for example, mentioned in Acts 20, was possibly founded by Paul but Luke is silent on the subject. The congregations that Paul founded are his greatest measure of success as an evangelist. Each one of these Christian groups represented a number of lives that had been changed by the gospel through Paul's ministry.

In examining the evangelistic aspects of Peter and Paul's ministries, a couple of differences can also be noted. First of all, their target audience was different. On the whole, Peter's ministry was aimed at the Jews while Paul's ministry was aimed at the Gentiles. This is not to say that Peter never preached to a Gentile audience or that Paul never preached to a Jewish audience. Peter clearly did reach out to Gentiles in the account at Cornelius' house and Paul regularly reached out to Jews by always starting his ministry in a city by going to the synagogue first. As was discussed in chapter 2, however, in Galatians Paul referred Peter as the "apostle to the Jews" and himself as the "apostle to the Gentiles." Luke shows that Peter's primary focus in Acts is in taking the Gospel to the Palestinian Jews. Luke then shows Paul taking the Gospel to the Gentiles throughout the Greek world. Even in his synagogue ministry, Paul seemed to have more success among the God-fearing Gentiles than he did among the Jews that were present there.

Another difference between the evangelistic ministries of Peter and Paul was in the area of church planting. In discussing Paul's apostolic endeavors, it was clearly seen that a fundamental aspect of his ministry was in planting churches.[206] As was mentioned previously, the numerous Christian communities that Paul established were the greatest evidence of his success as an evangelist. Cook says that Paul, "was consumed by the idea of planting churches and spreading his understanding of the gospel . . ."[207] Paul and his team established congregations in at least ten different cities, often under the threat of persecution from both the Jews and the Gentiles. These Christian groups would be a safe haven for the new believers in the midst of this persecution.

Peter, on the other hand, is never shown in the role of a church planter, in spite of his great success as an evangelist. He was one of the founding apostles of the church in Jerusalem and it could be argued that a Christian community was established in Cornelius' home. Other than these two possible examples, however, there is nothing to indicate that Peter made a habit of establishing churches in the areas that he evangelized. Even in

---

[206] Bowers, 89.

[207] Cook, 86.

those two examples there is nothing to demonstrate Peter taking an active role in establishing or organizing the communities. Rather, Peter seemed comfortable working where others had laid the groundwork. In Samaria, for example, Philip had already been working there for some time, and had possibly already established Christian communities when Peter and John came down from Jerusalem. Another example is seen in Acts 9:32, where Luke records the details of another one of Peter's evangelistic/pastoral trips: "As Peter traveled about the country, he went to visit the saints in Lydda." The indication here is that Peter was visiting those who were already believers. There is no information given by Luke to believe that Peter had started these communities. Most likely, Philip had previously founded them. A last example of Peter building on someone else's foundation would be in Corinth. There is nothing in Acts to indicate that Peter had ever visited that city. It was pointed out, however, in chapter 2 of the study that Paul seemed to imply in 1 Corinthians that Peter had spent some time in Corinth. Acts clearly demonstrates, however, that Paul was the one who founded the church in Corinth.

A last difference in the evangelistic styles of Peter and Paul that will be mentioned has to do with the aspect of teamwork and fellow workers. Peter is shown ministering with John on two occasions, for the healing of the lame man in Acts 3 and the ministry in Samaria in Acts 8. Other than that, however, Peter is usually shown ministering alone. This is surprising considering the fact that Jesus made it a point to send His disciples out in pairs to evangelize, as well as the very fact that He spent three years developing a team of twelve men to continue His work after He was gone. Even on those occasions when Peter is with the other apostles, he occupies the center stage and there is no indication that Peter understood or made use of the concept of teamwork in his ministry. In his own writings, Peter only mentions three other people in his two letters, and one of them is Paul.

Paul, however, is very seldom seen working alone. He preferred to have others working with him. His letters confirm what Luke shows in Acts. Paul makes reference to over a hundred different people in his letters that worked with him in some capacity. In Acts, Luke shows Paul delegating assignments to Timothy, Silas, Luke, and Priscilla and Aquila. These, as well as many other people, played an active role in Paul's apostolic ministry. It is probably safe to conclude that Paul's great success can be linked with the team of quality people that worked with him. They allowed Paul to multiply his efforts and to accomplish more than he could have ever accomplished working alone.[208] Even though Luke clearly has his attention focused on Paul, it is impossible to miss the importance of the network of co-workers that Paul puts together.

---

[208] Hiebert, 4, "Paul revealed his powers of leadership by drawing around himself friends from diverse cultural backgrounds and with varied gifts and achievements and by molding them into a strong working team in the furtherance of the gospel."

5

Miracle Working and Healing

Iᴛ is in the miracles that they performed that Peter and Paul draw the closest to imitating Jesus' ministry. Part of Jesus' commission to the Twelve included an element of the miraculous:

> When Jesus had called the Twelve together, he gave them power and authority to drive out all demons and to cure diseases, and he sent them out to preach the kingdom of God and to heal the sick . . . So they set out and went from village to village, preaching the gospel and healing people everywhere.[1]

The two apostles are seen in a number of situations in Acts where they presumably did as Jesus would have done. In fact, almost every type of miracle or healing that is seen in the Gospels is duplicated in Acts.[2] Luke understands that Jesus, by His Spirit, was continuing to do His works through His chosen servants. In Luke's Gospel, the miracles that Jesus performed are evidence of the divine providence that was active in His life. In the same way, the miracles that are seen in the early church in Acts are testimony to the divine providence that was active in the lives of these believers.[3] The number of miracles that Luke records in Acts and the amount of space that he devotes to them indicate that he considered miracles, and especially healings, an integral part of the apostolic ministry. Hardon makes the point, "that at every point where the Gospel was first established among a certain people, the foundation was made in a miraculous context."[4] Samaria is a

---

[1] Luke 9:1-2, 6.

[2] John A. Hardon, "The Miracle Narratives in the Acts of the Apostles," *Catholic Biblical Quarterly* 16 (1954) 305.

[3] Squires, 97, "The wonders and signs performed by each of the major figures in Acts 1–15 thus attest to continuing divine activity in the early church."

[4] Hardon, 311. Hardon goes on to say, "Not only do the apostolic miracles help to explain the rise of the apostolic Church, but in themselves they are a witness to the continued presence in the Church of the living Spirit of Jesus Christ, who alone, ultimately, must

good example of this. It was in the context of the miraculous that Philip established the Gospel there. In the first half of Acts, Luke shows that Peter was one of the primary mediators of this miraculous power.

Peter the Miracle Worker

Luke provides a summary statement in Acts 2:43 in regards to the miraculous, stating that, "many wonders and miraculous signs were done by the apostles." As with the rest of Acts, however, Luke provides only a representative sampling of these miracles. The first miracle that will be examined is the healing of the lame man in Acts 3. This miracle is an example of the "many wonders and miraculous signs" that Luke mentioned in Acts 2. This healing is likely recounted because of the attention it aroused in the crowd and in the religious leaders.[5] Luke does not provide a chronology for when this incident took place, however, it was most likely not long after Pentecost. At any rate, the message that Peter preaches after this healing is similar in content to the one that he preached on Pentecost.[6]

One of the first things that can be noted about this incident is that it occurs in the normal context of life. The apostles were doing what they normally did. Peter and John were going to the temple to pray at the ninth hour as they did every day. It does not appear that Peter or John had any kind of agenda other than prayer as they were going to the temple on this day. They had continued to live according to the Law and to observe the specified times of prayer.

As they arrived at the temple, they encountered the lame man. Luke records that, "he was put there every day to beg from those going into the temple courts."[7] It is likely that Peter and John had encountered him before and it is possible that they had even given him money in the past. On this particular day, however, when he asked Peter and John for money, "Peter looked straight at him, as did John." The word that Luke uses here for "look" is *atenzio*.[8] It has a strongly intensive meaning and can also be translated, "to look towards, to take heed, to behold."[9] The word carries the

---

account for the growth of the Mystical Body to which He gave birth by His death on the cross," 316.

[5] Neil, 82.

[6] Dennis Ham, "Acts 3:1-10: The Healing of the Temple Beggar as Lucan Theology," *Biblica* 67 (1986) 305.

[7] Acts 3:2.

[8] Moulton, 71.

[9] Ibid. See also Danker, 179, ". . . to take in the sight of something, look at, observe."

idea of looking at something or someone for the purpose of examination.[10] Even though Peter had probably had contact with this man before, on this day there was something about him that caught Peter's attention. Perhaps Peter was looking to see if he could see or sense faith in the lame man. A similar incident took place later at Lystra in Acts 14:9 when Paul, seeing a lame man in the audience that he was preaching to, perceived that he had faith to be healed.[11] Luke uses similar language in both accounts.

After looking at the man, Peter then ordered him, "Look at us!" The man gave his attention to Peter and John, "expecting to get something from them." While there is no indication that the man expected to get healed, he did have faith that he was going to receive something from the apostles. This may have been all the faith that Peter needed to see. The lame man originally saw Peter and John going into the temple and asked for money.[12] At that point, he was only hopeful that someone would give him something. Now Peter has gotten his attention and he is looking at them with anticipation. Luke seems to be underscoring here the importance of the apostles as the mediators of Christ's healing power.[13] "At this moment, just before the healing, the focus is on Peter (with John, present but inactive)."[14]

The formula that Peter uses to heal the lame man needs to be considered. Peter told him, "In the name of Jesus Christ of Nazareth, walk."[15] Krodel states, "By issuing the command in Jesus' name Peter placed the lame beggar under the saving power of Jesus."[16] The name of Jesus signifies here all the authority and power of Jesus Himself.[17] As a representative of Jesus, Peter had the authority to use His name to do what Jesus himself had done before when He was physically on the earth.

In using the name of Jesus to heal the lame man, Peter used a formula that was similar to that found in ancient magic.[18] Instead of Peter saying the

---

[10] Wilhelm Michaelis, "Βλεψον," *Theological Dictionary of the New Testament*, 5: 343.

[11] Williams, 64.

[12] Richard I. Pervo, *Luke's Story of Paul* (Minneapolis: Fortress, 1990) 22, "The dramatically effective reference to money informs the readers that the apostles do not have community funds at their personal disposal. Healers with money in their pockets are liable to be magicians."

[13] Hamm, 311.

[14] Ibid.

[15] Acts 3:6.

[16] Krodel, 97.

[17] Arrington, 38.

[18] Marshall, 88.

right words to invoke the deity through magic, however, to bring healing, this miracle is based on faith in God. Peter's faith and ultimately, the lame man's faith were what brought the miracle about. Talbert points out that magic is, "human control of the divine powers to make them work for humans."[19] Peter's encounter with the lame man was a faith encounter; with faith being the, "human response to the divine initiative."[20] Peter knew that neither he nor John had healing power in themselves, but that through faith they had access to God's miracle working power.

The next aspect of this miracle that needs to be discussed is the fact that Peter did something tangible to help bring about the man's healing. "Taking him by the right hand, he helped him up." Not only did Peter speak the word of healing over the lame man he became physically involved. Peter pulled the man to his feet before he had a chance to think about what was happening to him. Rather than just commanding the man to get up and waiting to see what would happen, Peter helped to activate his faith by pulling him to his feet.[21] It was as Peter was pulling the man up that, "his feet and ankles became strong." It was the power of God that healed the lame man, but it was Peter's hand that pulled him to his feet.[22] This action highlighted Peter's role as an instrument that God could work through.[23] Peter was willing to do whatever needed to be done to see that the man received his healing. Peter's action of physically helping the man up was also something that he had seen Jesus do when He raised Jairus' daughter from the dead in Luke 7:54.[24] This miracle was a clear example of the way that Peter imitated Jesus in his apostolic ministry.

Luke's description of the healing itself is very vivid.[25] "He jumped to his feet and began to walk. Then he went with them into the temple courts, walking and jumping, and praising God."[26] The language that Luke uses seems to be designed to invoke a comparison with Isaiah 35:6, "Then will

---

[19] Talbert, 54.

[20] Ibid.

[21] Stott, 91.

[22] Ibid.

[23] Krodel, 98.

[24] Stott, 91.

[25] Williams, 65. Williams believes that this narrative is so vivid in the way that Luke describes it that it had to have come from an eyewitness. Luke may have gotten it directly from Peter.

[26] Acts 3:8.

the lame leap like a deer."[27] Luke uses this healing as another example of how Biblical prophecies were being fulfilled through Jesus' followers.

As the man accompanies the apostles into the temple, his joy cannot be contained. He is walking, jumping and praising God. It is obvious that his praise was not quiet. He had not received any money but now he did not have to beg anymore. A crowd quickly gathered as the word of his healing spread. For a few moments, the newly healed man was the center of attention as everyone wanted to watch him walk and listen as he told what had happened to him. It was after the crowd had gathered that Peter seized the opportunity to use the healing as an object lesson for an evangelistic message. Peter then shifted the crowd's attention from the lame man to Jesus, the one whose power had brought the healing. The sermon that Peter preached here was discussed in the previous chapter.

A second passage that refers to Peter as a miracle worker is found in Acts 5:15-16 where people would bring the sick into the street in the hope that Peter's shadow might fall on them as he passed by. Luke does not record any specific incidents of where Peter's shadow healed anyone. Instead he gives a summary statement that, "all of them were healed."

The first aspect of these verses that needs to be considered is that of the people believing that there was healing power in Peter's shadow. It was a common belief in antiquity that a person's shadow, especially that of a holy man or miracle worker's, contained healing power.[28] It would be easy to dismiss a passage like this as merely popular superstition. Luke, however, makes it difficult to do so. First of all, he clearly believes what he was writing.[29] Luke believes that many people were healed as a result of Peter's shadow passing over them. In his gospel, Luke presents the healing of a woman who pushed her way through the throng to touch the hem of Jesus' garment. The woman had faith that this would heal her.[30] Later in Acts, he will record the story of people taking handkerchiefs and aprons that Paul had touched and healing people with them. The implied element that brought the healing to pass in each of these accounts was that of faith. It can be argued that there was a strong superstitious element involved here in believing that Peter's shadow had healing power. In spite of that, however, God still honored the faith behind it, even if it was an imperfect faith.[31]

---

[27] Hamm, 312.

[28] Krodel, 125.

[29] P. W. Van Der Horst, "Peter's Shadow," *New Testament Studies* 23 (1977) 210. See also Hemer, 439–40.

[30] Stott, 113.

[31] Robertson, 203.

Clearly, this account of Peter's shadow fits in with other miraculous incidents that Luke recorded.

A second aspect of this passage that needs to be considered is that of Peter's popularity. It appears that Peter was well known by this time as a miracle worker. Word had traveled out of Jerusalem and through many of the surrounding towns and villages about Peter and the things that had happened through his ministry. Bruce states, "Peter's reputation evidently stood specially high in this regard."[32] Peter's popularity and the type of ministry that he was performing is reminiscent of the early days of Jesus' Galilean ministry when people would bring the sick and demon possessed to where he was staying. Peter was once again following Jesus' example and doing the things that he had seen Jesus do.

The next place where Peter is seen performing miracles is in Acts 9:32-42. This passage concerns the healing of Aeneas and the resuscitation of Tabitha. The context for the healing at Lydda was that Peter was conducting a missionary tour through Judea. There is no indication that Peter founded these groups. Philip had preached throughout that area according to Acts 8:40 and he may have been responsible for the formation of these groups of Christians in Western Palestine.[33] Peter's visit to Lydda may have been pastoral as well as evangelistic.[34] Luke records that Peter, "went to visit the saints in Lydda."[35] While in Lydda he encountered Aeneas. It is probable that he was a member of the Christian community there, but Luke does not expressly state this.[36] Krodel, who doubts the historicity of much of Acts, believes that this narrative is based on a genuine tradition. He bases this on the amount of detail that Luke provides. Luke gives the man's name, a description of his illness, and the length of time that he had been sick.[37]

Luke does not provide much detail about the healing itself. He does not state where Peter's encounter with Aeneas took place. If he was a member of the church there, it is conceivable that the encounter could have occurred in the context of a church service. Luke's description of the healing is brief. Peter addressed Aeneas by name and told him, "Jesus Christ heals

---

[32] Bruce, *The Book of the Acts*, 109.

[33] Arrington, 106.

[34] Stott, 182, "Peter's purpose was not only to preach the gospel, but also *to visit the saints* (32b), in order to teach and encourage them." See also Luter, 155, ". . . the Apostle Peter was involved in traveling around to build up '"the church throughout all Judea and Galilee and Samaria.'"

[35] Acts 9:32.

[36] Bruce, 197–98.

[37] Krodel, 184.

you. Get up and take care of your mat."[38] The result of Peter's command was, "Immediately Aeneas got up."[39] The testimony Aeneas' healing was such that, "All those who lived in Lydda and Sharon saw him and turned to the Lord."[40] A miracle was once again responsible for turning people to Christ.

In describing this healing it is apparent that Luke saw parallels between it and Jesus' healing of a paralytic in Luke 5:17-26.[41] The language used in the respective miracles is also similar. Jesus told the paralytic, "Get up, take your mat and go home."[42] Peter's command to Aeneas was very similar. The ability of the lame man to now be able to make up his bed symbolized a, "transition from dependence to self-sufficiency."[43] While some would argue that Luke deliberately crafted Peter's encounter with Aeneas to resemble what Jesus did, it is much more likely that Peter was merely following Jesus' example. He did and said what he had seen Jesus do. This pattern will be seen in the next incident as well.

After describing Aeneas' healing, Luke then transitions to Joppa. He states that at the same time Peter was in Lydda, a disciple in Joppa named Tabitha became sick and died. She was not buried, but rather, "her body was washed and placed in an upstairs room."[44] It appears that Tabitha had a special ministry to the widows in the community. She clothed them with garments that she made with her own hands. It is possible that the church there had commissioned her to serve the widows.[45] The believers heard that Peter was in nearby Lydda so a delegation was sent to request that he come to Joppa. This request for Peter to come suggests that they had some hope that Tabitha might be raised from the dead.[46] At the very least, a visit from the Apostle Peter would have brought comfort in a difficult time.

When Peter arrived, he was taken to the room where Tabitha had been laid. The picture that Luke paints of this scene is a vivid one. "All the widows stood around him, crying and showing him the robes and other clothing that Dorcas had made while she was still with them."[47] It is implied in

---

38 Acts 9:34.

39 Ibid.

40 Acts 9:35.

41 Neil, 135.

42 Luke 5:24.

43 Pervo, 36.

44 Acts 9:37.

45 Arrington, 106.

46 Marshall, 179.

47 Acts 9:39.

the Greek that the widows were actually wearing some of the garments that Tabitha (also called Dorcas) had made for them.[48] Anderson draws attention to the fact that Tabitha was no ordinary disciple. "She is active and wakeful as an antelope, full of good works as well as alms, and even though a person of distinction, suitably humble, working in company with the widows and saints."[49]

As Peter met with the widows, "he was made aware of how great a loss the church in Joppa had sustained."[50] Peter then sent everyone out of the room. He was left alone with Tabitha's body. This was something that Peter had seen Jesus do when He raised Jairus' daughter from the dead. He had only allowed the girl's parents and three of His disciples to witness the miracle. Luke's picture of Peter here is not that of a self-confident miracle worker, but that of a humble man desiring to do God's will.[51]

After Peter cleared the room, Luke records that, "he got down on his knees and prayed." By making everyone leave the room, Peter was able to pray without distraction. A room full of crying women would create an extremely emotional atmosphere! The result of Peter's prayer was that he spoke to the body, "Tabitha, get up." She then opened her eyes and sat up. Only then did he take her by the hand and help her to her feet. This is in contrast with Peter's healing of the lame man at the temple in Acts 3. In that situation, Peter helped to facilitate the healing by pulling him to his feet. The raising of Tabitha from the dead took place through verbal command, not bodily contact.[52] After helping her up, Peter called the believers back into the room and presented Tabitha to them alive. Luke wrote that this miracle, "became known all over Joppa, and many people believed in the Lord."[53]

In discussing this miracle it bears mentioning that this was the first recorded time that one of the apostles had raised someone from the dead. It becomes even more significant to see that a woman was the recipient of the miracle.[54] Women play a prominent role in Luke-Acts and Tabitha is no exception. The amount of detail that Luke provides about Tabitha seems to

---

[48] Blaiklock, 94.

[49] Janice Capel Anderson, "Reading Tabitha: A Feminist Reception History, " in *The New Literary Criticism and the New Testament*, ed. Edgar V. McKnight and Elizabeth Struthers Malbon (Valley Forge, Pa.: Trinity, 1994) 117.

[50] Williams, 181.

[51] Robertson, 224.

[52] Tannehill, 127.

[53] Acts 9:42.

[54] Anderson, 130.

indicate that she occupied an important position in the church in Joppa.[55] It seems clear that she was involved in some type of a leadership role, especially among the widows.

The raising of Tabitha from the dead is the last recorded miracle for Peter in Acts. Luke demonstrates how the four other miracles that Peter performed culminated in this one.[56] This can be seen as the high point of Peter's ministry. Luke has painted a vivid portrait of a man who imitated Jesus in the miracles that he performed.

Paul the Miracle Worker

This section will examine the miracles that took place through Paul's ministry in Acts.[57] Paul understood the working of miracles to be a confirmation of his own apostolic ministry when he said,

> I will not venture to speak of anything except what Christ has accomplished through me in leading the Gentiles to obey God by what I have said and done—by the power of signs and miracles, through the power of the Spirit. So from Jerusalem all the way around to Illycrium, I have fully proclaimed the gospel of Christ.[58]

Paul considered the miraculous to be an indispensable part of the gospel that he preached.[59] He also understood that there were definite signs that confirmed and authenticated his apostleship.[60] In 2 Corinthians 12:12 Paul tells them, "The things that mark an apostle—signs, wonders, and miracles- were done among you with great perseverance." Even though he makes mention of signs and wonders in general terms here and in Romans, Paul never provides any specific examples of miracles that he performed in his letters. Perhaps his modesty would not permit it, or it was not something he wanted to emphasize. Luke, however, provides several accounts in Acts where Paul did work miracles. The presentation is such that, "Paul's life and work encompassed with exorcisms, healings, raisings of the dead, and other miracles of various kinds."[61] As was also seen in Peter's ministry, the miraculous would often create an environment for evangelism in Paul's

---

[55] Ibid.

[56] Gill, 166.

[57] Jervell, 10, "Acts portrays Paul as a miracle worker in order to demonstrate his preaching as the divine word."

[58] Romans 15:18-19.

[59] Jervell, 10.

[60] Schmithals, 36.

[61] Jervell, 71.

ministry. Koh points out that these power encounters in Acts almost always happen in the context of the preaching of the Kingdom of God, and they are marked by the presence of the Holy Spirit.[62] Peter and Paul both followed Jesus' example of proclaiming the Kingdom of God, while at the same time performing signs and wonders that confirmed their message. "The power encounters described in Luke-Acts clearly represents the reality of the spiritual conflict against Satan in proclamation of the Kingdom of God."[63]

The first account of the miraculous in Paul's ministry is found in his confrontation with Bar-Jesus the sorcerer in Acts 13. This story has often been compared with Peter's encounter with Ananias and Sapphira in Acts 5.[64] While there are some parallels between the two accounts, the differences seem to outweigh the similarities. The main similarity is the fact that in both stories, an apostle pronounces judgment on someone. Hardon refers to these as "punitive miracles."[65] In the case of Ananias and Sapphira, their judgment is death. In Bar-Jesus' case, his punishment is that he is blinded for a time. Acts demonstrates that at least in some cases, the filling of the Holy Spirit does not just allow the Christian to do good things. It also allows them to be instruments of God's judgment.[66] The biggest difference in these two accounts lies in the fact that Ananias and Sapphira were members of the Christian community and were judged for sinning against God and the community. Bar-Jesus, however, was not a believer. He was judged for attempting, "to turn the proconsul from the faith."[67] He was himself a stumbling block to Sergius Paulus.

Another account from Peter's ministry that is similar to this one is his confrontation with Simon in Acts 8.[68] In both of these narratives, Peter with Simon and Paul with Bar-Jesus, the apostle has a confrontation with a magician. Also, in both of these accounts, the apostles speak harsh words of judgment to the magicians. While Peter's confrontation with Ananias and Sapphira resulted in their death, that is not the case in his encounter

---

[62] Chu Fat Koh, "Power Encounters in Luke-Acts," Th. M. thesis, Fuller Theological Seminary (1996) 3.

[63] Ibid., 52.

[64] Foakes-Jackson, 112. See also Krodel, 229.

[65] Hardon, 306.

[66] Munck, *The Acts of the Apostles*, 119.

[67] Acts 13:8. See also Garrett, 81, ". . . Paul also charges Bar-Jesus with 'making crooked the straight paths of the Lord' (v. 10), which is the opposite of what the true prophet John the Baptist had done (Luke 3:4)."

[68] Bruce, 249. See also Krodel, 229, "As Jesus had been confronted by the devil, so Peter and Paul were confronted by magicians."

with Simon or Paul's encounter with Bar-Jesus. They were both judged and Bar-Jesus was blinded for a time, but they did not die as a result of their encounter with the apostles.

There are also several notable differences in the two encounters. First of all, before Peter has his confrontation with Simon in Acts 8, Luke notes that he had believed and been baptized. To some degree, Simon had become a part of the new Christian community in Samaria. Luke alludes to the fact that he was traveling with Philip and was possibly a part of the leadership team in Samaria. Bar-Jesus, on the other hand appeared to belong to the retinue of the proconsul, Sergius Paulus, and possibly served as some type of spiritual advisor to him.[69] There is no indication given by Luke that Bar-Jesus ever embraced the gospel that Paul and Barnabas were preaching.

Another difference between Simon and Bar-Jesus is the fact that not only is Bar-Jesus referred to as a sorcerer, he is also called a false prophet.[70] Simon was only referred to in the context of his sorcery. Arrington believes that Bar-Jesus was a Jewish astrologer that Sergius Paulus relied on for counsel and advice.[71] He probably would receive more respect as a Jewish seer than would a Greek. Bar-Jesus would claim divine inspiration when he gave the proconsul advice. In this way, Bar-Jesus would have had some measure of control over Sergius Paulus by the advice that he gave him.

This idea of control leads to the third difference between the two sorcerers. Bar-Jesus appears to have been very concerned with keeping his control over the proconsul. He attempted to turn him from the faith that Paul and Barnabas were preaching. This was what led to the confrontation with Paul. Simon, on the other hand, was more concerned with making money from the Gospel. He attempted to buy the ability to bestow the Holy Spirit from Peter. The implication was that he could then earn money for himself by laying his hands on people and giving them the Holy Spirit.

The language that Paul uses in his judgment of Bar-Jesus is similar to that of Peter's to Ananias. In both cases, Satan is acknowledged as being the force behind the person. Peter asked Ananias, "How is it that Satan has so filled your heart that you have lied to the Holy Spirit . . . ?"[72] Paul told

---

[69] Ramsay, 79–80.

[70] Bruce, 249, "Luke calls him a false prophet, not (probably) in the sense that he foretold things which did not come to pass, but in the sense that he claimed falsely to be a medium of divine revelation."

[71] Arrington, 133–34.

[72] Acts 5:3.

Bar-Jesus, "You are a child of the devil and an enemy of everything that is right!"[73] Paul's encounter with the sorcerer, like Peter's, is portrayed in terms of spiritual warfare. Bar-Jesus was the representative of the kingdom of Satan and Paul was the representative of the Kingdom of God.[74]

The judgment that Bar-Jesus received was blindness. This was a traditional punishment for wickedness.[75] It is important to note that this took place after Paul was, "filled with the Holy Spirit." He was not acting in his own power or passing his own judgment. Paul was the vessel for God's anger against someone who would attempt to block another from finding the truth. The judgment itself was fitting. As Bar-Jesus attempted to keep the proconsul in the darkness, so he himself would know a time of darkness.[76] In the midst of his punishment, however, grace is extended. The blindness is only going to be, "for a time." It may have been that Bar-Jesus' blindness would be removed when he repented.[77]

Paul's encounter with Bar-Jesus is significant for one final reason. This account shows the shift of Paul from being a subordinate to Barnabas to being the dominant of the two men. The next time that Luke refers to the missionaries, it as, "Paul and his companions."[78] From here on out, with the exception of the Jerusalem Conference, Paul's name is always mentioned first. Luke punctuates the shift in leadership here also by beginning to use "Paul" instead of "Saul" in referring to the apostle.

The result of the confrontation with Bar-Jesus was that, "When the proconsul saw what had happened, he believed, for he was amazed at the teaching of the Lord."[79] This verse has caused some confusion among scholars. Some would argue that Sergius Paulus only experienced a superficial conversion because of the power encounter between Paul and Bar-Jesus.[80] Others would see a valid conversion account here of the proconsul.[81] Luke makes no mention of the proconsul being baptized and there is no further mention of him in Acts. It appears that Luke is more interested in describ-

---

[73] Acts 13:10.

[74] Arrington, 134. See also Garrett, 80, Luke described Paul as being, "filled with the Holy Spirit." Paul referred to Bar-Jesus as a, "child of the devil. Thus the confrontation between Bar Jesus and Paul is also a confrontation between the Holy Spirit and the devil."

[75] Talbert, 128.

[76] Stott, 220.

[77] Williams, 226.

[78] Acts 13:13.

[79] Acts 13:12.

[80] Neil, 156. See also Foakes-Jackson, 112–13.

[81] Arrington, 134. See also Krodel, 230.

ing Paul's victory over the magician than he is in providing details about Sergius Paulus' conversion.[82]

The second account of miracles in Paul's ministry is found in Acts 14:3: "So Paul and Barnabas spent considerable time there, speaking boldly for the Lord, who confirmed the message of his grace by enabling them to do miraculous signs and wonders." While Luke does not give any specific examples of signs or wonders, it is clear from this passage that the miraculous was a very important component of Paul and Barnabas' evangelistic ministry in Iconium as well as the other cities of Galatia. Luke states that the apostles, "spent considerable time," in Iconium and that that time was marked by displays of God's power. "Their verbal testimony was confirmed by God who enabled them to do miraculous *signs and wonders,* just as the apostles had done in Jerusalem."[83] This passage also serves to provide a context for the miraculous healing that Paul will perform in Lystra.

Paul would later write to the churches in Galatia that he had founded on this trip and ask them, "Does God give you his Spirit and work miracles among you because you observe the law, or because you believe what you heard?"[84] The issue that he was dealing with in the letter was whether or not obedience to the law brought salvation. In making his point Paul reminds them of the miracles that had been performed in their midst. Their good works had not wrought any of the miracles that they had seen. God had given them freely through His grace.

The next account of Paul as a miracle worker that will be examined is in Acts 14:8-10. It is the narrative of a lame man who was healed. Luke sets up the story by describing the man to be healed and his condition, "In Lystra there sat a man crippled in his feet, who was lame from birth and had never walked." In describing the man's condition, Luke emphasizes that he was incurable. He was crippled, lame from birth, and had never walked. Luke says the same thing three different ways to make his point.

The healing in Lystra occurs in the context of Paul's preaching. "He listened to Paul as he was speaking."[85] Marshall suggests that the content of Paul's message included references to the healing ministry of Jesus.[86] Whether or not that is the case, something that Paul said triggered faith in the lame man. "Paul looked directly at him, saw that he had faith to be

---

[82] Marshall, 220.

[83] Ibid., 233. This passage is a parallel to the summary statement in Acts 2:43 where, ". . . many wonders and miraculous signs were done by the apostles."

[84] Galatians 3:5.

[85] Acts 14:9.

[86] Marshall, 236.

healed and called out, 'Stand up on your feet!'"[87] This is the only place in Acts where the faith of the person being healed is mentioned.[88] This contrasts with the Gospels, which frequently make mention of an individual's faith. The result of this miracle was that, "the man jumped up and began to walk."

While the faith of the man healed was a vital component of this healing, Paul's ability to detect it is also significant. As Paul spoke, he evidently supernaturally discerned that the man was ready to be healed. This same discernment was reflected in the previous encounter with Bar-Jesus in a negative sense. There, he had discerned that Bar-Jesus was a false prophet and was attempting to hinder the spread of the Gospel. In this case, Paul is able to see into the lame man's heart that he is ready to be healed physically and spiritually.

Paul's own faith is also notable here. He "did not whisper the command as an experiment. Everyone in the vicinity heard him. There was no going back if the man did not respond."[89] At Paul's word, however, the man jumped to his feet and began walking. This was the evidence of both the apostle's and the lame man's faith: he unfolded his crippled legs, climbed to his feet, and then began to walk.

Comparisons are naturally drawn between this healing and the one performed by Peter in Acts 3. Luke's language here is reminiscent of the way he described the lame man that Peter healed at the temple, "a man crippled from birth was being carried to the temple gate." Luke also emphasizes in that account the fact that the man was incurable. He had been crippled from birth and had to be carried everywhere he went.

Another similarity between the two accounts is in the way that Paul looked directly at the lame man and was able to detect his faith. In Acts 3, "Peter looked straight at him." The difference is that Peter then ordered the lame man to look at them, which he did, hoping to get some money from them. There was an expectation or some level of faith in the lame man that Peter and John would give him money. Peter evidently was able to perceive even that meager faith and bring healing to the man. In this story with Paul, however, the lame man in that story was already looking at Paul and listening to him speak. This was what created faith in his heart to be healed.

Another difference between these two accounts is where they took place. When Peter healed the lame man, it took place at the gate to the

---

87   Acts 14:9-10.

88   Krodel, 256. See also Foakes-Jackson, 126.

89   Guthrie, 105.

temple. Luke does not specifically say where Paul healed the man in Lystra. There is no indication that there was a synagogue there. From the subsequent events that occurred in this chapter in the aftermath of the healing, it is very likely that Paul and Barnabas were speaking to a group of people who had no knowledge of the Mosaic Law and could be classified as idol worshipping pagans. The crowd recognized that the healing was the result of divine power, yet they attributed it to their own gods, Hermes and Zeus, rather than the Lord God.[90]

A last difference that will be mentioned is the manner in which the healings were performed. In Peter's case, he made the declaration, "Silver and gold I do not have, but what I have I give you. In the name of Jesus Christ of Nazareth, walk."[91] Peter then physically took the man by the hand and helped him up. As he was being pulled up, his feet and ankles became strong. By way of contrast, Paul simply told the man, "Stand up on your feet!" He does not use the name of Jesus as a formula here. The most important element for the healing to take place is faith, not a certain formula that has to be used every time. There is no evidence that Paul helped the man up as Peter did. In this case, it was evidently important that the man get up in his own power.

At some point after this first missionary journey, Barnabas and Paul were in Jerusalem for the conference to determine whether or not the Gentiles would be required to obey the Law. Paul and Barnabas discussed the miracles that they had performed among the Gentiles during their missionary trip. After Peter made his speech to the delegates, "The whole assembly became silent as they listened to Barnabas and Paul telling about the miraculous signs and wonders God had done among the Gentiles through them."[92] This recounting of signs and wonders that Paul and Barnabas had seen on their missionary tour, as well as those that they had seen in Antioch, was designed to confirm what Peter had already said.[93] The miraculous was seen as validating the success of the Gospel among those who were uncircumcised.

The next account of the miraculous in Paul's ministry that will be examined is the healing of the demon possessed girl in Acts 16:16-18. This story follows right after the account of Lydia's conversion. Paul and his team had met Lydia at the designated place of prayer for Jews and God-fearers outside the city gates of Philippi. It was as he was going to this place

---

[90] Thompson, 358.

[91] Acts 3:6.

[92] Acts 15:12.

[93] Stott, 246.

of prayer on another occasion that Paul first met a slave girl that Luke described as having, "a spirit by which she predicted the future."[94] Literally, Luke said that she had, "a spirit, a python."[95] This was often referred to as ventriloquism or fortune telling.[96] Luke had possibly witnessed the girl functioning as a ventriloquist, and understood that this ability was the result of the spirit that inhabited her.[97] She would probably go into a trance and allow the spirit to take control of her. The utterances that would come out of her would be regarded as the voice of the god.[98] This would cause the slave girl to be in great demand from those who wished to know the future or to ask the god for something. This ability to communicate directly with the god would have allowed the girl's owners to charge a fee for her services, and Luke informs the reader that, "She earned a great deal of money for her owners by fortune-telling."[99]

Luke records that for many days this girl followed them, shouting, "These men are servants of the Most High God, who are telling you the way to be saved."[100] This appeared to be harmless enough and there is no indication that Paul initially did anything to dissuade the girl. She was giving them free publicity. The girl had evidently listened to the apostles' preaching and now began following them as a sort of demonic John the Baptist, preparing the way for them.

Blaiklock even sees that her following the apostles around and crying out as she did was her way of seeking the help that only they could give.[101] Paul eventually discerned that the girl's proclamation did not proceed from faith, however, but from demonic possession.[102] Arrington understands this as a clear example of Paul using the spiritual gift of discerning of spirits, which he writes about in 1 Corinthians 12:10.[103] Paul's ability to discern the demonic is comparable with his encounter with Bar-Jesus, with the exception that in that case Paul cursed him with temporary blindness. In

---

94 Acts 16:16.

95 Neil, 182.

96 Marshall, 268.

97 Ibid.

98 Bruce, 312.

99 Acts 16:16.

100 Acts 16:17. See also Williams, 286, "Her cries bear a striking resemblance to those of the demoniacs encountered by Jesus, even to the use of the title the Most High God."

101 Blaikock, 126.

102 Krodel, 308.

103 Arrington, 170.

the case of this slave girl, Paul cast the demon out and set her free. She was healed of the demonic possession.

In casting the spirit out of the girl, Paul invoked the Name of Jesus: "In the name of Jesus Christ I command you to come out of her."[104] The result was, "At that moment the spirit left her."[105] This is a clear example of Paul doing the same types of things that Jesus had done in His earthly ministry. A crucial component of Jesus' ministry involved setting free those oppressed by Satan. In freeing this slave girl from the evil spirit that bound her, Paul is again shown to be perpetuating the Kingdom of God and doing damage to the kingdom of Satan.

Luke does not specify whether or not the girl became a convert or a member of the Christian community in Philippi. The placement of the story between Lydia's conversion and the conversion of the jailer and his family, however, do seem to infer that she did become a part of the church there.[106] As has been seen previously, Luke seems to delight in showing the role that women played in the early church. In this case, he shows a girl who is triply oppressed. She is estranged from society because she is a woman, a slave, and is demon possessed.[107] She has been exploited financially by her owners. By healing her, Paul has removed one of the barriers that has hindered the girl in becoming integrated in society.[108] In recording this story, Luke not only is showing the power of the Gospel over the devil's power, he is also providing a snapshot of the way that the early church grew.

The next example of Paul the Miracle Worker that will be discussed is found during his extended ministry in Ephesus. Acts 19:11-12 says, "God did extraordinary miracles through Paul, so that even handkerchiefs and aprons that had touched him were taken to the sick, and their illnesses were cured and the evil spirits left them." There are, however, no specific accounts of miracles ascribed to Paul in this chapter. Luke does indicate that Paul's ministry time in Ephesus was very intense. God performed "extraordinary miracles through Paul." Miracles had been a part of Paul's apostolic ministry from the beginning. However, the type and quantity of the miracles that took place in Ephesus were of such a nature that Luke could not regard them as typical.[109]

---

104 Acts 16:18.

105 Ibid.

106 Stott, 265.

107 Brawley, 166.

108 Ibid.

109 Stott, 306.

In describing these miracles in Ephesus, Luke says that they involved people being healed and being delivered from evil spirits. This is reminiscent of Peter's description of Jesus' ministry in Acts 10:38, "how God anointed Jesus of Nazareth with the Holy Spirit and power, and how he went around doing good and healing all who were under the power of the devil, because God was with him." As a miracle worker, Paul is again being shown expanding the Kingdom of God. This is also consistent with the message that Paul preached in the synagogue in Ephesus. In 19:8 he argued, "persuasively about the kingdom of God." Paul's ministry combined both word and deed, just as those of Jesus and the other apostles.[110]

One of the most interesting facets of Paul's healing ministry in Ephesus was the fact that handkerchiefs and aprons that had touched Paul were taken and applied to those who were sick or demon possessed and brought them healing or deliverance. This is reminiscent, first of all, of the woman who touched the edge of Jesus' cloak and was healed in Luke 8:44. Luke could also be drawing a parallel here to Peter's ministry, when his shadow was considered to have healing power (Acts 5:15).

Bruce believes that the handkerchiefs that are referred to here are the sweat-rags that Paul wrapped around his head while he was working at his trade as a leather worker. The aprons would have been worn around his waist while he was working.[111] This provides an interesting insight into one of the ways that Paul conducted his apostolic ministry. If the handkerchiefs and aprons that Paul used while he was working were the ones that people took and applied to sick people, it seems likely that Paul's workshop was a place in which he evangelized and taught.[112] The workshop would have been a natural social setting in which Paul would have met people and had ample opportunities to share the Gospel with them. It would also have been natural for Paul to pray for people in the workshop as they made their needs known. It appears that in those cases where someone was in another location and had a need for healing or deliverance, the use of an apron or a handkerchief became a conduit of God's healing power.

Paul's miraculous ministry in Ephesus parallels the ministries of Jesus and Peter. It is also not hard to see comparisons in Paul's miracles and those who were involved in the occult.[113] The use of sweat-rags that had touched

---

[110] Krodel, 361.

[111] Bruce, 367.

[112] Ronald F. Hock, "The Workshop as a Social Setting for Paul's Missionary Preaching," *Catholic Biblical Quarterly* 41 (1979) 440. Hock makes the case that the workshop was just as much a social setting for Paul's apostolic ministry as were the synagogue and the home.

[113] Marshall, 310. See also Krodel, 361, "It is precisely Luke's point that, to the naked eye,

Paul's body, for example, being used to bring healing and deliverance has a ring of pagan magic to it. The magician would use amulets, potions, and spells in an attempt to control his god and force him to do his bidding. Jesus, however, told the woman who had gotten healed after touching the hem of His cloak, "Daughter, your faith has healed you."[114] It was her faith, not Jesus' garment, that brought about her healing. In a similar way, Peter's shadow did not have any healing power resident in it. The people that were healed when his shadow passed over them were healed because of their faith. The implication then is that faith is a component of every healing that takes place in Acts. If an apron or handkerchief from Paul was what used to facilitate the healing, that object became a point of contact for the person in need to trigger their faith. The object itself did not bring healing. The piece of cloth from Paul, the hem of Jesus' garment, and Peter's shadow all merely served as a conduit for the power of God.

The next miracle that will be examined is found in Acts 20:9-12, which records Paul raising Eutychus from the dead. This miracle is presented in the context of Paul's pastoral ministry. While Paul is speaking to the Christian community in Troas, Luke records that a young man named Eutychus was sitting in a window. As Paul, "talked on and on," however, the young man, "was sinking into a deep sleep. When he was sound asleep, he fell to the ground from the third story and was picked up dead."[115] Luke was evidently an eyewitness to what happened as this narrative is one of the "we" passages in the book. After Eutychus fell, Paul went down and, "threw himself on the young man and put his arms around him."[116] Paul then said, "Don't be alarmed, He's alive!"[117]

One of the first things that catches the reader's attention in this account is the humanness of it. Luke's presentation seems to indicate that he was watching the young man struggle to stay awake. As he listened to Paul, Luke also kept an eye on Eutychus. Luke refers to Paul's message as going "on and on." Perhaps he was struggling to stay awake himself. When the boy fell out of the window, it is likely that everyone ran outside to check him. As a doctor, Luke's verdict was that it was too late. He was dead.[118]

---

magic and miracle are in fact indistinguishable."

[114] Luke 8:48.

[115] Acts 20:9.

[116] Acts 20:10.

[117] Ibid.

[118] C. S. C. Williams, 230, "Luke did not mean that Eutychus was unconscious but dead, as he himself may have verified."

Paul's verdict, however, was that it was not too late, even though the boy was evidently dead. Paul threw himself on the young man and wrapped his arms around him. In a manner reminiscent of both Elijah and Elisha, Paul physically pressed himself onto Eutychus. As Paul embraced him, his life returned.[119] After giving the boy back alive, the believers returned to the meeting and Paul picked up where he left off.

While it is evident that Luke seeks to draw parallels between Peter's apostolic ministry and Paul's, the account given here of Paul raising Eutychus is very different from the account of Peter raising Tabitha. First of all, Paul had a crowd around him when he performed this miracle. When Peter raised Tabitha from the dead, he put everyone out of the room and then knelt down and prayed before speaking to her body. He had a quiet environment in which to seek the will of God. It was not so with Paul. It is easy to imagine the chaotic scene around Eutychus. His parents were probably present in the meeting and grief-stricken over what they have just seen. In the midst of the chaos, however, Paul took charge of the situation and stepped out in faith.

Another difference between the raising of Tabitha and the raising of Eutychus was the fact that Peter only spoke to her and commanded her to rise. He did not touch her until after she had sat up. Paul, on the other hand, physically wrapped himself around the boy. The healing occurs through bodily contact, not by Paul's words.[120] As mentioned above, Paul's healing has an Old Testament ring to it.

> And He [Elisha] went up and lay on the child, and put his mouth on his mouth and his eyes on his eyes and his hands on his hands, and he stretched himself on him; and the flesh of the child became warm. Then he returned and walked in the house once back and forth, and went up and stretched himself on him; and the lad sneezed seven times and the lad opened his eyes.[121]

Unlike Peter, Paul had never seen Jesus raise anyone from the dead. He did, however, know this story from the Old Testament. Paul imitates Elisha, rather than Jesus, when he resuscitates Eutychus.

After the miracle involving Eutychus, Paul and the congregation "broke bread and ate." The service continued until daybreak. The implication is that they celebrated the Lord's Supper together in the early hours

---

[119] Bruce, 385. Bruce acknowledges the possibility that Paul may have performed some type of artificial respiration on the lad. See also, Williams, 348.

[120] Tannehill, 248.

[121] 2 Kings 4:34-35. See also, 1 Kings 17:21-23.

of the morning.[122] The celebration of the Eucharist would have been even more meaningful since Eutychus was enjoying it with them, alive and doing well.

The last account of the miraculous in Paul's ministry is recorded in Acts 28:1-10 on the island of Malta. The first incident that is mentioned is the account of Paul being bitten by a poisonous snake and being miraculously protected from harm. As Paul was gathering firewood, "a viper, driven out by the heat, fastened itself on his hand."[123] The islanders that saw what happened said to themselves, "This man must be a murderer; for though he escaped from the sea, Justice has not allowed him to live."[124] The people interpreted the snakebite in the context of their pagan religion.[125] Paul, however, "shook the snake off into the fire and suffered no ill effects."[126] The local people watched Paul, waiting for him to drop dead. Eventually, when it became obvious that he was fine and the bite from the snake had not affected him, they went from thinking he was a murderer to thinking he was a god.

Paul's encounter with the snake sounds very similar to the verse in the long ending of Mark 16:18, where it says, "they will pick up snakes with their hands."[127] Luke may also have understood this incident in the light of Luke 10:19: "I have given you authority to trample on snakes and scorpions and to overcome all the power of the enemy; nothing will harm you." As a doctor, Luke of all people would understand the seriousness of a bite from this type of snake. He knew how deadly it could be. He was probably as amazed as the natives as he watched Paul fling the snake off into the fire and then not show any effects at all from the venom.

When Paul did not drop dead, the natives "changed their minds" about Paul. They began to think of him as a god. This shift in thinking is reminiscent of the incident in Lystra, where after healing a lame man, Paul and Barnabas were mistaken for the Greek gods, Zeus and Hermes, in Acts 14. The irony of that account, however, was that the crowd soon turned on the apostles and stoned Paul. In this incident, the irony lies in the fact that the crowd originally thought that Paul was a murderer who could not escape justice. After the incident with the snake, they changed their minds

---

[122] Neil, 212.

[123] Acts 28:3.

[124] Acts 28:4.

[125] Krodel, 479.

[126] Acts 28:5.

[127] Marshall, 417, Marshall believes that the promise in Mark 16:18 is based on this incident.

and said that he must be a god.[128] To some degree, this shows the ambiguity of miracles. In the incident at Lystra, the miracle led to Paul being stoned. The miracle on Malta culminated in the natives thinking that Paul was a god.[129] The miracle at Lystra also served as a catalyst for evangelism in the city. There is no record that Paul used the incident with the snake as a tool to preach the Gospel on the island.

Shortly after Paul was protected from the viper's venom, Luke records another incident of healing on the island. The chief official of the island, Publius, entertained the apostle and others for three days. It then came to Paul's attention that Publius' father, "was sick in bed, suffering from fever and dysentery."[130] Paul went to see him, "and after prayer, placed his hands on him and healed him."[131] There is no indication that this man was a believer or that Paul attempted to convert him. It is likely that Paul shared the Gospel with him in some way or other; however, Luke does not see a need to elaborate on it.

When news of this healing got around, "the rest of the sick on the island came and were cured."[132] Again, there is no mention of any type of evangelism, just the healings. As Tannehill says, "Paul is simply showing the same human kindness that the islanders showed him."[133] This narrative at the end of Acts is very similar to Luke's account of Jesus' first miracle recorded in his Gospel.[134] In Luke 4:38-41, Jesus first healed Peter's mother-in-law. When the news of that miracle became public, many sick and demon possessed people were brought to Jesus so that He might heal them. As these miracles on Malta are the last recorded ones for Paul, it is significant that it parallels Jesus' first recorded miracle.[135]

In comparing the miracles of Peter and Paul, it seems clear that throughout Acts Luke draws deliberate parallels between the type of miracles that they performed. For example, Luke shows both of them healing the lame. Peter actually heals two lame men. The first healing that Peter performs is done in the context of the temple in Jerusalem. This miracle led to an opportunity for Peter to preach an evangelistic message in which many people responded to the gospel. He also healed a second lame man while visiting the believers in Lydda. The implication from Luke is that the

---

128 Krodel, 480.
129 Ibid.
130 Acts 28:8.
131 Ibid.
132 Acts 28:9.
133 Tannehill, 340.
134 Williams, 444.
135 Tannehill, 342, "A scene from the beginning of Jesus' ministry is echoed in the last description of healing in Acts, suggesting a chiastic relationship."

man who was healed, Aeneas, was a member of the local Christian community. This miracle caused, "All those who lived in Lydda and Sharon" to turn to the Lord.[136]

Paul's healing of a lame man took place while he was speaking to a pagan audience in Lystra. It resulted in he and Barnabas being mistaken for the Greek gods Zeus and Hermes. While Luke does not specify that this miracle led to conversions, a church was planted in Lystra. One of Paul's lifelong companions, Timothy, was evidently converted at this time and was a part of the church there. These healings by Peter and Paul, despite their different contexts, are presented in very similar terms and have similar results.

While Luke provides only a few examples of miracles for both apostles, he alludes to the fact that they both performed many more. In Acts 5:12 it says, "The apostles performed many miraculous signs and wonders among the people." Peter's reputation as a healer was such that people would lay their sick in the street on mats so that Peter's shadow might touch them. In a similar way, when Paul was in Ephesus, handkerchiefs and aprons that had touched him were taken to the sick and those tormented by evil spirits and they were healed. In Iconium, God confirmed the message of Paul and Barnabas through "miraculous signs and wonders."[137]

In examining the miraculous aspects of the apostles' ministries, Luke also shows both men raising someone from the dead. Peter resuscitates Tabitha after she died of apparent natural causes. Paul resuscitates Eutychus after he falls from the third floor window. In both of these cases, the person that was resuscitated was a member of the local Christian community. While Peter resembles Jesus in the way that he raises Tabitha from the dead, Paul more closely resembles the Old Testament prophets Elijah and Elisha when they stretched themselves out on the widow's son and raised him from the dead.

The difference in the manner that these two miracles were performed has to do with the background of the two apostles. Peter had followed Jesus for three years and had watched him perform many different kinds of miracles. His miracles naturally resemble those that Jesus performed. There is no indication, however, that Paul had ever seen Jesus during his earthly ministry. As a Pharisee, Paul's background involved a lifetime study of the Hebrew Scriptures. It is no surprise then, that Paul's resuscitation of Eutychus follows the example of the Old Testament prophets.

---

[136] Acts 9:35.

[137] Acts 14:3.

The miracles that the apostles perform in Acts are used by Luke to highlight the fact that they are both in continuity with Jesus.[138] They are continuing His ministry of establishing the Kingdom of God on the earth. The miracles demonstrate God's ongoing participation in human history.

---

[138] Squires, 101.

6

Mystical and Supernatural Experiences

THIS SECTION will examine both the corporate and the individual supernatural experiences that Luke records for Peter and Paul. Mysticism can be defined as,

> The doctrine of an immediate spiritual intuition of truths believed to transcend ordinary understanding or a direct intimate union of the soul with God through contemplation and love.[1]

Mysticism, for the purpose of this study, will refer to those supernatural experiences that are outside the realm of the normal experiences of the Christian life. Tannehill provides a similar definition when he says that mysticism is, "the doctrine that the individual can come into immediate contact with God through subjective experiences which differ essentially from the experiences of daily life."[2] It could be argued that the entire Christian experience is supernatural to some degree. A person is saved by faith in something that He cannot see. They are then called to live the rest of their earthly life by that same kind of faith. For His part, God promises to send the Holy Spirit to indwell His followers. The Holy Spirit works to lead, guide, change, comfort, and help the believer to live their life. Mysticism, however, has to do with intense supernatural experiences in which a person is able to connect with God beyond their normal Christian experience.[3] In Acts, mystical experiences involve visions, dreams, angelic encounters, and various manifestations of the Holy Spirit. These supernatural encounters allow the believers to step out of what is considered normal and to experience the eternal realm for a few moments, to receive

---

[1] *Random House Dictionary of the English Language* (New York: Random House, 1966) 946.

[2] Robert C. Tannehill, *Dying and Rising with Christ*, as quoted by Bruce in *Paul: Apostle of the Heart Set Free*, 147.

[3] Margaret Smith, *The Way of the Mystics* (New York: Oxford University Press, 1978) 2.

a supernatural insight into spiritual truths, or specific divine guidance.[4] These experiences will be examined in the context of both corporate and individual realms. Both apostles had supernatural experiences in a group context as well as by themselves.

Peter the Mystic

Corporate Mystical Experiences

Peter's corporate mystical experiences in Acts were those that he had in conjunction with other believers. The first one that will be discussed is that of the Ascension of Jesus, as recorded in Acts 1:9-11. The significance of this event is seen in the fact that Luke also ends his Gospel by describing the Ascension in Luke 24:50-51. He uses this supernatural experience to tie his two books together.[5] While Luke does not explicitly say that Peter witnessed the Lord's Ascension, the implication is strong that he was there with the other disciples. The Gospel account says that after Jesus led His disciples, "out to the vicinity of Bethany, he lifted up his hands and blessed them. While he was blessing them, he left them and was taken up into heaven." In Acts, the Ascension took place right after Jesus had told the disciples that they would be receive power from on high and be His, "witnesses in Jerusalem, and in all Judea and Samaria, and to the ends of the earth."[6] After this, "he was taken up before their very eyes, and a cloud him from their sight." While the disciples were staring into heaven watching Jesus go, two angels appeared to them. Luke describes them as "men dressed in white." They said, "Men of Galilee, why do you stand here looking into heaven? This same Jesus, who has been taken from you into heaven, will come back in the same way you have seen him go into heaven." Their commission was emphasized and underlined through this corporate mystical experience.

It was only after Jesus had made his commission and mandate clear to the disciples that He was taken back into heaven. Jesus' followers had had the opportunity to interact with Him for a period of forty days after the resurrection. They had been around their resurrected Savior and had eaten and drank with Him, enjoying His fellowship. Now the time has come for Him to go back to His Father in heaven. While the Ascension is unique to the New Testament, the Old Testament also included an example of

---

[4] Ibid., 4.

[5] Keathley, 14.

[6] Acts 1:8.

the rapture of a living person. Elijah was transported to heaven by a fiery chariot before the eyes of his disciples.[7]

This last view that the disciples have of Jesus, however, is described in the language of a theophany.[8] Peter, James, and John had seen Jesus transfigured once before and were there when the cloud overshadowed them. They had heard the Divine Voice speak. At Jesus' Ascension, a cloud enveloped Him and hid Him from their sight. In both cases, this cloud can be understood as the glory of God, His *shekinah*.[9] So, in this last moment of the disciples seeing Jesus on earth, the entire group is allowed to see Him transfigured once again, giving them a vision of His heavenly glory.

The next corporate mystical experience that will be examined is the outpouring of the Holy Spirit on Pentecost. Luke records that Peter was in prayer with a group of 120 other believers. Together, they all experienced the infilling of the Holy Spirit.

> Suddenly, a sound like the blowing of a violent wind came from heaven and filled the whole house where they were sitting. They saw what seemed to be tongues of fire that separated and came to rest on each of them. They were all filled with the Holy Spirit and began to speak in other tongues as the Spirit enabled them.[10]

Peter and those who were with him heard something, saw something, and evidently felt something. They also found that they were able to speak in other languages that they had not learned. It appears that everyone who was present in the house experienced the same phenomenon. They all shared in the experience. Later on, Peter could defend his actions at Cornelius' house by reminding some of the Jewish Christians, "As I began to speak, the Holy Spirit came on them as he had come on us at the beginning."[11] This was an experience that would have impacted them all greatly. The fact that it was a shared experience made it that much more intense and lasting. This experience of being filled with the Holy Spirit becomes a reoccurring theme in Acts.[12] Luke does not present it as a singular occurrence.

Stronstad compares this outpouring of the Holy Spirit to what happened when Jesus was baptized. There were visible and audible signs present when John baptized Jesus, which attested to God having anointed

---

[7] Hans-Josef Klauck, 6.

[8] Bruce, *The Book of the Acts*, 37–38.

[9] Ibid., 38.

[10] Acts 2:2-4.

[11] Acts 11:15.

[12] Stronstad, 55.

Jesus for His work. "Just as the anointing of Jesus is attested to by visible and audible signs, so the transfer of the Holy Spirit to the disciples on the day of Pentecost is also attested by visible and audible signs."[13] The wind is an obvious symbol for the Holy Spirit.[14] It is interesting that Luke says they heard what sounded like, "the blowing of a violent wind." This sound of a powerful wind was probably symbolic of the Holy Spirit's power.[15] There is no indication that there was an actual wind blowing through the house, the disciples only heard the noise. In the same way, Luke describes, "what seemed to be tongues of fire that separated and came to rest on each of them." They saw something that looked like tongues of fire coming to rest on each other. The fire is likely symbolizing the purifying aspects of the Holy Spirit's work.[16] When they all began to speak in other languages, this probably represented the universal message of the Gospel and the universality of the church.[17] Speaking in tongues was not limited to this one incident in Acts. It will occur a later in Acts and Paul will later write to the Corinthians providing them with some instructions on how to use the gift.

While 120 people shared the Pentecost experience, the effects of it were much more far-reaching than that. Jerusalem was full of pilgrims who had come to attend the festival. They heard 120 people speaking in different languages. "Each one heard them speaking in his own language."[18] A crowd soon gathered and Peter had his first opportunity to preach the Gospel. His message was discussed in an earlier chapter. This mystical experience provided an opportunity for thousands of people to hear the Gospel and for 3,000 of them to come to faith.

While this corporate supernatural experience was dramatic, it was certainly not the last that Luke would record. The next one that will be discussed is mentioned in Acts 4:31: "After they prayed, the place where they were meeting was shaken. And they were all filled with the Holy Spirit and spoke the word of God boldly." The context of this experience is again a prayer meeting. Peter and John had been arrested after the healing of the lame man in Acts 3. After their hearing before the Sanhedrin they were warned to quit preaching in Jesus' name and released. They, "went back to their own people and reported all that the chief priests and elders had said

---

13 Ibid., 78.

14 Neil, 72.

15 Stott, 63.

16 Ibid.

17 Ibid.

18 Acts 2:6.

to them."[19] This led to a corporate prayer meeting. Luke does not indicate who was present other than Peter and John and "their own people."

The result of this prayer meeting, however, was that they felt the room or house that they were meeting in to be shaken and they were all filled again with the Holy Spirit. The result of being filled again with the Holy Spirit was that they, "spoke the word of God boldly." As Arrington describes it, there was an external manifestation of God's power, the meeting place was shaken, and an internal manifestation, they were filled with the Spirit.[20]

The way that Luke describes the place being shaken could be understood as an earthquake. In the Old Testament, an earthquake often indicated a theophany.[21] God was present and would answer their prayer. The fresh filling of the Holy Spirit was a further confirmation of His Presence. Again, the corporate nature of this mystical experience seemed to add to its intensity.

A fourth corporate supernatural experience involving Peter that will be examined is in Acts 5:17-42. In this account, the Sadducees have the apostles arrested. During the night, an angel sets them free and commands them to go back to the temple and keep preaching. Luke does not specify as to whether or not Peter is present when the apostles are arrested. When they are rearrested and brought before the Sanhedrin, however, Peter is the spokesman for the group. The implication is that all of the apostles had been arrested, including Peter.

There are parallels between this account and Peter's miraculous escape from prison in Acts 12. There are also parallels between this account and the earlier arrest of Peter and John. Some scholars believe that Luke took one or two traditions and turned them into three or four stories. This will be dealt with more in-depth when Peter's escape from prison is discussed.

This narrative of an angel setting the apostles free lacks the detail of many of Luke's other stories. Luke's account of the event is brief. "But during the night an angel of the Lord opened the doors of the jail and brought them out."[22] Neil speculates that the apostles may have been set free, "by a secret sympathizer among the guardroom staff."[23] Luke, however, clearly believed that this was a case of divine and not human intervention. The fact that when the Jewish officials went to bring the apostles before the

---

[19] Acts 4:23.

[20] Arrington, 50.

[21] Marshall, 107. Two Old Testament examples are Exodus 19:18 and Isaiah 6:4.

[22] Acts 5:19.

[23] Neil, 97.

Sanhedrin, they found the cell door locked and the guards standing in place outside seems to indicate that a supernatural, rather than a natural, event had taken place. For Neil's view to be correct, there would have needed to be a number of people involved in the plot to free the apostles, including the guards standing at the door to their cell. A lone "secret sympathizer" could not have pulled it off. There is no indication from Luke that there was an elaborate plot among the guards to free the apostles.

The apostles that were set free clearly believed that they were the recipients of divine intervention. If a human agent had set them free it is not likely that they would have stayed in Jerusalem. The more prudent course would have been to leave while the opportunity existed. However, the fact that an angel freed them and commanded them to go into the temple and keep preaching, gave them the boldness to face whatever repercussions might come their way.[24] They were set free so that they could continue the work that they had been called to.

The last corporate mystical experience that will be examined for Peter is the outpouring of the Holy Spirit on a Gentile audience at Cornelius' house. Both Peter and Cornelius had individual mystical experiences that prepared them for this event. Cornelius received an angelic visit instructing him to call for Peter to come to his house. Peter had a vision while praying that prepared him for the visit by the messengers from Cornelius. Peter's vision will be discussed in more detail later in the chapter as an individual mystical experience.

This account of the outpouring of the Holy Spirit is very similar to what was seen on the day of Pentecost. Luke records, "While Peter was still speaking these words, the Holy Spirit came on all those who heard the message."[25] Luke goes on to say that Peter and those Jewish believers who were with him heard the Gentiles, "speaking in tongues and praising God."[26] Luke describes this event is such a way that the reader would immediately recall Pentecost and understand that the Gentiles have been chosen by God to receive the same gift of the Holy Spirit that was initially poured out on Jesus' first followers.[27] This is also the way that Peter understood what was happening. When he defended his actions in chapter 11, he said, "As I

---

[24] Guthrie, 51.

[25] Acts 10:44.

[26] Acts 10:46.

[27] Tannehill, *The Narrative Unity of Luke-Acts A Literary Interpretation,* Volume Two: *The Acts of the Apostles,* 143.

began to speak, the Holy Spirit came on them as he had come on us at the beginning."[28]

While the experience at Cornelius' house was reminiscent of Pentecost, there were also some notable differences. First of all, there was no sound of a rushing wind or tongues of fire. The Gentiles received the Holy Spirit in a slightly more subdued manner. Another difference in the two events is the fact that on Pentecost, the Holy Spirit was poured out on those who were already believers. At Cornelius' house, there is no indication that these people were believers when Peter got there. However, it appears that they all came to faith at the same time as Peter preached. God then sealed their faith by filling them all with the Holy Spirit.[29]

In this corporate mystical experience, Peter was a facilitator for the Gentiles to receive the gift of the Holy Spirit. He was present as a representative of Jewish Christianity. The fact that that God used one of the leading apostles to bring the Gentiles into the church served to validate their experience.

Individual Mystical Experiences

The next type of mystical experiences that will be examined are those that Peter had by himself. The first of these that will be examined is the vision that he had while he was in Joppa. It is recorded in Acts 10. This was evidently a very important story to Luke.[30] He provides a significant amount of detail in his descriptions of what happened. Luke then repeats the story in chapter 11, as Peter has to defend his actions before the Jewish believers. There is also a brief summary of the incident in chapter 15. It was not that the vision itself was so important, but the issue that it represented was. The recognition of the Gentiles as being participants in the Gospel on the same level as the Jews, yet without having to follow the Law was an extremely important and far-reaching issue. Krodel sees this entire incident of vision and subsequent ministry at Cornelius' house to be the climax to Peter's apostolic ministry.[31]

This vision, like many others in Scripture, occurs in a very ordinary setting. Around noon Peter had gone to Simon's roof to pray. During prayer he became hungry and requested something to eat. He then fell into a trance and saw his vision. Several scholars believe that Luke is implying

---

[28] Acts 11:15.

[29] Marshall, 193–94.

[30] Ibid., 181. See also, Arrington, 108. See also note 108 above.

[31] Krodel, 187.

that Peter fell asleep and had a dream.[32] Blaiklock describes the situation as "touchingly human."[33] Peter, tired from his travels around the area, falls asleep while attempting to pray. The last thing that Peter would have seen before sleep set in would have been an awning over him to protect him from the sun, or a ship in the harbor letting down its sail.[34]

In Peter's vision, he saw heaven opened and something that looked like a large sheet being let down by its four corners. The open heaven that Peter saw signaled divine revelation.[35] The fact that the sheet was lowered from heaven has led some scholars to speculate that a ship letting down its sail in the harbor below Peter inspired the image. It contained many different types of animals, both clean and unclean. In the vision, Peter heard a voice tell him, "Get up, Peter. Kill and eat."[36] His answer was, "Surely not, Lord! I have never eaten anything impure or unclean."[37] The voice replied, "Do not call anything impure that God has made clean."[38] This was repeated twice for a total of three times and then the sheet was taken back into heaven.

Several aspects of this vision will be examined. First of all, the vision came while Peter was in prayer. Even if he did fall asleep praying, it was the prayer that seemed to prepare him for the vision.[39] In Luke-Acts, prayer often seems to be one of the contributing factors to receiving a vision.[40] Prayer makes the individual receptive to receive a message from God. Zechariah was in prayer when the angel appeared to him in Luke 1. Jesus was at prayer when He was transfigured. The 120 believers were praying when the Holy Spirit fell on them in Acts 2. Cornelius was praying when he had his vision of an angel in Acts 10. This pattern will also be seen later in the Apostle Paul's life and ministry.

A second aspect of Peter's vision that needs to be addressed is the manner in which God spoke to him. God spoke to Peter in the context of

---

32 Neil, 138. See also Williams, 187.

33 Blaiklock, 95.

34 Neil, 138.

35 Bobby Jay Kelly, "Divine Guidance in Luke-Acts: The Function of Commissioning as Encouragement and Apology," Ph.D. diss., Southwestern Baptist Theological Seminary (1998) 204.

36 Acts 10:13.

37 Acts 10:14.

38 Acts 10:15.

39 Tannehill, 129.

40 Talbert, 107, "This is in line with the Lukan belief that prayer is the means by which God makes the divine will known for new departures in the unfolding of His plan for history."

his own situation. As Guthrie puts it, "Subconsciously his sense of hunger contributed to the shape of the dream, for it centered on food."[41] As he was hungry and waiting on his food, he received a vision of impure animals and was told to eat them. This vision was especially poignant for Peter because of his hunger. He seems to treat the vision like it were a test.[42] He would not violate the Law, no matter how hungry he was. When the voice commanded Peter to eat, he was vehement in his protest, "Surely not, Lord! I have never eaten anything impure or unclean." Peter's response here is also consistent with the picture that is presented of him in the gospels.[43]

The importance of the vision is also seen in the fact that the sheet with the animals on it was lowered three times. On each occasion, Peter was commanded to, "Kill and eat." He refused each time and was told by the voice not to, "call anything impure that God has made clean." Blaiklock sees the three-fold repetition as a parallel to the time when Jesus asked Peter three times, "Do you love me?"[44] While this is possible, it is much more likely that the vision was repeated three times to emphasize its importance and to make a suitable impression on Peter. If Peter had only seen the sheet coming down from heaven once, and had only had one encounter with the voice that told him to eat from it, it would have been quite easy to dismiss the incident. When the encounter was repeated three times, however, Peter could not dismiss it. It was obvious that God was speaking to him about something important.

Peter's reluctance to obey the voice from heaven very likely has to do with the nature of what he is being asked to do. The Voice is commanding Peter to violate the Law of God. Peter had obeyed the Law his entire life. Now he was being asked to disobey it.[45] "Suddenly all of Peter's understanding of God is challenged in a dream concerning the kind of food he should eat."[46] Normally, Luke cites appropriate passages of Scripture to support what is taking place in Acts. Here, however, he shows that a higher authority than the Scriptures has stepped in to annul the dietary regulations. In

---

[41] Guthrie, 81.

[42] Talbert, 107. Could Peter have thought he was being tempted in some way like Jesus was? During Jesus' forty day fast He was tempted by the devil. One of the temptations that Satan attacked Him with was that of turning stones into bread to satisfy His hunger. Peter could have perceived, at least initially, that he, too, was being tempted in the vision to satisfy his hunger in a forbidden way.

[43] Compare with John 13:8, "Never shall you wash my feet!"

[44] Blaiklock, 96.

[45] Tyson, "The Gentile Mission and the Authority of Scripture in Acts," 629.

[46] Denton Lotz, "Peter's Wider Understanding of God's Will—Acts 10:34-48," *International Review of Mission* 77 (1988) 201.

this instance, it is the Holy Spirit, Who, "reveals alterations in scripture or annulments of long-standing commands."[47]

The next aspect of Peter's vision that needs to be discussed is that of Peter's response. Luke records that Peter was, "wondering about the meaning of the vision."[48] A couple of verses later, Luke says that, "Peter was still thinking about the vision."[49] Peter was trying to work out in his mind what the vision might mean. He was unable to reach any conclusions about how this vision should be interpreted. As Tannehill puts it, "visions are incomplete in themselves."[50] They need to be interpreted for their meaning to become clear. In Peter's case, the Holy Spirit played a prominent role in helping him to understand the vision. He was clearly unable to understand the vision's meaning apart from the Holy Spirit's help. The vision left Peter feeling confused. These dietary laws that Peter was being commanded to break, "functioned as boundary markers for Jews against Gentiles."[51] He would shortly learn that the vision he had seen had nothing to do with food and everything to do with people.[52]

The mystical experience of the vision ended and Peter awoke wondering what it meant. While he was still thinking about what the vision could mean, the Holy Spirit spoke to him and told him that the three men from Cornelius were downstairs looking for him. Peter expected an explanation to the vision. Instead he was instructed to go with the men that had called on him.[53] The Holy Spirit told Peter, "Do not hesitate to go with them, for I have sent them."[54] Luke differentiates this indication of the Spirit speaking to Peter from the vision.[55] It appears that Peter heard the Holy Spirit speaking by an inward monition. There is no indication that he heard the audible voice of God.[56] The vision was clearly over but the Spirit's words would have indicated that the vision had come from God and its meaning would be made clear in due time. For now, Peter must accompany, without misgivings, the Gentile men who had come for him.

---

47   Ibid., 630.

48   Acts 10:17.

49   Acts 10:19.

50   Tannehill, 130.

51   Kelly, 204.

52   Ibid., 205.

53   Krodel, 190–91, "So, for the immediate present, Peter has to obey and forgo a solution to the problem of his own vision."

54   Acts 10:20

55   Marshall, 187.

56   Bruce, 207.

The meaning of Peter's vision starts to become clear as he speaks with the men from Cornelius. They indicate that Cornelius had had a mystical experience himself and had seen an angel. Later, Peter will hear from Cornelius himself about his vision in which an angel appeared to him.[57] In talking with Cornelius and hearing about his experience, the meaning of Peter's own vision is unlocked.[58] God has opened the door of faith to the Gentiles and He used supernatural experiences to make His will known to those involved. Peter's vision led him to Cornelius' house where he was instrumental in bringing the message of the Gospel to a Gentile audience. While this in and of itself was groundbreaking, what was even more significant was the fact that Peter's vision enabled him to live and eat with a group of Gentiles.[59] God used the vision to change Peter's understanding of the way that God saw the Gentiles.

The second individual mystical experience that will be examined in Peter's apostolic ministry is his deliverance from jail by an angel in Acts 12. This story has a parallel in Acts 5. There, Luke writes that the Sadducees, "arrested the apostles and put them in the public jail."[60] He goes on to say that during the night, God sent an angel who freed them and told them to go into the temple courts and keep preaching. Some scholars see this story and the account of Peter's deliverance in Acts 12 to be referring to the same event. Others would see the account of the apostles' arrest in Acts 5 to be a repetition of Peter and John's arrest in Acts 4.[61] There is no reason, however, to doubt the uniqueness of each of these accounts. As Munck puts it,

> A seeming repetition is not, necessarily, another account of the same event. Events may also be repeated and this fact must be remembered because for some time there has been a tendency in New Testament research to identify persons, events, or parables that might or perhaps might not be identical.[62]

John wrote that if everything that Jesus had done had been written down, "the whole world would not have room for the books that would be written."[63] The same thing could probably be said for the church that Luke wrote about in Acts. Luke was very selective in what material he presented,

---

[57] Acts 10:30-33.

[58] Talbert, 107–8.

[59] Kelly, 207.

[60] Acts 5:18.

[61] Williams, 105. See also Bruce, 109–10.

[62] Munck, 50.

[63] John 21:25.

yet there were probably still some incidents that he recorded that were similar to other incidents.

The story that Luke relates in Acts 12 is told with vivid detail, possibly indicating that he got the account from Peter himself.[64] Herod had won favor with the Jews by having James, the brother of John executed. He then had Peter arrested during the Feast of Unleavened Bread with the intention of trying him publicly after the feast had ended. Peter was heading towards the same fate as James. His situation certainly looked hopeless. Luke emphasizes the gravity of Peter's predicament by mentioning the prison, the guards, chains, and soldiers. Luke then contrasts these measures with what was going on behind the scenes, "the church was earnestly praying for Peter."[65] "Surrounded by bars, walls, and guards, the imprisoned Peter was also surrounded by earnest prayer on his behalf."[66] For his part, however, Peter is not awake praying for a miracle or plotting an escape.[67] He is sleeping, chained between two soldiers. He seems to have accepted that Jesus' prophecy of his martyrdom was about to take place.[68] He is at peace and does not seem to be dreading what will come the next morning.

When the angel appeared in the cell, he actually had to strike Peter on the side to wake him up. As Peter was becoming awake, the angel said, "Quick, get up!"[69] The chains then fell off Peter's hands. The angel then commands Peter, "Put on your clothes and sandals . . . Wrap your cloak around you and follow me."[70] Tannehill points out the significance of these commands. They correspond to the regulations for the Passover.[71] Whether intentional or not, Luke records Peter's deliverance from prison by the angel in a manner that is reminiscent of the children of Israel being led out of Egypt by the Angel of the Lord. "As the Israelites were delivered from the hand of the Pharaoh, so Peter was delivered from the hand of Herod Agrippa I."[72]

---

[64] Blaiklock, 99.

[65] Acts 12:5.

[66] Krodel, 218.

[67] Arrington, 124. See also Stott, 209.

[68] John 21:18, "I tell you the truth, when you were younger you dressed yourself and went where you wanted; but when you are old you will stretch out your hands, and someone else will dress you and lead you where you do not want to go."

[69] Acts 12:7.

[70] Acts 12:8.

[71] Tannehill, 155.

[72] Kelly, 210.

As Peter was being led out of prison, Luke writes that Peter, "had no idea that what the angel was doing was really happening; he thought he was seeing a vision."[73] It is interesting to note that Peter was willing to obey, even believing that he was only seeing a vision. He did not argue with the angel or ask any questions. He merely did as he was told.[74] It was only after he found himself outside on the streets of Jerusalem that Peter came to himself and realized he was really free. Peter then went to the house of Mary, the mother of John Mark.

This mystical experience of Peter's is different from some of his others in the way that he was involved. Peter was an active participant in all of his other mystical experiences. Peter was completely passive in this experience. The angel directed Peter and gave him instructions. All he had to do was follow those instructions. It is also interesting to note that while in Acts 10 Peter's prayer seemed to prepare him for his vision, his deliverance from prison in chapter 12 is in answer to the church's prayers and not his own.[75]

Peter's response to this supernatural experience is interesting and needs to be commented on. He evidently thought he was dreaming and seeing a vision.[76] He was not expecting to be set free. As mentioned previously, he is completely at peace and is willing to accept his fate. Peter must feel that he is about to get his opportunity to follow Jesus to death.[77] He actually appears surprised when he realizes that he has been set free. "Now I know without a doubt that the Lord sent his angel and rescued me from Herod's clutches and from everything the Jewish people were anticipating."[78] Peter was just as surprised to be free as those who were praying for his deliverance.

There is a significant difference between Peter's deliverance here in chapter 12 and the deliverance of all the apostles in chapter 5. In chapter 5, after the angel released the apostles, he told them to go into the temple and keep preaching the gospel. This led to their being arrested again and subsequent flogging. After the angel escorted Peter out of the prison in chapter 12, he left him without giving him any instructions. Peter evidently felt that this was a good opportunity to leave Jerusalem. He went to Mary's

---

73 Acts 12:9.

74 Calvin, 341.

75 Talbert, 119.

76 Williams, 212, Williams points out that Luke uses the same word here in verse 9 for *vision* that he uses in 10:17.

77 Luke 22:33, "Lord, I am ready to go with you to prison and to death."

78 Acts 12:11.

house where the church there was still praying for his release. After showing them that their prayers had been answered, Luke records that Peter, "left for another place."[79] Bruce comments that Peter, "went underground so successfully that no one to this day has discovered for certain where he went."[80] Other than a brief appearance at the Jerusalem Council in chapter 15, Peter steps out of Acts for good. This last mystical experience serves as an exclamation point to Peter's apostolic ministry. Even though Peter's ministry in Acts is about to come to a close, Luke uses his deliverance from jail by the angel to show that his apostolic ministry is not finished yet.[81] The supernatural deliverance from Agrippa's hand leaves the reader with the understanding that Peter's ministry will continue, only in "another place."

Paul the Mystic

Acts consistently shows that Paul was, "guided directly from heaven, by God, by Jesus, or the Spirit with the help of visions, auditions, different ecstatic experiences, heavenly inspiration, etc."[82] In discussing Paul's mysticism, however, Bruce points out that Paul's own writings give a much clearer picture than Acts of his mystical leanings.[83] In fact, Paul's understanding of the believer being "in Christ" is found throughout his writings and points to the possibility of a constant spiritual communion with God.[84] The clearest account in which Paul describes his own mystical experiences is in 2 Corinthians 12:2, where he refers to being, "caught up to the third heaven." It is possible, though unlikely, that Paul was speaking of his conversion experience in that passage.[85] This is the same passage where Paul mentions the "visions and revelations" that he had received from the Lord in 12:1. A final example of where Paul describes his own supernatural experiences is in Galatians 1:12, where he said that he received the Gospel that he was preaching "by revelation from Jesus Christ." Paul's gospel was not something he worked out in his own mind. God supernaturally revealed it to him. Acts does not provide the depth of detail that Paul's letters do about

---

79 Acts 12:17.

80 Bruce, 238–39.

81 Kelly, 212.

82 Jervell, 71.

83 Bruce, *Paul: Apostle of the Heart Set Free*, 136–39.

84 Ibid. See also Sandmel, 75, "Paul was a mystic who encountered God—in the form of Christ."

85 Alan F. Segal, *Paul the Convert: The Apostolate and Apostasy of Saul the Pharisee* (New Haven: Yale University Press, 1990) 36.

his mysticism. Acts does demonstrate, to some degree, however, the mystical side of Paul from the viewpoint of an associate and admirer.[86]

Corporate Mystical Experiences

In Acts, Paul, like Peter, had both corporate and individual mystical experiences. The corporate experiences will be examined first. After Saul/Paul's vision of Jesus on the Damascus Road (an individual mystical experience), he was ministered to by a disciple from Damascus named Ananias. God spoke to him in a vision and told him to go to a certain house and ask for Saul of Tarsus, who was praying. "In a vision he has seen a man named Ananias come and place his hands on him to restore his sight."[87] The reputation of Saul as a persecutor of the church was such that it took a vision from God to convince Ananias to go. Luke will use this technique of a vision within a vision again in the next chapter of Acts to direct Peter to Cornelius' house.[88]

After overcoming his initial hesitancy, Ananias went to the house and found Saul. Ananias placed his hands on him and said, "Brother Saul, the Lord- Jesus, who appeared to you on the road as you were coming here- has sent me so that you may see again and be filled with the Holy Spirit."[89] The result of Ananias' prayer was that, "Immediately, something like scales fell from Saul's eyes, and he could see again."[90] Later in Acts, Paul recounts the story of his conversion before the Jewish mob in Jerusalem and again before King Agrippa and the Roman governor Festus. In Acts 22:13 Paul elaborates on Ananias' visit. "He stood beside me and said, 'Brother Saul, receive your sight!' And at that very moment I was able to see him." The opening of Saul's physical eyes was symbolic of what had happened to his spiritual eyes on the Damascus Road. His spiritual blindness was healed there. Because he had seen Jesus, now he could see humanity in a new light.[91] He could see like he had never seen before. Of the three accounts that Luke provides for Paul's conversion, it is the one in Acts 9 that places more emphasis on his healing.[92] The other two accounts are more concerned with Paul's call and commission.

---

[86] Bruce, 145.

[87] Acts 9:12.

[88] Krodel, 176.

[89] Acts 9:17.

[90] Acts 9:18.

[91] Stagg, 112.

[92] Charles W. Hedrick, "Paul's Conversion and Call: A Comparative Analysis of the Three Reports in Acts," *Journal of Biblical Literature* 100 (1981) 419.

Saul not only had his eyes opened during Ananias' visit. Ananias also came to pray for him so that he might be filled with the Holy Spirit. That was one of the things that he told Saul that was going to happen when he prayed for him. As Saul's eyes were opened he was filled with the Holy Spirit.[93] There is no question that God could have filled Saul with the Holy Spirit and healed his eyes without any human contact. He chose, however, to use Ananias as an intermediary.[94] In a very real way, Saul's life and all that he had believed up to that point had been shattered. This was a time when he needed human contact. To be welcomed as a brother by one of those that Saul had come to arrest was an additional confirmation that God had truly forgiven him.[95]

While this mystical experience that Saul had with Ananias, as Luke records it, is not as intense as some others that he had, it nevertheless was extremely important. First of all, this was his first post-conversion contact with another believer. The first words that Saul hears from Ananias are these: "Brother Saul." Ananias is warmly welcoming him into the Christian community.[96] Saul has now become a part of the community that he went to Damascus to destroy.[97]

This experience was also important because it pointed past Saul's conversion to his commission. The laying on of hands was symbolic of healing. Saul's eyes were healed when Ananias laid his hands on him.[98] In the larger context, however, the laying on of hands here represented the call of God on Saul's life and Ananias, as a devout follower of God, was acknowledging it.[99] In retelling the story later to the Jewish mob in Jerusalem, Paul quotes Ananias as saying to him, "The God of our fathers has chosen you to know his will and to see the Righteous One and to hear words from his mouth. You will be his witness to all men of what you have seen and heard."[100] While Saul's commission came to him directly from Jesus on the Damascus Road, it was confirmed through the ministry of Ananias.

The next corporate mystical experience that is seen in Paul's life is found in Acts 13:2, and deals with the call of Paul and Barnabas to mission-

---

[93] Talbert, 99.

[94] Hengel and Schwemer, 41.

[95] Stott, 175–176. See also Guthrie, 270. Guthrie speculates that Ananias may very well have been on Paul's list of people that he was coming to Damascus to arrest.

[96] Williams, 172.

[97] Bruce, 76.

[98] Marshall, 172.

[99] Bruce, *The Book of the Acts*, 189.

[100] Acts 22:14-15.

ary work. "While they were worshipping the Lord and fasting, the Holy Spirit said, 'Set apart for me Barnabas and Saul for the work to which I have called them.'" When this call came, the two men were still laboring together in some type of leadership capacity at the Antioch church. Luke opens this chapter by providing a small glimpse into the church at Antioch. He lists prophets and teachers: Barnabas, Simeon called Niger, Lucius of Cyrene, Manaen, and Saul. It is significant that Barnabas heads the list, probably indicating his position of authority in the church there.[101]

When this supernatural experience took place, the church was together in some type of corporate service. Luke also makes mention of fasting, indicating that the congregation had decided to conduct a fast in conjunction with their worship. Fasting seldom occurs alone. It is usually done in conjunction with prayer, or as it is here, done in the context of worshipping the Lord.[102]

There seems to be the implication that the church was in prayer for something specific, which could be related to the type of direction that they received. It is possible that the church was praying and fasting about the possibility of a missionary trip and were asking for guidance as to who should be involved.[103] In the early days of the Jerusalem church there did not appear to be much of a strategy involved in their evangelism. In actively seeking God's will about whom they should commission as missionaries, the church in Antioch was moving into the realm of intentional and deliberate planning for a full-scale mission.[104] The believers were waiting on God to speak and they had prepared themselves to listen.[105] The message of the Holy Spirit evidently came through one of the prophets that were mentioned in verse one. Luke has shown in other places in Acts that prophets brought direction and revelation from the Holy Spirit to the church, as well as to individuals (Acts 11:27-30; Acts 21:10-11). Here, the Holy Spirit indicates His choice as to who should be a part of this new work. Luke emphasizes the point that the initiative for this new work did not originate from Barnabas and Saul themselves, but from the Holy Spirit who was active in the Antioch church.[106]

---

[101] Raymond E. Brown and John P. Meier, *Antioch and Rome: New Testament Cradles of Catholic Christianity* (New York: Paulist, 1982) 35.

[102] Stott, 217.

[103] Williams, 222.

[104] Kelly, 213.

[105] Marshall, 216.

[106] Tannehill, 160.

While the Holy Spirit was the one who called Barnabas and Saul to a new task, it was the church in Antioch that laid hands on them and sent them out.[107] After the two men had been set apart by God, the church fasted and prayed again before commissioning them and sending them out. Bruce makes the point that the two men that the Antioch church released into missionary service were probably, "the two most eminent and gifted leaders in the church."[108] The most talented and gifted leaders were the ones that were sent out.

Acts 16:25-28 contains Paul's next corporate supernatural experience. He shares this one with Silas, a Philippian jailer, and unnamed prisoners. Paul and Silas had been arrested, beaten, and then thrown into jail after healing the demon possessed slave girl who was following them. They were placed in the inner cell and their feet were fastened in stocks. Luke says that around midnight, "Paul and Silas were praying and singing hymns to God."[109] The result was that, "Suddenly, there was such a violent earthquake that the foundations of the prison were shaken. At once all the prison doors flew open, and everybody's chains came loose."[110] This supernatural experience led to the conversion of the jailer and his family.

Parallels can be drawn between this mystical experience and the one in which Peter was delivered from jail by an angel, as well as the earlier account in which all of the apostles were delivered from jail by an angel. While the accounts are similar in the sense that they all involve deliverance from jail and the authorities, there are also significant differences. First of all, Peter was asleep when the angel entered his cell to release him. Paul and Silas were praying and singing hymns. Arrington believes that they were actually praying for deliverance and vindication.[111] Williams, on the other hand, believes that Paul and Silas were praying and worshipping without any thought of deliverance.[112] In either case, they were probably not able to sleep because of the injuries incurred from the beating that they had endured. They were using their time to turn their attention to the Lord.

A second difference between Peter's deliverance from jail and the account here is the fact that in the story about Peter, an angel took an active role in releasing him. The angel woke him up, told him to get dressed and then led him out of the jail. Here, God moved in a sovereign way

---

[107] David L. Bartlett, *Ministry in the New Testament* (Minneapolis: Fortress, 1993) 12.

[108] Bruce, 246.

[109] Acts 16:25

[110] Acts 16:26.

[111] Arrington, 171.

[112] Williams, 288.

through the earthquake to open the doors of the cells and cause the chains to come free from the walls. The earthquake itself is reminiscent of another corporate mystical experience involving the apostles in Acts 4:31, where, "After they prayed, the place where they were meeting was shaken."

The third difference between Peter and Paul's deliverance stories is the fact that in Peter's situation, he actually did escape. He was scheduled to be executed the next day and the angel took him all the way out of the jail. Paul and Silas, however, did not escape when they had the opportunity. By choosing to stay, it gave them the opportunity to save the jailer's life.[113] This mystical experience, like many of the miracles in the apostle's lives, provided an opportunity for someone to come to faith.

The next corporate mystical experience that will be examined in Paul's apostolic ministry is found in Acts 19:1-7. When examining Paul's encounter with these disciples in Ephesus, the first issue that should be dealt with is whether or not these twelve were actually Christians. When Luke refers to someone as a "disciple" in Acts, he always means that they are a Christian.[114] Luke's perception of whether or not these people were Christians or not is very important. If his understanding of them as disciples was only, "a first impression,"[115] it changes the dynamics of the encounter from one that is pastoral in nature to one of evangelism. This does not appear to be the case, however. Paul treats these disciples as believers, and there is no indication by Luke that they were converted through Paul's ministry.

It should be noted that the story detailing Priscilla and Aquila's dealings with Apollos in Ephesus preceded this one. Apollos, like the twelve disciples in Ephesus that Paul dealt with, only knew the baptism of John. Priscilla and Aquila, "explained to him the way of God more adequately."[116] It seems likely that Apollos had not experienced the Pentecostal filling of the Spirit, either. Whatever his deficiencies were, Priscilla and Aquila corrected them and then helped him on his way.[117]

This account also has the same basic ingredients as the Samaritan narrative.[118] First of all, in both accounts there are disciples who have believed but have not yet received the Pentecostal gift of the Holy Spirit. A second

---

[113] Tannehill, 204.

[114] Arrington, 191. See also Williams, 329.

[115] Krodel, 356.

[116] Acts 18:26.

[117] Williams, 325, Williams thinks that even though Luke does not explicitly state that Apollos was rebaptized like the twelve disciples that Paul dealt with, he implies that it happened. See also Neil, 201.

[118] Stronstad, 68.

similar ingredient is that an apostle was the mediator of this gift. In the Samaritan account it was Peter and John, here it is Paul. The last similarity is the fact that there were physical manifestations when they were filled with the Holy Spirit. In Acts 8, these manifestation are only implied, but Simon Magus saw something happen when the apostles laid their hands on the people. He then attempted to buy the ability from Peter. Here in Acts 19, Luke writes, "When Paul placed his hands on them, the Holy Spirit came on them, and they spoke in tongues and prophesied." Their supernatural experience also corresponded to the believers in Jerusalem on the Day of Pentecost, as well as the Gentiles who received the gift of the Holy Spirit at Cornelius' house.

It is no surprise that Luke places this narrative at the beginning of Paul's Ephesian ministry. This corporate mystical experience was indicative of the supernatural aspect of Paul's apostolic ministry there. As was mentioned previously, these twelve disciples were very likely foundational members of the church in Ephesus. The supernatural experience that they had at the hands of Paul served to solidify their faith and to prepare them for future ministry.

The last corporate mystical experience that is seen in Paul's ministry is found in Acts 21:10-14. It concerns the encounter that Paul had with Agabus the prophet. It took place during Paul's last journey to Jerusalem. He and his companions had stopped in Caesarea to visit with Philip the evangelist. Luke records that Agabus came down from Judea, presumably by prophetic mandate. He took Paul's belt and tied his own hands and feet with it and said, "The Holy Spirit says, 'In this way the Jews of Jerusalem will bind the owner of this belt and will hand him over to the Gentiles.'"[119] This prophetic message led Paul's companions to beg him to cancel his trip to Jerusalem. Paul responded that he was, "ready not only to be bound, but also to die in Jerusalem for the name of the Lord Jesus."[120]

One of the first things that is seen in this encounter is the way in which Agabus resembles an Old Testament prophet in the manner in which he delivers the prophetic message to Paul. The word that Agabus brings is not just verbal. He performs a prophetic sign by using Paul's belt to tie his own hands and feet. The Hebrew Scriptures provide many examples of God instructing His prophets to do a physical act as a sign. Isaiah was told to go around naked and barefoot as a sign against Egypt and Cush.[121] God told Jeremiah to wear a yoke on his neck to symbolize the fact that Judah

---

[119] Acts 21:11.

[120] Acts 21:13.

[121] Isaiah 20:2-3.

would be defeated by Babylon and would be in bondage to them.[122] Ezekiel was told to lay on his side for over a year to show the depth of Judah's iniquity.[123] God had these Old Testament prophets perform a physical act and then had them interpret what it meant.[124] This is exactly what Agabus does with Paul. After tying himself up, Agabus tells Paul what the sign means and what he can expect in Jerusalem.

It also bears pointing out here that after Agabus had prophesied over Paul, he does not tell Paul what he should do. Agabus does not interpret the prophecy. He has told Paul what his destiny was but he does not give him any guidance as to whether he should cancel his trip to Jerusalem or not. He leaves that decision up to Paul. This is in contrast with the disciples at Tyre that Paul had visited shortly before coming to Caesarea. While he spent a week with them, they evidently also had a prophetic word for Paul. "Through the Spirit they urged Paul not to go on to Jerusalem."[125] Paul however, understood that his destiny lay in Jerusalem. On the surface, this appears to be a conflict in the Holy Spirit's guidance. Paul feels that the Holy Spirit is guiding him to Jerusalem but his friends believe that the message that they have from the Holy Spirit is that Paul should not go.[126] In reality, however, what appears to be contradictory messages is much more likely to be a case in which Paul's friends received a similar prophetic message to that which Agabus had. Paul's friends in Tyre, however, attempted to interpret the message for Paul based on their love for him.[127]

In examining this corporate mystical experience, it seems clear that Luke draws parallels between Paul's trip to Jerusalem and Jesus' last trip to Jerusalem.[128] The language that he uses is similar to that of his gospel. For example, Agabus' statement that Paul would be handed over to the Gentiles is reminiscent of Luke 18:31-32, where Jesus says, "We are going up to Jerusalem, and everything that is written by the prophets about the Son of Man will be fulfilled. He will be handed over to the Gentiles."

Paul's response to his friends also needs to be considered. When they attempted to change Paul's mind about going to Jerusalem he said, "Why are you weeping and breaking my heart? I am ready not only to be bound,

---

[122] Jeremiah 27:1-6.

[123] Ezekiel 4:4-5.

[124] Krodel, 394.

[125] Acts 21:4.

[126] Tannehill, 263.

[127] Ibid.

[128] Krodel, 395.

but also to die in Jerusalem for the name of the Lord Jesus."[129] Luke may be drawing a comparison here between Peter and Paul. On the night before Jesus' crucifixion, Peter said, "Lord, I am ready to go with you to prison and to death."[130] Paul's statement of willingness to die for Jesus, if need be, in Jerusalem sounds very much like Peter's pledge to follow Jesus to the death. The difference, however, is that, "Peter fails to keep his pledge; Paul does not."[131]

Luke also seems to make a comparison here between Paul's inner conflict about whether or not to go to Jerusalem and Jesus' spiritual conflict in Gethsemane.[132] He was recently given the prophetic word in Tyre and now hears a similar message from Agabus about what awaits him in Jerusalem. The tension between what Paul knows is God's course for him and that of his friends' entreaties is making it difficult for Paul. C. S. C. Williams notes that the verb that is being used here when Paul says that his friends are breaking his heart is used in describing a woman pounding her laundry on a rock.[133] "Paul felt their request like a blow at his heart, quite apart from his natural fears."[134]

When Paul's friends realize that Paul will not be dissuaded, they remark, "The Lord's will be done."[135] This is reminiscent of Jesus' prayer, "Father, if you are willing, take this cup from me; yet not my will, but yours be done."[136] Like Jesus, Paul is willing to pay whatever price is required of him to fulfill his destiny. In the same way that Jesus' disciples did not understand His instance on going to Jerusalem, where death awaited Him, neither can Paul's friends understand his choice. Paul's friends do understand, however, that Paul is striving to do God's will and in their statement to him about God's will, they are acknowledging that.

---

[129] Acts 21:13.

[130] Luke 22:33.

[131] Tannehill, 265, Tannehill goes on to say that, "Jesus' followers have moved beyond the faithlessness and blindness of the disciples prior to Jesus' resurrection. What Peter then promised but did not do, Paul now promises and will do. In this way he will also fulfill the destiny of suffering announced by the Lord in the narrative of Paul's conversion (9:16)."

[132] Williams, 362.

[133] C. S. C. Williams, 237.

[134] Ibid.

[135] Acts 21:14.

[136] Luke 22:42.

Individual Mystical Experiences

The first individual experience that will be discussed is Paul's conversion. This was obviously an extremely important event for Paul. Luke emphasized just how important by restating the account three times in Acts (9:1-9; 22:5-11; 26:11-18). It could be argued that this was a corporate mystical experience because there were other people with Paul when it happened. It appears, however, that even though Paul's traveling companions heard something and saw a light, they themselves did not have any type of spiritual experience. Paul is clearly the central figure in the story.

In discussing Paul's conversion, the experience itself will be examined using the three accounts that are in Acts. There appear to be slight contradictions in these different accounts. This would seem to indicate three different traditions that Luke has drawn his material from. If this is the case, "The first source is Paul himself, the second is the tradition of the church in Jerusalem, and the third is the tradition handed down in the church at Antioch."[137] Instead of harmonizing these different accounts, Luke used them as he received them.[138] It is also possible that in the two situations in which Paul's retells his story, he modified it according to the needs of his audience.[139]

Paul's conversion is different from that of all the original Twelve apostles. They became followers of Jesus and were converted through His teaching. Paul, however, was converted through a revelatory experience in which the risen Christ appeared to him.[140] This event, more than any other, shaped the rest of Paul's life.

The first aspect of this experience that will be examined is the light that flashed from heaven. Luke records in 9:3, "suddenly a light from heaven flashed around him." In 22:6, Paul says basically the same thing when he was recounting the story to the Jewish mob. In 26:13, however, Paul describes the light as, "brighter than the sun, blazing around me and my companions." Paul said that this happened about noon providing some indication of how bright the light that flashed around them was. It was brighter than the midday sun.

---

[137] Munck, 17.

[138] Hengel and Schwemer, 38–41.

[139] Krodel, 172, Krodel understands the differences in the three accounts to stem from the different nature of them. The first one in Acts 9 is a conversion and healing narrative. The other two focus on Paul's call and commission.

[140] Segal, 3.

The "light from heaven" is a standard feature in many of the theophanies that are recorded in the Old Testament.[141] It appears that Luke deliberately follows that pattern in describing Paul's conversion. One account that Luke clearly sees as somewhat of a parallel to Paul's experience is that of Ezekiel. Ezekiel spoke in similar terms about heavenly light. He says that he saw, "a great cloud with fire flashing forth continually and a bright light around it."[142] In Ezekiel's vision, the light symbolized the coming of the Presence of God. Luke also uses similar language when describing what happened on the Mount of Transfiguration. Luke says that as Jesus was praying, "the appearance of his face changed, and his clothes became as bright as a flash of lightning."[143]

In Paul's encounter, the bright light blinded him. While Peter was not blinded on the Mount of Transfiguration and Ezekiel was not blinded by the bright light that he saw, Paul the persecutor lost his sight. It was in temporarily losing his natural eyesight, however, that Paul's darkened heart was illuminated and he received the ability to see spiritually.[144]

Paul was very likely referring to this experience in 2 Corinthians 4:6 where he says that God has, "made his light shine in our hearts to give us the light of the knowledge of the glory of God in the face of Christ." Acts 22:14 indicates that Paul did see Christ in the divine light. Paul would later ask the Corinthians, "Have I not seen Jesus our Lord?"[145] Evidently, it was in the divine light that blinded him that Paul saw the glorified Christ with his spiritual eyes. There was never any question in Paul's mind that he had actually seen Jesus. This image of the exalted Christ would forever be stored in his mind's eye.[146]

The next thing that happened after the light flashed around Paul was that he fell to the ground. It was while he was on the ground that he heard the Divine voice speak to him. The first thing that he heard was a reproach: "Saul, Saul, why do you persecute me?"[147] Saul asked who the speaker was and was told, "I am Jesus, whom you are persecuting . . . Now get up and go into the city, and you will be told what you must do."[148] According to the account in chapter 22, Paul received his commission a few days later

---

141 Talbert, 98.

142 Ezekiel 1:4.

143 Luke 9:29.

144 Hengel and Schwemer, 42.

145 1 Corinthians 9:1.

146 Williams, 376.

147 Acts 9:4.

148 Acts 9:5-6.

from Ananias. Chapter 26 shows him receiving his commission directly from Jesus on the Damascus Road. It is likely that both accounts are accurate. Paul did receive his call and commission directly from Jesus however it was reaffirmed and explained to him by Ananias.[149] The laying on of hands by Ananias confirmed God's call and commission on Paul.

This is again reminiscent of Ezekiel's mystical experience by the Kebar River. When Ezekiel saw the glory of the Lord, he fell facedown. It was then that Ezekiel heard God speak and commission him as a prophet. Where Ezekiel was commissioned as a prophet to his own people, however, Paul's commission would be sending him to the Gentiles.[150] By showing the parallels between Ezekiel's call and Paul's conversion and call, Luke is introducing Paul as a new prophet.[151] The biggest difference between the call that Paul received and those that Old Testament prophets received was that the Old Testament prophets were presumably believers already. Paul, however, was an opponent of God and an enemy of the church.[152] Even though his conversion preceded his call only by a moment, it still closely fits the pattern of the call of many of the Old Testament prophets.

It was this life altering conversion experience and divine commissioning that led Paul into his missionary endeavors. It would be wrong to think of him as merely a traveling missionary who had mystical experiences. It would be correct to say that Paul understood, "his prophetic-like commission to be that of a traveling missionary."[153] It was Paul's encounter with Christ on the Damascus road that drove him forward for the rest of his life.

A second mystical experience of Paul's evidently occurred on his first trip to Jerusalem after his conversion. This experience is only referred to by Paul as he was addressing the Jewish mob in Jerusalem in Acts 22:17-21. He says that as he was praying at the temple in Jerusalem, he fell into a trance and saw the Lord speaking to him. "'Quick!' he said to me. 'Leave Jerusalem immediately, because they will not accept your testimony about me.'" Paul protested, reminding the Lord that his opponents knew his past as a persecutor of the church, as well as how he had supported the ston-

---

[149] Krodel, 415.

[150] Segal, 9.

[151] Ibid., 11, "Luke provides the first interpretation of Paul's conversion by figuring it in terms of Ezekiel's prophetic commissioning: as a conversion, commission, or vocation, Paul's movement to Christianity is interpreted as the result of a revelation of the image of God's Glory."

[152] Munck, 29.

[153] Sandmel, 77.

ing of Stephen. The Lord's reply was, "'Go; I will send you far away to the Gentiles.'"

The first thing that stands out about this spiritual experience was its location. Paul was in the temple performing his loyal duty as a Jew.[154] He had just been accused of defiling this same temple by the mob that he is now addressing. Paul testifies to the crowd that his commission as an apostle to the Gentiles came while he was in the temple. This narrative sounds similar to Isaiah's inaugural commission that he received in the temple in Isaiah 6:1-13. For Paul, however, it was not his inaugural commission but a reminder of what God had called him to.[155]

Paul objected to being told to leave Jerusalem. He felt that he was the very person that the Jews would listen to.[156] Surely they would listen to the one who was previously the foremost persecutor of the church. If anyone could persuade his countrymen, Paul believed that it was him.[157] The Lord was insistent, however, and told Paul that he was being sent far away, to the Gentiles. One reason for sending him away from Jerusalem was for his own protection. Luke recorded in Acts 9:29 that the Grecian Jews that Paul had been debating in Jerusalem had tried to kill him. Sending Paul away from Jerusalem was more than just for Paul's protection, however. It was part of the divine plan for Paul's life. Even though his heart burned to share the Gospel with his fellow Jews, God had called him to take the message, "to the ends of the earth."[158]

Another individual mystical experience that Luke presents is found in Acts 14:19-20 from the first missionary journey. This is the account of Paul being stoned and dragged out of the city as dead in Lystra. It is not clear that this is actually a mystical experience or not. At the very least, however, the way that Luke describes this event gives it the, "flavor of a miracle."[159] The reason that this incident is dealt with as a mystical experience is because if Paul did, in fact, die from this stoning, which can be implied, he could not have raised himself from the dead. It would take a supernatural intervention to raise him up.

This episode shows the extremes of pagan religion.[160] After Paul had healed the lame man, the crowd had attempted to offer sacrifices to he and

---

[154] Neil, 224.

[155] Bruce, 418.

[156] Marshall, 357.

[157] Krodel, 418.

[158] Acts 1:8.

[159] Bruce, 279.

[160] Krodel, 259.

Barnabas. Because of the language barrier, however, it took the apostles a little while to realize that this is what was happening. When they did, the process was well under way, with the local priest of Zeus bringing bulls that were to be slaughtered and sacrificed.

When Paul and Barnabas did realize what was happening, they tore their clothes and rushed in among the people. Their message was examined in the previous section, "Paul the Evangelist and Church Planter." Klauck points out that in tearing their clothes the apostles were showing their horror at the blasphemy of being mistaken for gods and in rushing in among the crowd to stop them, the apostles were showing that they were on the same level as these people.[161] Luke records that even after they had spoken to the people, "they had difficulty keeping the crowd from sacrificing to them."[162]

Luke does not provide a clear chronology here. At some point around this time, however, hostile Jews came from Antioch and Iconium and "won the crowd over." The Jews possibly convinced the Lystrans that the apostles were imposters and that their power came from evil forces.[163] The crowd was probably also upset about the fact that the sacrificial meal that they had been looking forward to was not going to take place.[164] At any rate, the Jews were able to provoke the Lystran mob to go after Paul.

The stoning that is described here is also referred to by Paul in 2 Corinthians 11:25, "once I was stoned." Luke's description make it sound more like an attempted lynching than a Jewish stoning, which would have been performed as an actual execution.[165] The mob scored enough with their stones, however, that Paul fell down and appeared to be dead. He was then dragged out of the city and possibly dumped in the refuse pit. The people who dragged him out of the city certainly thought he was dead.

Luke then records the apparent miracle/mystical experience: "But after the disciples had gathered around him, he got up and went back into the city." The disciples had probably come to see that Paul received a proper burial. Even though Luke does not specifically say it, it also seems implied that the disciples prayed for Paul. Possibly in response to this united prayer of faith, Paul got up. This narrative has all the markings of a resurrection

---

[161] Klauck, 59.

[162] Acts 14:18.

[163] Williams, 251.

[164] Klauck, 56.

[165] Ibid., 61.

story. Luke could also be using this story to illustrate the fact that even in tribulation, there is always the promise of resurrection.[166]

This incident serves as an example of a mystical experience only if it is understood that Paul was actually killed by the stoning and then brought back to life by God. If Paul did die in Lystra, it is possible that this was the time that he wrote about later when he, "was caught up to the third heaven . . . caught up to paradise."[167] He writes that he, "heard inexpressible things, things that man is not permitted to tell."[168] In telling the Corinthians of this experience, Paul said that it occurred 14 years earlier. That would have placed this vision sometime around the time of the first missionary journey. With that being the case, the possibility exists that when Paul was attacked and stoned by the Lystrans, he did actually die and was caught up to the third heaven and saw Paradise. His work was not finished on earth, however, and God miraculously raised him up to continue his apostolic ministry.

The next of Paul's individual mystical experiences that will be discussed is found near the beginning of the second missionary tour. After being prevented by the Holy Spirit from preaching in Asia and Bithynia, Paul and his team ended up in Troas. "During the night Paul had a vision of a man of Macedonia standing and begging him, 'Come over to Macedonia and help us.'"[169] This vision provided Paul and his team with the divine guidance that was needed for the next phase in their missionary journey.

This vision came to Paul at the time when it was needed the most. Paul's original goal seemed to have been to preach in Asia after they left Galatia.[170] The Holy Spirit did not allow them to minister at all in Asia, even though they passed through it. They continued North and then attempted to go into Bithynia. This time, "the Spirit of Jesus" would not even allow them to enter the region. Luke does not specify how the Holy Spirit communicated with Paul and his team. It could have come through a dream, vision, prophetic utterance, or an inner prompting. It is also possible that circumstances dictated the direction the team took.[171] In actuality, it was probably a combination of these factors that helped Paul to understand the direction in which he was being led.

---

[166] Ibid.

[167] 2 Corinthians 12:2, 4.

[168] Ibid.

[169] Acts 16:9.

[170] Arrington, 166.

[171] Neil, 179.

Bruce notes that, "Paul's missionary trips display an extraordinary combination of strategic planning and keen sensitiveness to the guidance of the Spirit of God."[172] This is seen clearly in the second missionary journey. Paul had plans for where he wanted to go. Luke provides no details for the first part of the trip. He just makes note of the fact that Paul and his team preached throughout Syria, Cilicia, and Galatia, "strengthening the churches." The next part of Paul's plan called for the team to go to Asia, with Ephesus probably being his target city. After being prevented by the Holy Spirit from preaching there or in Bithynia, Paul found himself in Troas probably wondering what to do. It was obvious that his own plans and itinerary had not worked out.

It was at this point that Paul received the vision of the Macedonian man during the night. The previous guidance that the team had received, even though it had been negative in telling them where not to go, had prepared them for the guidance that God gave through the vision.[173] This mystical experience eased any tension that Paul may have felt and let him know that he was indeed being guided by the Holy Spirit. The vision then became more than just a turning point for the second missionary trip. In Luke's opinion it provided the true starting point of this trip.[174] This is made clear by the fact that Luke provides very minimal information about the start of this trip, in spite of the issue that by this point in their journey, Paul and his team had already ministered in several locations in Syria, Cilicia, and Galatia.

The next mystical experience that will be examined is another vision that Paul received. This one came to him while he was in Corinth and is recorded in Acts 18:9-11:

> One night the Lord spoke to Paul in a vision: "Do not be afraid; keep on speaking, do not be silent. For I am with you, and no one is going to attack and harm you, because I have many people in this city." So Paul stayed for a year and a half, teaching them the word of God.

Paul's ministry in Corinth was discussed in the previous sections, "Paul the Pastor" and "Paul the Evangelist and Church Planter." Up until this point, Paul's time in Corinth had been very successful. Many had been converted and baptized, including Crispus, the synagogue ruler. It was right after he

---

[172] Bruce, 306.

[173] Arrington, 167.

[174] Neil, 180.

mentioned how well the work in Corinth was going that Luke included this narrative about Paul's vision.

It appears that Paul was struggling with fear. So far, the second missionary journey had been very difficult. Churches had been planted in Philippi, Thessalonica, Berea, and possibly Athens. There had also been intense persecution in each of those cities. While the work in Corinth was going well and a thriving church had been established, it was clear that there was also opposition. It seems that this constant battle with the opponents of the gospel had begun to wear Paul down. He confesses in 1 Corinthians 2:3, "I came to you in weakness and fear, and with much trembling."

It was evidently while Paul was struggling with fear and discouragement that he had the mystical experience of the vision that is described here in Acts 18. This vision came to Paul at night. In this it is similar to the one that he received in Troas in Acts 16. The implication seems to be that he also received this vision in a dream. The first thing that the Lord told Paul was, "Do not be afraid," or literally, "Stop being afraid."[175] The language that is used in this vision is very similar to that of the Old Testament theophanies in which the recipient would be told not to be afraid because God was addressing them.[176] In this case, however, Paul was told not to fear those who opposed him.

Paul was then told to, "keep on speaking, do not be silent." The Lord was reminding Paul of the commission that he had been given to be a, "witness to all men," of what he had seen and heard. Even though suffering is understood to be included in Paul's commission (Acts 9:16), Jesus makes promises to Paul to assure him that he is going to be protected for the remainder of his time in Corinth.

The first thing that we notice when examining this vision is the fact that the Lord assures Paul that He will be with the apostle. "For I am with you." This promise is again reminiscent of Old Testament language in which God promised to be with His people.[177] This promise leads to the next statement that the Lord makes, "no one is going to attack and harm you." Because the Lord is with him, Paul is going to be protected to continue his ministry in Corinth. This was probably very reassuring after the beating he and Silas suffered in Philippi and the stoning he received on the first missionary journey in Lystra.

The last thing that the Lord tells Paul in this vision is that He has, "many people in this city." God had gathered a large number of people

---

[175] Williams, 316.

[176] Marshall, 296.

[177] Stott, 298.

to Himself in Corinth, even many who had not believed yet.[178] It would be through Paul's continued ministry that they would come to faith. This statement from the Lord that He has many people in Corinth also has Old Testament overtones. When Elijah was despairing and asking God to take his life, God spoke to him and said, "I reserve seven thousand in Israel—all whose knees have not bowed down to Baal and all whose mouths have not kissed him."[179] God reassures Elijah and reminds him that he is not alone. In a similar way, the Lord lets Paul know that he is not alone either. God has many people besides him in the city.

The result of this vision was that, "Paul stayed for a year and a half, teaching them the word of God." This supernatural experience provided Paul with the encouragement that he needed to stay in Corinth longer than he had stayed in any other city. When he first came to Corinth there is no indication that he saw Corinth becoming one of the main centers for his missionary work.[180] It is obvious based on this vision, however, that God viewed Corinth as a strategic center for the spread of the Gospel. It is possible that the Corinthian church even became Paul's largest congregation.[181]

Another vision that Paul had came while he was in custody awaiting trial. This mystical experience is recorded in Acts 23:11: "The following night the Lord stood near Paul and said, 'Take Courage! As you have testified about me in Jerusalem, so you must also testify in Rome.'" This vision is very similar to the one that he received in Corinth. Paul had had three brushes with death in the previous two days, and a new plot would be unfolding shortly. If ever the apostle needed assurance, it was now.[182] At this point, it seemed doubtful that Paul would even leave Jerusalem alive, much less make it all the way to Rome.[183]

As in previous visions this one also came at night. The language is different in this one, however, saying that, "the Lord stood near Paul." This does not rule out the possibility that the vision came through a dream, but Luke is drawing attention to the physical nearness of the Lord in this encounter. The Lord tells Paul to, "Take courage!" This phrase is unique to Jesus in the New Testament and it is the same thing that He told his

---

178 Williams, 316.

179 1 Kings 19:18.

180 Williams, 317.

181 Arrington, 185.

182 Williams, 386–387.

183 Stott, 353.

disciples in their storm-driven boat as He walked across the water to them in Mark 6:50.[184]

The Lord then assured Paul that just as he had testified about Him in Jerusalem, so he would also testify in Rome. It is significant to note that Paul is not told that he will defend himself in Rome, or what the result will be, but only that he will be a witness for Jesus. His appearance before the emperor will be for the purpose of testifying about the Lord.[185]

This encouraging vision, "goes far to account for the calm and dignified bearing which from now on marks him out as a master of events rather than their victim."[186] Now, no matter how the storms (literal and physical as will be seen next) rage around Paul, he has the assurance that he will make it to Rome. Over the next two years of imprisonments, it is likely that Paul returned again and again in his mind to this encouraging vision.[187]

The last individual mystical experience that is seen in Paul's life took place on his ill-fated journey to Rome to appear before Caesar. This was the trip that resulted in a shipwreck and is recorded in Acts 27. After being driven along by the storm for many days, everyone aboard the ship was captured by feelings of hopelessness and despair. Paul then stood up and addressed those with him on the boat. He begins by telling them that this entire episode could have been avoided if only they had listened to him. Paul continues,

> But now I urge you to keep up your courage, because not one of you will be lost; only the ship will be destroyed. Last night an angel of the God whose I am and whom I serve stood beside me and said, 'Do not be afraid, Paul. You must stand trial before Caesar; and God has graciously given you the lives of all who sail with you.' So keep up your courage, men, for I have faith in God that it will happen just as he told me. Nevertheless, we must run aground on some island.[188]

One of the first things that is observed about this spiritual experience is that even though Paul is on a crowded ship, he is evidently the only one who saw and spoke with the angel. It had been about two years since his previous vision in Jerusalem in which the Lord promised him that he would testify in Rome. Again, at a time when it would be easy to give in to fear and despair, God provides the encouragement and reassurance that

---

184 Williams, 387.

185 Marshall, 366–367.

186 Bruce, 430.

187 Stott, 353.

188 Acts 27:22-26.

Paul needed. In the previous vision the Lord Himself appeared to Paul to reassure him. Here, He sends an angel to give Paul essentially the same message as before. Paul would stand before Caesar.

There is also one new element in what the angel tells Paul. He tells him that, "God has graciously given you the lives of all who sail with you." The implication is that Paul had interceded for those who were on the ship with him and God was letting him know that this prayer had been answered.[189] For Paul, it was not enough that only his life be spared. He was a pastor to the very end and never stopped praying and caring for others.[190]

As Paul begins to speak to the others on the ship to tell them about his vision, he starts off with a bit of, "I told you so."[191] There is no indication of vindictiveness in Paul's tone, however. He had warned them in Acts 27:10, "Men, I can see that our voyage is going to be disastrous and bring great loss to ship and cargo, and to our own lives also." They had put themselves through needless tribulation. Even as Paul rebukes, it is only to add weight to the encouragement that he would be bringing.[192] Paul then told them of his encounter with the angel and relayed his message to those on the ship with him. God had agreed to spare them. Because of Paul's previous accurate prediction, the people were probably more likely to listen to what he said.

Most of Paul's mystical experiences were only meant for him alone or for him and his team, as with the vision of the Macedonian man he saw at Troas. This mystical experience, however, is unique in the sense that the angel's message, while primarily for Paul, also included encouragement for all the unbelievers who were on the ship with him. Kilgallen states that, "to be associated with the man who is close to God is to enjoy life."[193] By saving them physically from the sea, God was giving them a picture of the reality of His saving power.

In comparing and contrasting the mystical experiences between Peter and Paul, it was observed that both men had a number of different types of experiences. They both had angelic encounters, visions, dreams, as well as various physical manifestations of the Holy Spirit. Luke, for example,

---

[189] Arrington, 260. See also Marshall, 410. Marshall sees a parallel here between Paul and Abraham from Genesis 18 where he interceded with God for the people of Sodom.

[190] Bruce, 488, Bruce notes, "Human society has no idea how much it owes, in the mercy of God, to the presence in it of righteous men and women."

[191] Ibid.

[192] Guthrie, 289.

[193] John J. Kilgallen, *A Brief Commentary on the Acts of the Apostles* (New York: Paulist, 1988) 215.

shows both apostles having a vision/dream that provided specific direction for their ministry. Peter had the vision of the sheet containing both clean and unclean animals. This vision coupled with the inner prompting of the Holy Spirit prepared him for ministry in Cornelius the Gentile's house. Peter would refer back to this vision later as the determining factor in his taking the message of the gospel to a Gentile audience. When defending his actions in Acts 11, Peter carefully recounted in order everything that had happened, especially the vision and inner prompting of the Holy Spirit.

Paul, on the other hand, on the second missionary journey, received specific guidance about where not to preach before he saw his vision, which would show him where he was to evangelize. He was, "kept by the Holy Spirit from preaching the word in Asia."[194] Later, "the Spirit of Jesus would not allow him to,"[195] preach in Bithynia. Luke is not specific on how this direction came. It could have been through an inner prompting, a prophetic utterance, circumstances, or a combination of the three. However, after being directed where he was not to preach, Paul received a vision/dream of Macedonian man asking him to, "Come over to Macedonia and help us."[196] This vision led to one of the most successful periods of Paul's ministry.

While Luke shows both Peter and Paul having both corporate and individual supernatural experiences, he presents many more for Paul than he does for Peter. The likely reason for this is because if Luke, the companion of Paul, is the author of Acts, he would have had much more access to Paul than he would have had to Peter. As one of Paul's traveling companions, Luke would have been able to hear first-hand about many of Paul's mystical experiences.

Luke clearly shows that both apostles are on the same level spiritually. They both had the ability to hear the inner prompting of the Holy Spirit. They both received visions and dreams which provided direction for their ministries. Peter and Paul both had angelic encounters as well. In Peter's case, the angels set him free from prison on two different occasions. In Paul's case, the angels appeared to him to assure him that he would be spared from harm so that he could stand before Caesar.

One of the main differences in the mystical experiences between Peter and Paul is that while Peter is never shown having a vision of Jesus after the Ascension, Paul has a number of visions/dreams in which he does see the Lord. The first of these is at his conversion on the Damascus road. This encounter with the risen Lord set the tone for Paul's entire ministry. Jesus

---

[194] Acts 16:6

[195] Acts 16:7.

[196] Acts 16:9.

then appeared to Paul at least three other times in Acts providing encouragement and direction at crucial times in Paul's apostolic ministry. Paul had not had a relationship with Jesus as Peter had. Luke, then, goes to great lengths to establish the fact that Paul's relationship with the Lord Jesus was just as real and just as valid as that of Peter and the other apostles'.

Conclusions

This study has examined the apostolic ministries of Peter and Paul, as seen through the eyes of Luke in Acts. Their ministries were compared and contrasted through the lenses of several different apostolic functions. The functions that were examined were leadership, evangelism and church planting, miracle working, and mystical or supernatural experiences. These particular functions provide a way to analyze how Peter and Paul conducted their individual apostolic ministries so that they can be studied in greater detail. As was discovered in the study, there are many similarities as well as many differences in the way that the two men went about fulfilling their ministries.

We began by establishing the credibility of Luke as a writer, historian, and theologian. The case was made that the author of Acts is Luke, the companion of Paul. There are many scholars who do not hold to this traditional view of Acts and question the historical reliability of the author's work. While acknowledging that this issue will never be fully resolved, I believe that we built a case for the acceptance of the traditional view. The internal evidence as well as the strong early church tradition held that Luke wrote both volumes of Luke-Acts. The traditional view also usually holds to an early dating of the book. We also built a case for an early dating of Acts.

The relationship between Luke's gospel and Acts was discussed. There are many parallels and similarities between the two books. They are essentially two parts to the same story. One will not be able to fully understand Acts apart from Luke's gospel. What God began to do in Jesus (Luke's gospel), He continued to do through His people (Acts).[1] The first few chapters of Luke's gospel establish the fact that Jesus is the fulfillment of the Old Testament prophecies. Rather than bringing a "new" message,

---

[1] Keathley, 11, "Luke did not separate the work of Christ from the work of those described in Acts; they were two parts of one grand plan of salvation."

Jesus' teaching was in essential continuity and agreement with that of the Hebrew Scriptures. Luke quotes and then interprets extensively from the Old Testament to establish Jesus as the One that the writers were talking about.

The bulk of the book was devoted to examining, comparing, and contrasting the apostolic ministries of Peter and Paul. In the early chapters of Acts, Luke demonstrates that Jesus' followers are in essential continuity with Him. In 1:8 Jesus commissions them as His witnesses and is then transfigured before all of them as He ascends back to heaven. Their commission is provided in the context of a corporate mystical experience. The first half of Acts is devoted to the apostolic ministry of Peter. In the first example that Luke presents of his leadership role, Peter uses the Hebrew Scriptures to establish the need to fill the vacancy left by Judas' defection. Luke also shows Peter quoting extensively from the Hebrew Scriptures in some of his evangelistic speeches/sermons to establish the fact that Jesus was the fulfillment of the prophecies and the long awaited Messiah. There are clear parallels between Peter's evangelistic ministry and that of Jesus. Jesus was known as a powerful teacher and preacher. In a similar way, Peter's first two sermons in Acts were responsible for 5,000 conversions.

Luke presents Peter's apostolic ministry in such a way that he is shown doing the same kinds of things that Jesus had done in His earthly ministry. This is especially evident in the area of miracle working. Jesus healed a lame man; Peter heals two of them. A woman was healed by touching the hem of Jesus' robe; in Acts people were healed as Peter's shadow passed over them. Jesus raised people from the dead; Peter raises Dorcas from the dead.

In the same way, however, that Jesus endured opposition and conflict in His ministry, so did His followers in Acts. Peter and John were arrested after healing the lame man in the temple. All of the apostles were arrested and then flogged in Acts 5. Stephen was falsely accused and then stoned to death in Acts 7. In Acts 12, James, the brother of John is beheaded. Peter was arrested immediately after that and would have met the same fate had he not been delivered by an angel. This miraculous escape from prison was examined as an individual mystical experience for Peter. Other than a brief appearance at the Jerusalem Council, Peter steps out of the pages of Acts. His supernatural release from prison serves as an exclamation point to his ministry.

The second half of Acts focuses on the ministry of the Apostle Paul. Luke's presentation of Paul does not show him to be an innovator who is starting a new religion. Rather, he is shown to be in essential unity with Peter and the Twelve, as well as the Hebrew Scriptures. Paul had not been a disciple of Jesus as Peter had. Instead, his conversion is presented in terms of an Old Testament prophetic call. Luke draws clear parallels between Paul's conversion and call with that of Ezekiel. Paul's conversion experience is an individual mystical experience and is described using language that is reminiscent of the Old Testament theophanies. The implication here seems to be that the God of the Hebrew Scriptures is still acting in history and He chose Paul as a prophet to fulfill His plan. The personal appearance of Jesus to Paul serves to validate his conversion and call.

In the same way that Luke drew parallels between Peter's ministry and that of Jesus, he now does the same between Peter and Paul. They are both shown to be strong leaders. In Peter's ministry, this is expressed, for a time, in a governmental role in the Jerusalem church. He provides foundational leadership in the early days of the church. Peter also clearly functions as the leader of the Twelve apostles. Peter's ministry will eventually go though a transition and he will become more of a traveling evangelist. Paul's leadership role, on the other hand, is expressed in terms of that of a pastor. Luke presents Paul over and over again functioning in that capacity. Paul is seen spending at least a year working with Barnabas in a pastoral setting in Antioch. After founding the church in Corinth, he spent a year and a half there as a pastor. In Ephesus, Paul spent three years working with the church that he had founded, functioning in a pastoral role.

The parallels that Luke draws between the two apostles are especially evident in the miracle working aspect of Paul's ministry. Peter has a confrontation with Simon the magician; Paul has an encounter with the false prophet, Elymas, and pronounces temporary blindness on him. Peter healed lame people; Paul healed the lame man in Lystra. Luke records that Peter's shadow brought healing to people. He records that handkerchiefs and aprons that had touched Paul were taken to sick and demon possessed people and they were healed. Peter raised Dorcas from the dead; Paul raised Eutychus. In raising Eutychus, however, Luke seems to also draw a pointed comparison between Paul and the Old Testament prophets, Elijah and Elisha, in the way that he performed the miracle. Whereas Peter clearly resembles Jesus in the way that he resuscitates Dorcas, Paul wraps himself physically around Eutychus like both Elijah and Elisha did in their ministries.

Where Peter is shown as a powerful evangelist, responsible for thousands of people turning to Christ, Paul is shown as the consummate missionary/evangelist responsible for leaving behind a group of Christian communities throughout the Roman Empire. The message that the two apostles preach is essentially the same. Paul preaches a message in the synagogue at Pisidian Antioch that is very similar in content to Peter's sermon on Pentecost and the one that he preached in the temple after healing the lame man. In this sermon, Paul quotes extensively from the Hebrew Scriptures to establish the fact that Jesus was the fulfillment of the prophecies. When Peter speaks to the delegates at the Jerusalem Council in Acts 15, his message sounds very much like something that Paul would have preached with its emphasis on justification by faith. Luke clearly shows that there is a basic continuity in their message and theology. They are not preaching two different messages; Peter and Paul are both preaching the same gospel.

Luke also showed that Peter and Paul were in continuity with respect to their target audiences. Even though Paul later referred to Peter as the, "apostle to the Jews," and to himself as the, "apostle to the Gentiles," in Galatians, it was Peter who initially preached the gospel to a Gentile audience at Cornelius' house. Peter was the one who was supernaturally directed through a vision to, "not call anything impure that God has made clean," in Act 10. Even though Peter's primary ministry in Acts was among Palestinian Jews, he still led the way in taking the message to a non-Jewish audience. Luke also makes a point of showing Paul's ministry to be one in which he never stopped trying to reach Jews as well. In Acts, Paul's ministry always starts in the synagogue where there was one available. The main thrust of his ministry was directed towards the Gentiles, yet he never stopped trying to reach his own people as well.

Luke also shows that Paul suffered opposition and persecution as Jesus, Peter and others did. Peter is arrested several times and delivered by an angel on two occasions, once with all of the apostles and once by himself. During one of these arrests, the apostles were all flogged. Luke records that Paul was stoned and left for dead by the mob in Lystra. He and Silas were arrested and beaten with rods in Philippi. It was in this Philippian jail that Paul and Silas experienced the earthquake that caused their chains to fall off. Paul was later seized and beaten by the mob in Jerusalem on his last trip there. Luke seems to be emphasizing the point that Paul suffered unjustly in the same way that the apostles and Jesus before them had.

Acts ends without any final resolution about what happens to Peter or Paul. Peter has, "left for another place,"[2] and Paul is in custody in Rome awaiting trial where, "Boldly and without hindrance he preached the kingdom of God and taught about the Lord Jesus Christ."[3] It was argued in Chapter One that this open ending of Acts is evidence for an early dating of the book, as well as the possibility that Paul was still alive when it

---

[2] Acts 12:17.

[3] Acts 28:31.

198

was written. It could also be, however, that whether Peter and Paul were still alive when Acts was written or not, that this was the message that Luke wanted to communicate. The message that came through the Hebrew Scriptures and was fulfilled in the Person of the Lord Jesus continued to be proclaimed through the apostles and others in the early church. Later, Paul, through a supernatural encounter and direct commission from Jesus, also, became a witness and a chosen vessel that God could work through. The essential continuity of the message that was present between Jesus and the original apostles was also present in Paul's ministry. As Acts ends, Luke seems to be making the point that the message that Jesus, Peter, and Paul have been declaring will continue to spread and grow because ultimately it is eternal and cannot be stopped. As Paul quotes from Isaiah 6 in Acts 28, the message in Acts has come full circle. Luke's work now ends with the fulfillment of the prophecies that it began with.[4]

---

[4] Squires, 151.

Bibliography

Achtemeier, Paul J. "An Elusive Unity: Paul, Acts, and the Early Church." *Catholic Biblical Quarterly* 48 (1986) 1–26.

Agnew, Francis H. "The Origin of the NT Apostle-Concept: A Review of Research." *Journal of Biblical Literature* 105 (1986) 75–96.

Akenson, Donald Harman. *Saint Paul: A Skeleton Key to the Historical Jesus.* New York: Oxford University Press, 2000.

Allen, Roland. *Missionary Methods: St. Paul's or Ours?* Grand Rapids: Eerdmans, 1962.

Alexander, Loveday. "Mapping Early Christianity: Acts and the Shape of Early Church History." *Interpretation* 57 (2003) 163–73.

Arrington, French L. *The Acts of the Apostles.* Peabody, Mass.: Hendrickson, 1988.

———. *Divine Order in the Church: A Study of 1 Corinthians.* Grand Rapids: Baker, 1978.

Ascough, Richard S. *What are They Saying About the Formation of Pauline Churches?* New York: Paulist, 1998.

Aune, David E. *The New Testament in its Literary Environment.* Library of Early Christianity. Philadelphia: Westminster John Knox, 1987.

Back, Peter. "Exegesis on Some Key Passages Relating to Mission: Part 1—Acts 13:1-4." *Evangel* 20 (2002) 15–20.

———. "Exegesis on Some Key Passages Relating to Mission: Part 2—Acts 14:21-28, Acts 15:36-41, and Acts 16:2." *Evangel* 20 (2002) 20–22.

Banks, Robert. *Paul's Idea of Community.* Peabody, Mass.: Hendrickson, 1994.

Barbero, Mario. "A First-century Couple, Priscilla and Aquila: Their House Churches and Missionary Activity." Ph.D. diss., The Catholic University of America, 2001.

Barclay, William. *The Acts of the Apostles.* The Daily Bible Study Series. Philadelphia: Westminster, 1976.

Barnett, Paul. *Behind the Scenes of the New Testament.* Downers Grove, Ill.: InterVarsity, 1990.

Barrett, C. K. "The Historicity of Acts." *Journal of Theological Studies* 50 (1999) 515–34.

———. *Paul: An Introduction to His Thought.* Louisville: Westminster John Knox, 1994.

———., *The New Testament Background.* San Francisco: HarperCollins, 1989.

———. *The Signs of an Apostle: The Cato Lecture—1969.* Carlisle: Paternoster, 1996.

Bartlett, David L. *Ministry in the New Testament.* Minneapolis: Fortress, 1993.

Beare, Frank W. "The Sequence of Events in Acts 9–15 and the Career of Peter." *Journal of Biblical Literature* 62 (1943) 295–306.

Beker, J. Christiaan. *Heirs of Paul: Their Legacy in the New Testament and the Church Today.* Grand Rapids: Eerdmans, 1991.

———. *The Triumph of God: The Essence of Paul's Thought.* Minneapolis: Fortress, 1990.

Best, Ernest. *Paul and His Converts.* Edinburgh: T. & T. Clark, 1988.

———. *A Commentary on the First and Second Epistles to the Thessalonians.* Harper's New Testament Commentaries. New York: Harper & Row, 1972.

———. "The Revelation to Evangelize the Gentiles." *Journal of Theological Studies* 25 (1984) 1–30.

Bibliography

———. "Paul's Apostolic Authority." *Journal for the Study of the New Testament* 27 (1986) 3–25.

Best, John Ernest. "Paul's Theology of the Corporate Life of the Local Church." Th.D. diss., Dallas Theological Seminary, 1984.

Blaiklock, E. M. *The Acts of the Apostles: An Historical Commentary*. The Tyndale New Testament Commentaries. Grand Rapids: Eerdmans, 1959.

Blomberg, Craig. *1 Corinthians*. The NIV Application Commentary. Grand Rapids: Zondervan, 1994.

Bock, Darrell L. *Luke*. The NIV Application Commentary. Grand Rapids: Zondervan, 1996.

Boice, James Montgomery. *Zondervan NIV Bible Commentary: Galatians*. Grand Rapids: Zondervan, 1994.

Bondi, Richard A. "Become Such as I Am: St. Paul in the Acts of the Apostles." *Biblical Theology Bulletin* 27 (1996) 164–76.

Borgen, Peder. "From Paul to Luke: Observations Toward Clarification of the Theology of Luke-Acts." *Catholic Biblical Quarterly* 31 (1969) 168–82.

Bornkamm, Günther. *Paul*. Minneapolis: Fortress, 1995.

Bowers, Paul. "Church and Mission in Paul." *Journal for the Study of the New Testament* 44 (1991) 89–111.

———. "Paul and Religious Propaganda in the First Century." *Novum Testamentum* 22 (1980) 316–23.

———. "Paul's Route Through Mysia: A Note on Acts XVI. 8." *Journal of Theological Studies* 30 (1979) 507–11.

Branick, Vincent. *Understanding the New Testament and Its Message*. New York: Paulist, 1998.

Brawley, Robert L. *Centering on God: Method and Message in Luke-Acts*. Literary Currents in Biblical Interpretation, Louisville: Westminster John Knox, 1990.

Brehm, H. Alan. "The Significance of the Summaries for Interpreting Acts." *Southwestern Journal of Theology* 33 (1990) 29–40.

Brown, Raymond E., editor. *Peter in the New Testament*. Minneapolis: Augsburg, 1973.

———. *The Churches the Apostles Left Behind*. New York: Paulist, 1984.

———. "*Episkope* and *Episkopos*: The New Testament Evidence." *Theological Studies* 41 (1980) 322–38.

———, and John P. Meier. *Antioch to Rome: New Testament Cradles of Catholic Christianity*. New York: Paulist, 1983.

Brown, Schuyler. "Apostleship in the New Testament as an Historical and Theological Problem." *New Testament Studies* 30 (1984) 474–80.

Bruce, F. F. *The Book of the Acts*. The New International Commentary on the New Testament. Grand Rapids: Eerdmans, 1988.

———. *Philippians*. New International Biblical Commentary. Peabody, Mass.: Hendrickson, 1989.

———. *1 & 2 Thessalonians*. Word Biblical Commentary. Waco, Tex.: Word, 1982.

———. *Paul: Apostle of the Heart Set Free*. Grand Rapids: Eerdmans, 1977.

———. *Peter, Stephen, James and John: Studies in Non-Pauline Christianity*. Grand Rapids: Eerdmans, 1979.

———. *The Pauline Circle*. Carlisle: Paternoster, 1985.

———. *New Testament History*. Garden City, N.Y.: Doubleday, 1980.

———. *The Message of the New Testament*. Grand Rapids: Eerdmans, 1972.

———. *The Spreading Flame: The Rise and Progress of Christianity*. Grand Rapids: Eerdmans, 1954.

———. "Is the Paul of Acts the Real Paul?" *Bulletin of the John Rylands Library* 58 (1976) 282–305.

———. "The Significance of the Speeches for Interpreting Acts." *Southwestern Journal of Theology* 33 (1990) 20–28.

———. "The Holy Spirit in the Acts of the Apostles." *Interpretation* 27 (1973) 166–83.

Callan, Terrance. "The Background of the Apostolic Decree (Acts 15:20; 21:25)." *Catholic Biblical Quarterly* 55 (1993) 284–87.

Cairns, Earle E. *Christianity Through the Centuries*. Grand Rapids: Zondervan, 1981.

Calvin, John. *The Acts of the Apostles: 1–13*. Calvin's New Testament Commentaries. Edited by David W. Torrance and Thomas F. Torrance. Translated by John W. Fraser and W. J. G. McDonald. Grand Rapids: Eerdmans, 1965.

———. *Acts 14–28*. Calvin's New Testament Commentaries. Edited by David W. Torrance and Thomas F. Torrance. Translated by John W. Fraser. Grand Rapids: Eerdmans, 1966.

Campbell, Thomas H. "Paul's 'Missionary Journeys' as Reflected in His Letters." *Journal of Biblical Literature* 74 (1955) 80–87.

Cannon, William R. "The Book of Acts." 1989 http://www.religion-online.org/showbook. asp?title=693 (May 22, 2003).

Carroll, John T. "Luke's Portrayal of the Pharisees." *Catholic Biblical Quarterly* 50 (1988) 604–21.

Carroll, John T. and Joel B. Green. *The Death of Jesus in Early Christianity*. Peabody, Mass.: Hendrickson, 1995.

Carson, D. A., Douglas J. Moo, and Leon Morris. *An Introduction to the New Testament*. Grand Rapids: Zondervan, 1992.

Catchpole, David R. "Paul, James and the Apostolic Decree." *New Testament Studies* 23 (1977) 428–44.

Clarke, Andrew D. *Serve the Community of the Church: Christians as Leaders and Ministers*. First-Century Christians in the Graeco-Roman World. Grand Rapids: Eerdmans, 2000.

Cole, R. Alan. *Galatians*. Tyndale New Testament Commentaries. Grand Rapids: Eerdmans, 1989.

Conzelmann, Hans. *The Theology of St. Luke*. Translated by Geoffrey Buswell. New York: Harper & Row, 1961.

———. *History of Primitive Christianity*. Translated by John E. Steely. Nashville: Abingdon, 1973.

———. *Gentiles, Jews, Christians: Polemics and Apologetics in the Greco-Roman Era*. Translated by M. Eugene Boring. Minneapolis: Fortress, 1992.

Cook, Richard B. "Paul the Organizer." *Missiology: An International Review* 9 (1981) 485–97.

Cousar, Charles B. *Galatians*. Interpretation: A Bible Commentary for Teaching and Preaching. Louisville: John Knox, 1982.

Craddock, Fred B. *First and Second Peter and Jude*. Westminster Bible Companion. Louisville: Westminster John Knox, 1995.

Craffert, Pieter F. "The Pauline Household Communities: Their Nature as Social Entities." *Neotestamentica* 32 (1998) 309–39.

Cullman, Oscar. *Peter: Disciple, Apostle, Martyr*. Translated by Floyd V. Filson. London: SCM, 1962.

Culver, Robert Duncan. "Apostles and the Apostolate in the New Testament." *Bibliotheca Sacra* 134 (1977) 131–43.

Cwiekowski, Frederick J. *The Beginnings of the Church*. New York: Paulist, 1988.

Danker, Frederick W., editor. *A Greek-English Lexicon of the New Testament and Other Early Christian Literature*. Chicago: University of Chicago Press, 2000.

Davies, Philip. "The Ending of Acts." *Expository Times* 94 (1983) 334–35.

Dawsey, J. "The Literary Unity of Luke-Acts: Questions of Style—A Task for Literary Critics." *New Testament Studies* 35 (1989) 48–66.

Detwiler, David F. "Paul's Approach to the Great Commission in Acts 14: 21–23." *Bibliotheca Sacra* 152 (1995) 33–41.

Dickerson, Patrick L. "The Sources of the Account of the Mission to Samaria in Acts 8:5-25." *Novum Testamentum* 39 (1997) 210–34.

Dodd, Brian J. *The Problem With Paul*. Downers Grove, Ill.: InterVarsity, 1996.

———. *Empowered Church Leadership: Ministry in the Spirit According to Paul*. Downers Grove, Ill.: InterVarsity, 2003.

Dodd, C. H. *The Apostolic Preaching and Its Developments*. http://www.religion-online.org/cgi-bin/relsearchd.dll 1964 (October 15, 2001).

Drury, John. *Tradition and Design in Luke's Gospel*. Atlanta: John Knox, 1976.

Dunn, James D. G. *Jesus, Paul and the Law*. Louisville: Westminster John Knox, 1990.

Dupont, Jaques. *The Salvation of the Gentiles: Studies in the Acts of the Apostles*. Translated by John R. Keating. New York: Paulist, 1979.

Ellis, E. Earle. "Paul and His Co-Workers." *New Testament Studies* 17 (1970–1971) 437–52.

———. *Paul and His Recent Interpreters*. Grand Rapids: Eerdmans, 1961.

Esler, Philip F., editor. *Modelling Early Christianity: Social-Scientific Studies of the New Testament in its Context*. London: Routledge, 1995.

Evans, Craig A. *Luke*. New International Biblical Commentary. Peabody, Mass.: Hendrickson, 1990.

Evans, C. F. *Saint Luke*. Trinity Press International New Testament Commentaries. Philadelphia: Trinity, 1990.

Fenton, John. "The Order of the Miracles Performed by Peter and Paul in Acts." *Expository Times* 77 (1965–66) 381–83.

Filson, Floyd V. "The Significance of the Early House Churches." *Journal of Biblical Literature* 58 (1939) 105–12.

Fitzmyer, Joseph A. *Acts of the Apostles*. Anchor Bible, New York: Doubleday, 1998.

———. *According to Paul: Studies in the Theology of the Apostle*. New York: Paulist, 1993.

Foakes-Jackson, F. J. *The Acts of the Apostles*. The Moffat Commentary. New York: Harper and Brothers, 1931.

Franklin, Benjamin. *Autobiography and Selected Writings*. Edited by Larzer Ziff. New York: Holt, Rinehart and Winston, 1965.

Frend, W. H. C. *The Early Church*. Minneapolis: Fortress, 1982.

Furnish, Victor Paul. "Fellow Workers in God's Service." *Journal of Biblical Literature* 80 (1961) 364–70.

Gager, J. G. "Some Notes on Paul's Conversion." *New Testament Studies* 27 (1980–1981) 697–704.

Garrett, Susan R. *The Demise of the Devil: Magic and the Demonic in Luke's Writings*. Minneapolis: Fortress, 1989.

Gasque, W. Ward. "The Historical Value of Acts." *Tyndale Bulletin* 40 (1989) 136–57.

————. "A Fruitful Field: Recent Study of the Acts of the Apostles." *Interpretation* 42 (1988) 117–31.

Gill, David W. *Peter the Rock: Extraordinary Insights From an Ordinary Man.* Downers Grove, Ill.: InterVaristy, 1986.

Glover, T. R. *Paul of Tarsus.* Peabody, Mass.: Hendrickson, 2002.

Gooding, David. *True to the Faith: A Fresh Approach to the Acts of the Apostles.* London: Hodder & Stoughton, 1990.

Goodwin, Frank J. *A Harmony of the Life of St. Paul.* Grand Rapids: Baker, 1951.

Goulder, Michael. *St. Paul Versus St. Peter: A Tale of Two Missions.* Louisville: Westminster John Knox, 1994.

Grant, Michael. *Saint Peter, A Biography.* New York: Scribner, 1994.

Green, Michael. *2 Peter and Jude.* Tyndale New Testament Commentaries. Grand Rapids: Eerdmans, 1968.

Gundry, Robert. *A Survey of the New Testament.* Grand Rapids: Zondervan, 1970.

Guthrie, Donald. *The Apostles.* Grand Rapids: Zondervan, 1975.

————. *New Testament Theology: A Thematic Study.* Downers Grove, Ill.: InterVarsity, 1981.

————. *Galatians.* The New Century Bible Commentary. Grand Rapids: Eerdmans, 1973.

————. *New Testament Introduction: The Pauline Epistles.* Chicago: InterVarsity, 1966.

Haenchen, Ernst. *The Acts of the Apostles: A Commentary.* Translated by Bernard Noble and Gerald Shinn. Philadelphia: Westminster, 1971.

Hall, Robert G. "The Rhetorical Outline for Galatians: A Reconsideration." *Journal of Biblical Literature* 106 (1987) 277–87.

Hamm, Dennis. "Acts 3.1-10: The Healing of the Temple Beggar as Lucan Theology." *Biblica* 67 (1986) 305–19.

Hardon, John A. "The Miracle Narratives in the Acts of the Apostles." *Catholic Biblical Quarterly* 16 (2001) 303–18.

Harrington, Daniel J. "Paul and Collaborative Ministry." *New Theology Review* 3 (1990) 62–71.

Harris, Horton. *The Tübingen School: A Historical and Theological Investigation of the School of F. C. Baur.* Grand Rapids: Baker, 1990.

Hawthorne, Gerald F., Ralph P. Martin, and Daniel G. Reid, editors. *Dictionary of Paul and His Letters.* Downers Grove, Ill.: InterVarsity, 1993.

Hawthorne, Gerald F. *Philippians.* Word Biblical Commentary. Waco, Tex.: Word, 1983.

Hay, David M. "Paul's Indifference to Authority." *Journal of Biblical Literature* 88 (1969) 36–44.

Hedrick, Charles W. "Paul's Conversion/Call: A Comparative Analysis of the Three Reports in Acts." *Journal of Biblical Literature* 100 (1981) 415–32.

Hemer, Colin J. *The Book of Acts in the Setting of Hellenistic History.* Winona Lake, Ind.: Eisenbrauns, 1990.

————. *The Letters to the Seven Churches of Asia in Their Local Setting.* Grand Rapids: Eerdmans, 1989.

Hengel, Martin, and Anna Maria Schwemer. *Paul Between Damascus and Antioch: The Unknown Years.* Translated by John Bowden. Louisville: Westminster John Knox, 1997.

Hengel, Martin. *Between Jesus and Paul.* Translated by John Bowden. 1983. Reprinted, Eugene, Ore.: Wipf and Stock, 2003.

————. *Acts and the History of Earliest Christianity*. Translated by John Bowden. 1979. Reprinted, Eugene, Ore.: Wipf and Stock, 2003.

————. *Property and Riches in the Early Church: Aspects of a Social History of Early Christianity*. Translated by John Bowden. Philadelphia: Fortress, 1974.

Hester, James D. "The Rhetorical Structure of Galatians 1:11—2:14." *Journal of Biblical Literature* 103 (1984) 223–33.

Hiebert, D. Edmond. *The Gospels and Acts. An Introduction to the New Testament: Volume One*. Chicago: Moody, 1975.

————. *The Pauline Epistles. An Introduction to the New Testament: Volume Two*. Chicago: Moody, 1977.

————. *An Introduction to the Non-Pauline Epistles. An Introduction to the New Testament: Volume Three*. Chicago: Moody, 1962.

————. *In Paul's Shadow: Friends and Foes of the Great Apostle*. Greenville, S.C.: Bob Jones University Press, 1992.

Hillyer, Norman. *1 and 2 Peter, Jude*. New International Biblical Commentary. Peabody, Mass.: Hendrickson, 1992.

Hock, Ronald F. "The Workshop as a Social Setting for Paul's Missionary Preaching." *Catholic Biblical Quarterly* 41 (1979) 438–50.

Holmberg, Bengt. *Paul and Power*. Philadelphia: Fortress, 1978.

Houlden, J. L. "The Purpose of Luke." *Journal for the Study of the New Testament* 21 (1984) 53–65.

Howard, R. E. *Galatians through Philemon*. Beacon Bible Commentary. Kansas City: Beacon Hill, 1965.

Hubbard, Benjamin J. "Commissioning Stories in Luke-Acts: A Study of Their Antecedents, Form and Content." *Semeia* 9 (1977) 103–26.

Hultgren, Arland J. "Interpreting the Gospel of Luke." *Interpretation* 30 (1976) 353–65.

Hurlbut, Jesse Lyman. *The Story of the Christian Church*. Grand Rapids: Zondervan: 1967.

Jervell, Jacob. *Luke and the People of God: A New Look at Luke-Acts*. Minneapolis: Augsburg, 1972.

————. *The Unknown Paul: Essays on Luke-Acts and Early Christian History*. Minneapolis: Augsburg, 1984.

Jervis, L. Ann. *Galatians*. New International Biblical Commentary. Peabody, Mass.: Hendrickson, 1999.

Johnson, Luke T. *The Writings of the New Testament: An Interpretation*. Philadelphia: Fortress, 1986.

————. *The Acts of the Apostles*. Collegeville: Liturgical, 1992.

Jonkman, Fred. "The Missionary Methods of the Apostle Paul." http://www.thirdmill.org/Paul2/missionarymethods.asp 1999 (Oct. 11, 2001).

Judge, E. A. *The Social Pattern of the Christian Groups in the First Century*. London: Tyndale, 1960.

Karris, Robert J. "Missionary Communities: A New Paradigm for the Study of Luke-Acts." *Catholic Biblical Quarterly* 41 (1979) 80–97.

Keathley, Naymond H. *The Church's Mission to the Gentiles: Acts of the Apostles, Epistles of Paul*. Macon, Ga.: Smyth & Helwys, 1999.

Kee, Howard Clark, and Franklin W. Young. *Understanding the New Testament*. Englewood Cliffs: Prentice-Hall, Inc., 1957.

Kelly, Bobby Jay. "Divine Guidance in Luke-Acts: The Function of Commissioning Narratives as Encouragement and Apology." Ph.D. diss., Southwestern Baptist Theological Seminary, 1998.

Kelly, J. N. D. *A Commentary on the Epistles of Peter and Jude*. Thornapple Commentaries. Grand Rapids: Baker, 1969.

Keener, Craig S. *New Testament*. The IVP Bible Background Commentary. Downers Grove, Ill.: InterVarsity, 1993.

Kilgallen, John J. "Acts 13:38-39: Culmination of Paul's Speech in Pisidia." *Biblica* 69 (1988) 480–506.

———. *A Brief Commentary on the Acts of the Apostles*. New York: Paulist, 1988.

Kittel, Gerhard, editor. *Theological Dictionary of the New Testament*. 10 vols. Translated and edited by Geoffrey W. Bromiley. Grand Rapids: Eerdmans, 1965–76.

Klauck, Hans-Josef. *Magic and Paganism in Early Christianity: The World of the Acts of the Apostles*. Translated by Brian McNeil. Minneapolis: Fortress, 2003.

Kobayashi, Teruo. "The Role of Peter according to the Theological Understanding of Paul, Mark, and Luke-Acts." Ph.D. diss., Drew University, 1963.

Koh, Chu Fat. "Power Encounter in Luke-Acts." Th.M. thesis. Fuller Theological Seminary, 1996.

Krodel, Gerhard. *Acts*. Proclamation Commentaries. Philadelphia: Fortress, 1981.

———. *Acts*. Augsburg Commentary on the New Testament. Minneapolis: Augsburg, 1986.

———, editor. *The General Letters*. Proclamation Commentaries. Philadelphia: Fortress, 1995.

Kung, Ronald Y. K. *The Epistle to the Galatians*. The New International Commentary on the New Testament. Grand Rapids: Eerdmans, 1988.

Lemaire, André. "The Ministries in the New Testament." *Biblical Theology Bulletin* 3 (1973) 133–66.

Lenski, R. C. H. *Interpretation of the Acts of the Apostles*. Minneapolis: Augsburg, 1961.

Levinskaya, Irina. *The Book of Acts in Its Diaspora Setting*. The Book of Acts in Its First Century Setting,—Volume 5. Grand Rapids: Eerdmans, 1996.

Lightfoot, J. B. *St. Paul's Epistle to the Galatians*. Peabody, Mass.: Hendrickson, 1999.

Lohse, Eduard. *The New Testament Environment*. Translated by John E. Steely. Nashville: Abingdon, 1976.

Longenecker, Richard N. *The Ministry and Message of Paul*. Grand Rapids: Zondervan, 1971.

Lotz, Denton. "Peter's Wider Understanding of God's Will—Acts 10:34-48." *International Review of Mission* 77 (1988) 201–7.

Luck, G. Coleman. *First Corinthians*. Chicago: Moody, 1958.

Lüdemann, Gerd. "The Acts of the Apostles and the Beginnings of Simonian Gnosis." *New Testament Studies* 33 (1987) 420–26.

Luter, A. Boyd, Jr. "A New Testament Theology of Discipling." Th.D. diss., Dallas Theological Seminary, 1985.

Malherbe, A. J. "Pastoral Care in the Thessalonian Church." *New Testament Studies* 36 (1990) 375–91.

Maness, Stephen. "The Pauline Congregations, Paul and His Co-workers: Determinative Trajectories for the Ministries of Paul's Partners in the Gospel." Ph.D. diss., Southwestern Baptist Theological Seminary, 1998.

Marshall, I. Howard. *The Acts of the Apostles*. Tyndale New Testament Commentaries. Grand Rapids: Eerdmans, 1980.

———. *Luke: Historian and Theologian*. Grand Rapids: Zondervan, 1970.

———. "Luke's View of Paul." *Southwestern Journal of Theology* 33 (1990) 41–51.

Martin, Ralph P. "Salvation and Discipleship in Luke's Gospel." *Interpretation* 30 (1976) 366–80.

———. *Philippians*. The New Century Bible Commentary. Grand Rapids: Eerdmans, 1985.

Martin, Vincent. *A House Divided: The Parting of the Ways Between Synagogue and Church*. New York: Paulist, 1995.

Mattill, A. J., Jr. "The Date and Purpose of Luke-Acts: Rackham Reconsidered." *Catholic Biblical Quarterly* 40 (1978) 335–50.

McKnight, Edgar V., and Elizabeth Struthers Malbon, editors. *The New Literary Criticism and the New Testament*. Valley Forge, Pa.: Trinity, 1994.

Meeks, Wayne A. *The First Urban Christians: The Social World of the Apostle Paul*. New Haven: Yale University Press, 1983.

———. *The Moral World of the First Christians*. The Library of Early Christianity. Philadelphia: Westminster, 1986.

Meyer, F. B. *The Life of Peter*. Lynnewood: Emerald, 1996.

Moessner, David P. "'The Christ Must Suffer': New Light on the Jesus-Peter, Stephen, Paul Parallels in Luke-Acts." *Novum Testamentum* 28 (1986) 220–56.

———. "Paul in Acts: Preacher of Eschatological Repentance to Israel." *New Testament Studies* 34 (1988) 96–104.

Morris, Leon. *The Gospel According to St. Luke*. Tyndale New Testament Commentaries. Grand Rapids: Eerdmans, 1974.

———. *1 Corinthians*. Tyndale New Testament Commentaries. Grand Rapids: Eerdmans, 1958.

———. *1 and 2 Thessalonians*. Tyndale New Testament Commentaries. Grand Rapids: Eerdmans, 1984.

———. *Galatians: Paul's Charter of Christian Freedom*. Downers Grove, Ill.: InterVarsity, 1996.

———. *The Cross in the New Testament*. Grand Rapids: Eerdmans, 1965.

Moulton, Harold K., editor. *The Analytical Greek Lexicon Revised 1978 Edition*. Grand Rapids: Zondervan, 1978.

Munck, Johannes. *The Acts of the Apostles*. Anchor Bible. New York: Doubleday, 1967.

———. *Paul and the Salvation of Mankind*. Richmond: John Knox, 1959.

———. "Paul, the Apostles, and the Twelve." *Studia Theologia* 3 (1949) 96–110.

Murphy-O'Connor, Jerome. "Paul and Gallio." *Journal of Biblical Literature* 112 (1993) 315–17.

Murray, George W. "Paul's Corporate Evangelism in the Book of Acts." *Bibliotheca Sacra* 155 (1998) 189–200.

Navone, John. "Three Aspects of the Lucan Theology of History." *Biblical Theology Bulletin* 3 (1973) 115–32.

Neil, William. *The Acts of the Apostles*. The New Century Bible Commentary. Grand Rapids: Eerdmans, 1981.

Nesbitt, Charles F. "What *Did* Become of Peter?" *Journal of Bible and Religion* 27 (1959) 10–16.

Nollant, John. "A Fresh Look at Acts 15.10." *New Testament Studies* 27 (1980–1981) 105–15.

O'Grady, John F. *Disciples and Leaders: The Origins of Christian Ministry in the New Testament*. New York: Paulist, 1991.

Osborne, Robert E. "Where Did Peter Go?" *Canadian Journal of Theology* 14 (1968) 274–77.

Oster, Richard. *The Acts of the Apostles—Part II: 13.1—28:31.* The Living Word Commentary. Abilene: Abilene Christian University Press, 1984.

Packer, J. W. *The Acts of the Apostles.* The Cambridge Bible Commentary on the New English Bible. Cambridge: Cambridge University Press, 1966.

Palmer, D. W. "The Literary Background of Acts 1.1-14." *New Testament Studies* 33 (1987) 427–38.

Parsons, Mikeal C. "Reading Talbert: New Perspectives on Luke-Acts." *Society of Biblical Literature Seminar Papers* (1987) 687–720.

Perkins, Pheme. *Peter: Apostle for the Whole Church.* Minneapolis: Fortress, 2000.

———. *Reading the New Testament: An Introduction.* New York: Paulist, 1978.

———. *Ministering in the Pauline Churches.* New York: Paulist, 1982.

Pervo, Richard I. *Luke's Story of Paul.* Minneapolis: Fortress, 1990.

Pfeiffer, Charles F., and Howard F. Vos and John Rea, editors. *The Wycliffe Bible Encyclopedia Volume 2: K-Z.* Chicago: Moody, 1975.

Picirilli, Robert E. *Paul the Apostle.* Chicago: Moody, 1986.

Pierard, R. V. "Tübingen School." http://www.mb-soft.com/believe/bxc/Tübingen.htm 2002 (May 22, 2003).

Pillette, Bard. "Paul and His Fellow Workers: A Study in the Use of Authority." Ph.D. diss., Dallas Theological Seminary, 1992.

Powell, Mark Allen, editor. *The New Testament Today.* Louisville: Westminster John Knox, 1999.

———. *What Are They Saying about Acts?* New York: Paulist, 1991.

Praeder, Susan Marie. "The Problem of First Person Narration in Acts." *Novum Testamentum* 29 (1987) 193–218.

Raisanen, Heikki. "Paul's Conversion and the Development of His View of the Law." *New Testament Studies* 33 (1987) 404–19.

Ramsay, W. M. *St. Paul the Traveller and the Roman Citizen.* Grand Rapids: Baker, 1951.

———. *Historical Commentary on Galatians.* Edited by Mark Wilson. Grand Rapids: Kregel, 1997.

———. *The Letters to the Seven Churches.* Grand Rapids: Baker, 1985.

Random House Dictionary of the English Language. New York: Random House, 1966.

Reed, Oscar F. *Corinthians.* Beacon Bible Expositions 7. Kansas City: Beacon Hill, 1976.

Richard, Earl. "Luke—Writer, Theologian, Historian: Research and Orientation of the 1970's." *Biblical Theology Bulletin* 13 (1983) 3–15.

Richardson, Peter. "Pauline Inconsistency: I Corinthians 9:19-23 and Galatians 2:1-14." *New Testament Studies* 26 (1979–1980) 347–62.

Riesner, Rainer. *Paul's Early Period: Chronology, Mission Strategy, Theology.* Grand Rapids: Eerdmans, 1998.

Robertson, A. T. *Epochs in the Life of Simon Peter.* Grand Rapids: Baker, 1974.

Rosenblatt, Marie-Eloise. *Paul the Accused: His Portrait in Acts of the Apostles.* Collegeville: Liturgical, 1995.

Sanders, E. P. *Paul, the Law, and the Jewish People.* Philadelphia: Fortress, 1983.

———. *Paul and Palestinian Judaism.* Philadelphia: Fortress, 1977.

Sanders, Jack T. "Paul's 'Autobiographical' Statements in Galatians 1–2." *Journal of Biblical Literature* 85 (1966) 335–43.

Sanders, Joseph N. "Peter and Paul in Acts." *New Testament Studies* 2 (1955) 133–43.

Sandmel, Samuel. *The Genius of Paul.* Philadelphia: Fortress, 1979.

Schmithals, Walter. *The Office of Apostle in the Early Church.* Translated by John E. Steely. Nashville: Abingdon, 1969.

Seccombe, David. "Luke's Vision for the Church." In *A Vision for the Church: Studies in Early Christian Ecclesiology*, edited by Markus Bockmuehl and Michael B. Thompson, 45–63. Edinburgh: T. & T. Clark, 1997.

Segal, Alan F. *Paul the Convert: The Apostolate and Apostasy of Saul the Pharisee*. New Haven: Yale University Press, 1990.

Sheeley, Steven M. "Narrative Asides and Narrative Authority in Luke-Acts." *Biblical Theology Bulletin* 18 (1988) 102–7.

Smalley, Stephen S. "Spirit, Kingdom and Prayer in Luke-Acts." *Novum Testamentum* 25 (1973) 59–71.

Smith, Margaret. *The Way of the Mystics*. New York: Oxford University Press, 1978.

Soards, Marion L. *The Apostle Paul*. New York: Paulist, 1987.

———. *1 Corinthians*. New International Biblical Commentary. Peabody, Mass Hendrickson, 1999.

———. *The Speeches in Acts: Their Content, Context, and Concerns*. Louisville: Westminster John Knox, 1994.

Squires, John T. "The Function of Acts 8.4—12.25." *New Testament Studies* 44 (1998) 608–17.

———. *The Plan of God in Luke Acts*. Cambridge: Cambridge University Press, 1993.

Stagg, Frank. *The Book of Acts: The Early Struggle for an Unhindered Gospel*. Nashville: Broadman, 1955.

Stambaugh, John E., and David L. Balch. *The New Testament in Its Social Environment*. Library of Early Christianity. Philadelphia: Westminster, 1986.

Stanley, David M. "Authority in the Church: A New Testament Reality." *Catholic Biblical Quarterly* 29 (1967) 555–73.

Sterling, Gregory E. "'Athletes of Virtue:' An Analysis of the Summaries in Acts (2:41-47; 4:32-35; 5:12-16)." *Journal of Biblical Literature* 113 (1994) 679–96.

Stott, John R. W. *The Message of Acts: The Spirit, the Church & the World*. The Bible Speaks Today. Downers Grove, Ill.: InterVarsity, 1990.

Stowers, Stanley. "Social Status, Public Speaking and Private Teaching: The Circumstances of Paul's Preaching Activity." *Novum Testamentum* 26 (1984) 59–82.

Stronstad, Roger. *The Charismatic Theology of St. Luke*. Peabody, Mass.: Hendrickson, 1984.

Suggs, M. Jack. "Concerning the Date of Paul's Macedonian Ministry." *Novum Testamentum* 4 (1960) 60–68.

Talbert, Charles H. *Reading Acts: A Literary and Theological Commentary on the Acts of the Apostles*. New York: Crossroad, 1997.

———. "Again: Paul's Visits to Jerusalem." *Novum Testamentum* 9 (1967) 26–40.

Tannehill, Robert C. *The Narrative Unity of Luke-Acts: A Literary Interpretation*, Volume One: *The Gospel According to Luke*. Minneapolis: Fortress, 1986.

———. *The Narrative Unity of Luke-Acts A Literary Interpretation*, Volume Two: *The Acts of the Apostles*. Minneapolis: Fortress, 1990.

———. "The Functions of Peter's Mission Speeches in the Narrative of Acts." *New Testament Studies* 37 (1991) 400–414.

Tenney, Merrill C. *New Testament Survey*. Grand Rapids: Eerdmans, 1961.

———. *New Testament Times*. Peabody, Mass.: Hendrickson, 1965.

———. *Galatians: The Charter of Christian Liberty*. Grand Rapids: Eerdmans, 1989.

Thompson, Richard P., and Thomas E. Phillips, editors. *Literary Studies in Luke-Acts: Essays in Honor of Joseph B. Tyson*. Macon, Ga.: Mercer University Press, 1998.

Thompson, Richard P. "Christian Community and Characterization in the Book of Acts: A Literary Study of the Lukan Concept of the Church." Ph.D. diss., Dedman College, Southern Methodist University, 1996.

Tyson, Joseph B. *A Study of Early Christianity*. New York: Macmillan, 1973.

———. *The New Testament and Early Christianity*. New York: Macmillan, 1984.

———. "The Emerging Church and the Problem of Authority in Acts." *Interpretation* 41 (1988) 132–45.

———. "John Knox and the Acts of the Apostles." *Society of Biblical Literature Seminar Papers* (1987) 669–86.

———. "Authority in Acts." *The Bible Today* 30 (1992) 279–83.

Van Der Horst, P. W. "'Peter's Shadow'" The Religio-Historical Background of Acts V.15." *New Testament Studies* 23 (1977) 204–12.

Van Ommeren, Nicholas M. "Was Luke an Accurate Historian?" *Bibliotheca Sacra* 148 (1991) 57–71.

Van Unnik, W. C. "The 'Book of Acts' the Confirmation of the Gospel." *Novum Testamentum* 4 (1960) 26–59.

Van Zyl, Hermie C. "The Evolution of Church Leadership in the New Testament—A New Consensus?" *Neotestamentica* 32 (1998) 585–604.

Vaughan, Curtis, and Thomas D. Lea. *1 Corinthians*. Founders Study Guide Commentary. Cape Coral: Founders, 2002.

Vine, Victor E. "The Purpose and Date of Acts." *Expository Times* 96 (1984) 45–48.

Vine, W. E., and C. F. Hogg. *Vine's Expository Commentary on Galatians*. Nashville: Thomas Nelson, 1997.

Vine, W. E. *Vine's Expository Dictionary of New Testament Words*. Peabody, Mass.: Hendrickson.

Wade, Rick. "The World of the Apostle Paul." http://www.probe.org/docs/apospaul.html 1997 (Sept. 24, 2001).

Wall, Robert W. "Successors to 'The Twelve' according to Acts 12: 1-17." *Catholic Biblical Quarterly* 53 (1991) 628–44.

Wand, J. W. C. *A History of the Early Church*. London: Methuen, 1937.

Williams, C. S. C. *A Commentary on the Acts of the Apostles*. Harper's New Testament Commentaries. New York: Harper & Brothers, 1957.

Williams, David J. *Acts*. New International Biblical Commentary. Peabody, Mass.: Hendrickson, 1990.

Willimon, William H. "Eyewitnesses and Ministers of the Word: Preaching in Acts." *Interpretation* 42 (1988) 158–70.

Wills, Lawrence M. "The Depiction of the Jews in Acts." *Journal of Biblical Literature* 110 (1991) 631–54.

Wilson, A. N. *Paul: The Mind of the Apostle*. New York: Norton, 1997.